Color Management for Packaging

A RotoVision Book

Published and distributed by RotoVision SA

Route Suisse 9

CH-1295 Mies

Switzerland

RotoVision SA

Sales & Editorial Office

Sheridan House, 114 Western Road

Hove BN3 1DD, UK

Tel: +44 (0) 1273 72 72 68

Fax: +44 (0) 1273 72 72 69

Email: sales@rotovision.com

Web: www.rotovision.com

10 9 8 7 6 5 4 3 2 1

ISBN 10: 2-940361-67-3
ISBN 13: 978-2- 940361-67-0

RotoVision Art Director: Tony Seddon

Creative Directors: John T. Drew and Sarah A. Meyer

Book Design: Matt Woolman

Book Layout and Production: Matt Woolman and Ann Ford

Acuity Color System: John T. Drew and Sarah A. Meyer

Diagrams and Illustrations: John T. Drew, Sarah A. Meyer, and Matt Woolman

Typeface: Trade Gothic Family

Text © 2008 John T. Drew and Sarah A. Meyer

Acuity Color System © 2008 John T. Drew and Sarah A. Meyer. For more information about Acuity 1.0 contact John T. Drew at jdrew@fullerton.edu or Sarah A. Meyer at sameyer@csupomona.edu

Reprographics in Singapore by ProVision Pte.

Printed in Singapore by Star Standard

Color Management for Packaging

A Comprehensive Guide for Graphic Designers

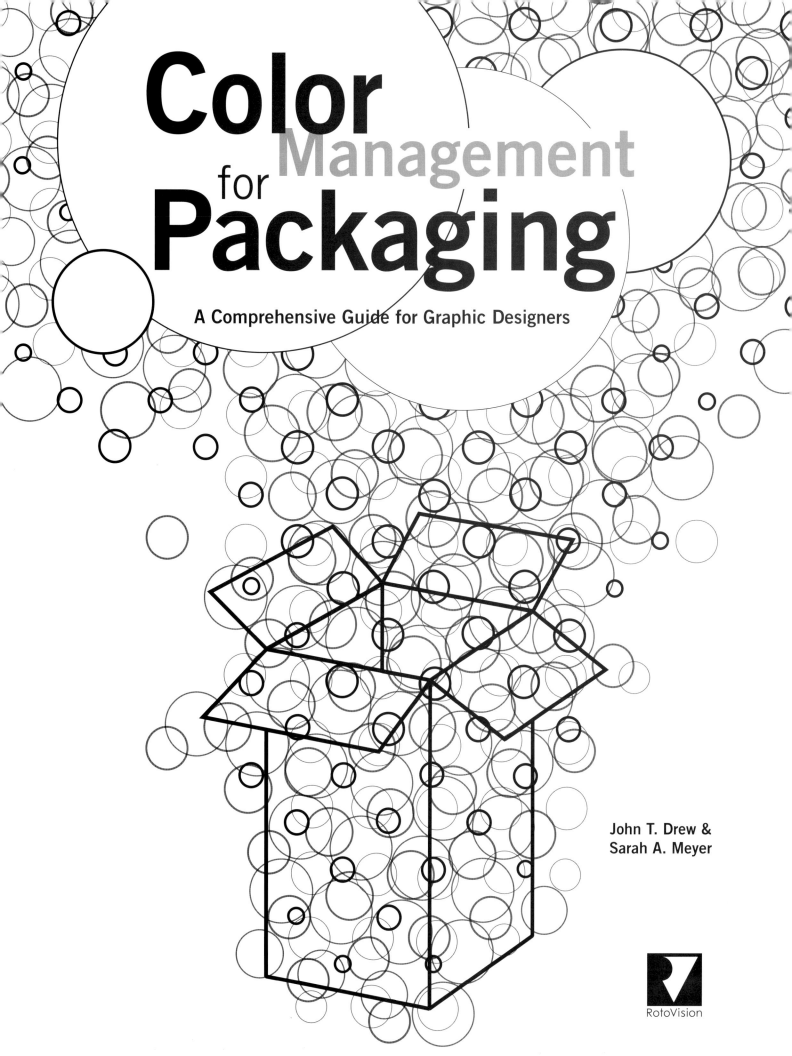

John T. Drew &
Sarah A. Meyer

RotoVision

Acknowledgments
We would like to thank all those who have contributed to and made this
book possible. So many people have shown generosity and insight that it
is impossible to list them all. Our deepest gratitude go to Christine Pickett,
for making us sound like geniuses; the International Council of Graphic
Design Association (ICOGRADA) and the American Institute of Graphic Artists
(AIGA), for supporting the international call for entries; Danny Giang, Jimmy
Khemthong, and Maho Sasai, for their help and all our students who have
inspired us to think differently; RotoVision, Simon Smith, and especially
Tony Seddon and Lindy Dunlop, for their continued support; and finally
everyone who answered the call and may or may not appear in this book.
*Color Management for Packaging: A Comprehensive Guide for Graphic
Designers* would not have been possible without your participation.

Contents

7      Introduction

8   **1**   One and Two Colors

26   **2**   Three Colors

44   **3**   Four Colors

64   **4**   Spot Colors

84   **5**   Specials and Finishing Techniques

98   **6**   Packaging Materials and Printing Stocks

112   **7**   Storage, Display, and Aging

130   **8**   Color Management for Print

164   **9**   Color Legibility

184   **10**   Color Association

210   Glossary

214   Bibliography

216   Contributors

218   Index

Introduction

Effective, practical color use is intrinsic to the process of solving a graphic design problem. Without color, packaged products would lack differentiation and standout. The materials and shapes of packaging designs are an important aspect of a given outcome, however, color is the force that holds a package together and acts as a conduit to engage and transfix the buyer.

Color sells a product—it has a physical shape and creates emotional responses that can communicate well beyond the size, shape, and scope of the product. Color has the ability to transform and translate meaningful messages, and to activate the human condition so that response can be measured.

Color Management for Packaging is a unique body of consolidated information that demonstrates both the pragmatic and the technical color issues involved in packaging design today, including the utilization of subtractive, additive, and 3-D color space. Through detailed case studies and a visually stimulating showcase, *Color Management for Packaging* will fill you with new ideas and provide you with the technical know-how for effective use of color in packaging design.

One and Two Colors

One- and two-color package design commonly has budgetary constraints limiting the amount of hues that can be used, either that or it is part of an overall campaign that utilizes both one-, two-, three-, and full-color packaging and collateral materials. However, as demonstrated in this chapter, one- and two-color packaging requires a greater use of creativity—a mastering of three-dimensional form, color, typography, image making, composition, and conceptual development. This is not to say that three- and four-color jobs do not possess the same qualities—often they do. However, frequently a full-color iconic photograph is used leaving no room for gestalt—the active participation of the audience to partake, engage, and imagine the sum of the parts as being greater than the whole.

Iconic packaging is a very direct form of communication. Most often, when dealing with one- and two-color packaging, symbolic and indexical information is used, which is a less direct form of communication that inherently leaves more to the imagination—and some stunning examples are found in this chapter. An underutilized marketing strategy for high-end design, one- and two-color package design can create striking visual separation on the shelf, and should be considered seriously every time a new design or design campaign is being developed.

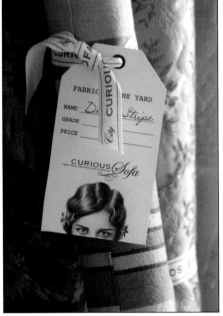

Curious Sofa
Studio: REFLECTUR.COM

Associative Color Response:
· white: cleanliness, purity, clean, sterling

Color Scheme: one hue

The typographic specimens chosen (Copperplate and a script typeface) reinforce the timeless and classical nature of the design.

Curious Sofa
Studio: REFLECTUR.COM

Associative Color Response:
· golden-yellow/beige family: harvest, classic, earthy, natural, soft
· blue-green family: pristine, pure, inner coolness, consistent
· earth-tone family: rustic, delicious, sheltering, warm

Color Scheme: two points of a triad with shading

In this simple, but elegant package design harmony is created through the use of overprinting to a colored substrate, creating a bridge between the light-colored brown and the turquoise green. The color palette chosen along with the typography and image convey a seamlessly timeless package design—one that is appropriate for the content.

Curious Sofa
Studio: REFLECTUR.COM

Associative Color Response:
· golden-yellow/beige family: harvest, classic, earthy, natural, soft
· blue-green family: pristine, pure, inner coolness, consistent
· earth-tone family: rustic, delicious, sheltering, warm

Color Scheme: two points of a triad with shading

Sparing no expense, the labeling system for Curious Sofa is masterfully done. To help convey a timeless quality, the photograph of the woman's hair and face is not only styled after a popular 1920s haircut, but also manipulated to appear as though the image is etched.

Curious Sofa
Studio: REFLECTUR.COM

Associative Color Response:
· golden-yellow/beige family: harvest, classic, earthy, natural, soft
· earth-tone family: rustic, delicious, sheltering, warm

Color Scheme: one hue with tinting

The hand-held fan is not only beautifully executed, but is also a brilliant concept, harking back to a time where there was no air conditioning—consistently reinforcing the idea of a timeless and elegant experience.

Curious Sofa
Studio: REFLECTUR.COM

Associative Color Response:
· golden-yellow/beige family: harvest, classic, earthy, natural, soft
· blue-green family: pristine, pure, inner coolness, consistent
· earth-tone family: rustic, delicious, sheltering, warm

Color Scheme: two points of a triad with shading

This simply constructed package design uses multiple layers to create a semiprecious object. Note that the sticker is attached to the cloth ribbon thus securing the contents during transportation. The additional layer of very thin and semitranslucent paper adds to the opening ritual before revealing the object inside.

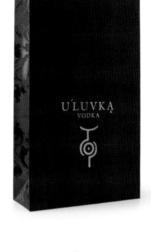

Elias & Grace
Studio: Aloof Design
Art Director: Sam Aloof
Designers: Andrew Scrase,
Jon Hodkinson

Associative Color Response:
· earth-tone family: pleasant, warm
· blue-green family: pristine, pure,
  serious, lively

Color Scheme: two-points of a triad

Elias & Grace provides a modern and
versatile approach to maternity and
children's wear. Aloof Design created
the brand identity, a range of playful
packaging and garment labeling,
business stationery, and a website.
Luggage labels were created to price
each garment and product, and to
adorn the store's carrier bags and
gift boxes. A die cut was utilized to
emulate the relationship between
parent and child, with colored glass
beads and metal bells strung with
brown linen thread to adorn the
concept further. Note: Inks were
mixed containing a high percentage
of opaque white to lift the colors on
the natural kraft material, and at the
same time retaining a match to the
brand-identity-specified hue.

Virgil's Fine Soaps
Studio: Fuelhaus
Art Director: Kellie Schroeder
Designer: Donovan Mafnas

Associative Color Response:
· high-chroma red family: active,
  cheer, joy, fun
· black: powerful, basic,
  neutral, classic

Color Scheme: one hue

Virgil's Fine Soaps is a classic
example of a low-budget job
superbly done. The design of the
band gives the soap an "old-timey"
feel without making the product look
too verbose or overcrowded. The color
palette is shifted from product to
product by using different-colored
paper—with the exception of red,
this is often a seasonal color that
printers have pre-mixed in stock,
thus incurring no additional cost.

U'Luvka Vodka
Studio: Aloof Design
Art Director: Sam Aloof
Designers: Andrew Scrase,
Jon Hodkinson

Associative Color Response:
· silver family: cool, expensive,
  money, valuable, classic

Appetite Rating:
· silver family: excellent

Associative Taste:
· no associative tastes

Color Scheme: incongruous

This package design was litho
printed using a solid custom ink
mixed to match other product
packaging within this line. A silkscreen spot-varnish UV pattern was
employed, adding elegance to the
design, and a silver foil was used
both for the logotype and mark. The
combination of these techniques
coupled with a black ribbon handle
creates a highly sophisticated bag
that is masterfully executed.

Alison Price
Studio: Aloof Design
Art Director: Sam Aloof
Designers: Andrew Scrase,
Jon Hodkinson

Associative Color Response:
· high-chroma pink family:
  stimulates, aggressive,
  excitement, attention-getting

Appetite Rating:
· high-chroma pink family: excellent

Associative Taste:
· high-chroma pink: very sweet

Color Scheme: one hue

By using high-quality materials and
printing, Aloof Design was able to
create a memorable food package
for private catering business Alison
Price & Company to use as a teaser
to entice prospective clients. The
multifaceted canapé box is an Aloof
in-house design. A solid magenta
with a type reversal was employed.
The logotype was then debossed
to create a subtle shadow-and-
texture effect. With a tabbed lid
and envelope base, the box can be
supplied flat and assembled by hand
without any use of glue.

Capsoles
Studio: Exhibit A: Design Group
Art Director: Cory Ripley
Designers: Cory Ripley,
Robert Spofforth

Associative Color Response:
· high-chroma red family: brilliant,
  intense, active, cheer, joy, fun

Color Scheme: one hue plus shading
(this includes the gray in the socks)

Color plays an important role for the
Capsoles™ brand. The corporate
colors (red and PANTONE® cool
gray) were selected as the best
combination to visually emote the
term "sportmedical." In addition,
these colors are easy to replicate
in different methods of print
production. The sleeve packaging
ensures consumer confidence by
soliciting/reassuring a qualitative
response of production confidence.

The 12 Bar
Art Director: John T. Drew
Designer: Steve Gonsowski

Associative Color Response:
· earth-tone family: delicious,
  deep, rich, warm
· golden-yellow beige family: rich,
  sun, buttery, classic, natural

Appetite Rating:
· earth-tone family: excellent
· mid-range orange family: good
  to excellent
· golden-yellow/beige family: excellent

Associative Taste:
· mid-range orange family: sweet

Color Scheme: analogous
with shading

This candy package is based
conceptually on the 12-bar blues.
The formal shape of the packaging
is meant to resemble a harmonica,
an instrument associated with
the genre.

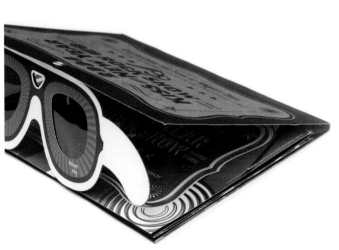

Interstate Paper
Art Director: Andrew Wong
Designers: Andrew Wong, Spy Lan
Copywriter: Andrew Wong

Associative Color Response:
· high-chroma red: brilliant, intense,
  energizing, sexy, dramatic,
  stimulating, joy, fun
· high-chroma green: motion,
  growth, fresh, lively, spring
· black: powerful, elegant,
  mysterious, heavy, basic
· silver: futuristic, cool, expensive,
  money, valuable, classic

Color Scheme: direct complementary
with neutral

This unique package exploits the use
of a three-dimensional color effects.
When attempting to create work in
this manner, the two plates—in
this case green and red—need to
be out of register in order for the
three-dimensional effect to work.
The more the image is out of register
the deeper the three-dimensional
illusion. However, at a certain point
this register effect will break down
and flatten back out. It is best to
work wearing three-dimensional
glasses when designing using
this effect. Note: The opposition in
color between the front and back
of this beautifully executed design
is masterfully done. The metallic
silver printed on black opens to an
orchestra of high-chroma colors
on the reverse side—an excellent
strategy for creating intrigue and
kinetic energy throughout the piece.

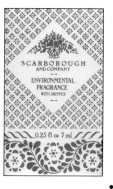 

Ashford Eye Drops
Studio: Midnite Oil
Art Director/Designer:
Mongkolsri Janjarasskul

Associative Color Response:
· pastel pink: intimate, active
· mid-range orange: gentle, entice, good spirits
· pastel green: innate, completely, calm, quiet, smoothing
· blue-green: pristine, pure, serious, cleanliness, incorruptible
· dark gray: cultured, professional, classic, expensive
· white: cleanliness, purity, clean

Color Scheme: one hue plus neutral

White is the dominant hue within this packaging series—an excellent choice for pharmaceutical products. In this case, white is created from the substrate's color, so technically this would be a two-color job. The other hues used within this system are for product identification.

Dahesh Museum of Art
Studio: Poulin + Morris

Associative Color Response:
· dark-red family: rich, elegant, refined, taste
· high-chroma yellow-orange: enterprise, drive, target, goal, luxuriance
· white: cleanliness, purity, clean, sterling, zeal, bright, awareness

Color Scheme: two points of a triad

This elegant and regal package design is a perfect color combination for the Dahesh Museum of Art. The oxblood red chosen was visually referenced from the museum's logotype—an academic artist's palette—and this is complemented by the yellow-orange, as the two colors harmonize through yellow and red. Note: visually referencing existing elements within a given environment is an excellent strategy for choosing colors within a color scheme or as a point of departure to invent a new palette.

Wild Bites
Studio: Exhibit A: Design Group
Art Director: Cory Ripley
Designers: Cory Ripley, Robert Spofforth

Associative Color Response:
· high-chroma red: brilliant, intense, energizing
· white: cleanliness, purity, clean
· earth tone: rustics, delicious, deep, rich, warm, folksy, rooted, life

Appetite Rating:
· high-chroma red: excellent
· white: excellent
· earth tone: good

Associative Taste:
· high-chroma red: very sweet

Color Scheme: monochromatic with tinting and shading

This packaging utilizes a vibrant, yet subtle color palette that conveys the character of the product—natural, fresh, organic, healthy, and gourmet. The four containers were printed simultaneously on a six-color press allowing each flavor its own specific PANTONE color. Each package uses a spot gloss varnish and dull aqueous coating for added visual depth.

Ciao Bella
Studio: Wallace Church, Inc.
Creative Director: Stan Church

Associative Color Response:
· high-chroma pink: stimulates, aggressive, genial, exciting, happy, high, fun, excitement
· high-chroma orange: healing, tasty, cleanliness, cheerfulness
· high-chroma reddish purple: sweet taste, subtle, restlessness, prolongs life

Appetite Rating:
· high-chroma pink: excellent
· high-chroma orange: excellent

Associative Taste:
· high-chroma pink: very sweet
· high-chroma orange: very sweet

Color Scheme: near analogous

This high-chroma package series is intensely executed through hue. A symmetrical design is used to create a strong focal point (a snowflake) keeping the consumer's eye lodged in the center of the package. High-chroma hues are utilized to counterbalance the symmetrical design, giving the packages a kinetic energy through the use of hue.

Becker Surf + Sport
Studio: Jefferson Acker
Art Director: Glenn Sakamoto

Associative Color Response:
· dark-red family: rich, elegant, refined, taste, expensive, mature
· black: spatial, powerful, elegant, mysterious, heavy, basic, neutral
· white: refreshing, antiseptic, perfect balance, zeal, bright
· earth tone: delicious, deep, rich

Color Scheme: one hue with tinting plus neutral and white

This is a superb package design, printed with three hues—black, white, and a brick red. The continuous-tone imagery was silkscreened using a crude halftone. The white and black hues are actually printed inks and have a distressed texture. White printed ink is uncommon—white is usually provided by the substrate—and thus can create a unique look and feel.

Scarborough and Company
Studio: Bohoy Design
Art Director: Johanna Bohoy, Susannah Jonas
Designer: Johanna Bohoy

Associative Color Response:
· pastel pink: soft, sweet, tender, joyful, beautiful, expressive, emotional
· pastel blue: pleasure, peace, calm, quiet
· mid-range red-purple: charming, elegant, select, refined, subtle
· high-chroma pink: stimulates, aggressive, genial, exciting, happy, high, fun, excitement
· dark green: nature, mountains, lakes, natural, mature growth
· dark orange: exhilarating, moving, inspiring, stirring, stimulating

Color Scheme: complementary with tinting, near complementary with tinting, and two points of a triad

This beautifully executed packaging references Art Nouveau styles. Many hues and color combinations are used to create this series, however, continuity is brought about through the consistent use of color tinting.

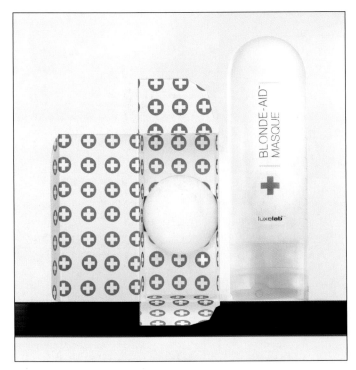

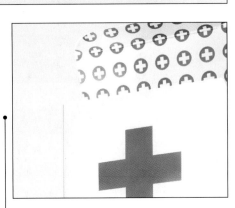

Luxelab Blonde-Aid Masque
Studio: Dustin Edward Arnold
Art Director/Designer:
Dustin E. Arnold

Associative Color Response:
· high-chroma red: brilliant,
  intense, energizing, hope
· black: powerful, elegant,
  classic, strong
· white: purity, clean, life,
  refreshing, perfect balance

Color Scheme: one hue plus neutral
and white

Blonde-Aid is a revitalizing
conditioner formulated specifically
for the special needs of blond hair.
Keeping in line both with the salon's
aesthetic and its strict modernist
tastes, Blonde-Aid Masque is a
salon-grade luxury product based
on the needs of both stylists and
their clients.

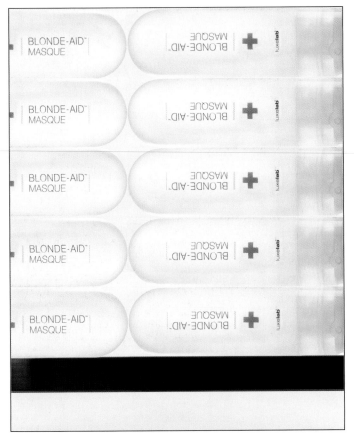

Shoot Better
Studio: milkxhake
Art Director/Designer: milkxhake

Associative Color Response:
· high-chroma red: surging, brilliant, intense, energizing, sexy, dramatic, stimulating
· high-chroma orange: communication, cheerful, lively, exciting, bright, luminous
· white: zeal, bright, refreshing

Color Scheme: analogous with white

The redesign of a 35mm roll of film for Cream, an alternative-pop-culture magazine from Hong Kong—the slogan "Shoot better!" is a simple reminder before you load the film and press the shutter. By using warm, high-chroma colors that are not usually associated with this product, it visually separates itself from other packaging.

Crew
Art Director/Designer: Marcos Chavez

Associative Color Response:
· earth tone: delicious, deep, rich, warm
· blue-green: pristine, pure, serious, cleanliness, incorruptible

Color Scheme: near complementary with shading and white

The Crew shampoo bottle incorporates a masculine color scheme while at the same time choosing individual hues that are excellent for packaging. Note how the simplistic design is skillfully executed using symmetrical typographic techniques to create a strong focal point.

Zenz Therapy
Studio: Greydient
Designer: Morten Nielsen

Associative Color Response:
· silver: cool, expensive, money, valuable, classic
· dark gray: wise, cultured, mature, professional, classic, expensive, sophisticated, solid, enduring

Color Scheme: achromatic

The Zenz Therapy Conditioner bottle is a simple design—but classic. Beautifully executed, the vibrating oval symbolizes a human head, and at the same time is an energetic mark. The choice of silver and dark gray is masterfully executed, implying a sense of sophistication and quality.

Wow
Studio: Mary Hutchison Design LLC
Art Director/Designer:
Mary Chin Hutchison

Associative Color Response:
· high-chroma red: active, cheer, joy, fun
· high-chroma orange: cheerfulness, energizing, gregarious, friendly

Appetite Rating:
· high-chroma red: excellent
· high-chroma orange: excellent

Associative Taste:
· high-chroma red: very sweet
· high-chroma orange: very sweet

Color Scheme: analogous with white

The Wow cookie-dough buckets are quite unusual—this type of container is seldom used for this kind of product, and therefore stands out on the shelf. The choice of a white opaque container is an excellent one—using a clear container for cookie dough would not be recommended, as the natural color of the dough may have unwanted connotations.

Aquatanica Spa
Studio: Doyle Partners

Associative Color Response:
· high-chroma bluish purple: expensive, regal, classic, powerful, tender, elegant
· black: powerful, elegant, mysterious
· white: refreshing, perfect balance, zeal, bright

Color Scheme: one hue plus tinting plus neutral

This specialty line of skincare products contains natural ingredients from the sea. A single strong color was chosen so the products would stand out visually from their competitors in a retail environment, where hundreds of bottles, jars, and tubes of skincare products compete for the buyer's attention. The imagery was inspired by Victorian cyanotypes.

Capsoles
Studio: Exhibit A: Design Group
Art Director: Cory Ripley
Designers: Cory Ripley, Robert Spofforth

Associative Color Response:
· dark green: nature, mountains, lakes, natural, mature growth
· white: cleanliness, purity, clean, sterling

Color Scheme: near analogous

An excellent example of simplicity, the Capsoles Foot Emulsion uses color association and/or learned behavioral effects to imbue the bottle with the appropriate colors. Note how the plastic bottle has a large end-cap so that it can be stored cap down—a perfect solution for any liquid.

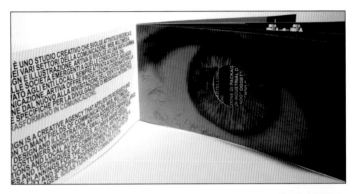

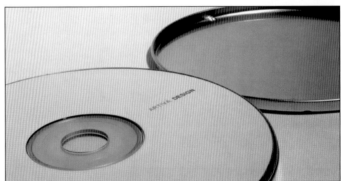

Artiva Design
Studio: Artiva Design
Art Directors/Designers:
Davide Sossi, Daniele De Batte
Illustrator: Daniele De Batte

Associative Color Response:
· white: cleanliness, purity,
  clean, sterling
· high-chroma red: brilliant,
  intense, energizing
· silver: cool, expensive

Color Scheme: one hue plus neutral,
white, and silver

This unique self-promotional
package is cleverly conceived and
wonderfully executed. The red-and-
black combination is a designer's
choice that conveys intrigue and
professionalism. The exterior tin has
great crush resistance and allows
for multiple items to be placed safely
and securely within.

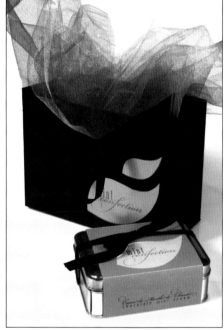

Rush
Art Director: Dan Hoy
Designer: Savio Alphonso

Associative Color Response:
· white: cleanliness, purity, clean, sterling
· high-chroma red: brilliant, intense, energizing
· silver: cool, expensive

Appetite Rating:
· white: excellent
· high-chroma red: excellent
· silver: excellent

Associative Taste:
· high-chroma red: very sweet

Color Scheme: one hue plus neutral, white, and silver

The Rush energy drink uses unique symbolism combined with an excellent color palette to create impact on the shelf. In this case, the symbolism is metaphorically derived and uses objects that have or create/generate some type of energy, shock, or explosion.

Vivr
Art Director/Designer: Boris Ljubicic

Associative Color Response:
· pastel pink: soft, sweet, tender, rarefied, cute, comfortable, snug, delicate
· high-chroma purple: deep, power, nostalgia, memories, spirituality

Color Scheme: two points of a triad plus neutral

The Vivr product is an excellent example of color sampling. In other words, the hue of the type is being sampled from the graphic being used. The white hue of the spray cans creates a neutral background in which the typography and graphics pop.

MacNeill Group
Studio: Gouthier Design
a brand collective
Creative Director: Jonathan Gouthier
Designers: Gouthier Design
Creative Team

Associative Color Response:
· high-chroma blue: electric, energetic, vibrant, happy, dramatic
· blue-green: expensive, regal, classic, powerful
· neutral gray: classic, corporate

Appetite Rating:
· high-chroma blue: poor to good
· blue-green: excellent
· neutral gray: poor to good

Color Scheme: analogous with neutral gray

This small case of M&Ms was the perfect gift to launch the new brand identity within the company. The two custom blue colors allowed the brand to start making an impact on the employees and their belief in the company. The cyan, blue, and turquoise hues convey a pristine and lively work environment.

Mint Confection
Art Director: John T. Drew
Designer: Kristine Yan

Associative Color Response:
· pastel green: empathy, innate, completely, smoothing, natural
· earth tone: delicious, deep, rich, warm

Appetite Rating:
· pastel green: excellent
· earth tone: excellent

Associative Taste:
· no associative tastes

Color Scheme: direct complementary with shading

Mint Confection is a wonderfully executed tin with accompanying bag. Designed for a high-end market, three layers of material are utilized (cloth bow, paper wrapper, and metal tin) to contain the product. Once the tin is open, two more layers of material separate the product—chocolate mints—from the consumer. This ritual of opening, or peeling away, the layers makes the chocolates seen semiprecious and well worth the money spent.

Confection Breath Mints
Art Director: John T. Drew
Designer: Kristine Yan

Associative Color Response:
· high-chroma bluish-green: pristine, cool, fresh, liquid, refreshing, healing, wholesome

Appetite Rating:
· high-chroma bluish-green: excellent

Associative Taste:
· no associative tastes

Color Scheme: analogous with tinting

A sister product to Mint Confection, left, the same layering strategy was employed with the packaging. However, due to the complexity of the product/package design, the color palette was restrained to a simple analogous color scheme. Turquoise hues were chosen because of their color association with mint, thus conveying a pristine and refreshing package and taste.

Egekilde
Studio: 3PART designteam

Associative Color Response:
· pastel blue: pleasure, peace,
  calm, quiet, hygienic, peaceful,
  refreshing, clean, cool, water
· dark blue: classic, conservative,
  strong, dependable

Appetite Rating:
· pastel blue: excellent
· dark blue: excellent

Associative Taste:
· no associative tastes

Dark blue: no associative taste

Color Scheme: monochromatic
with tinting

Simply incredible, this beautiful
design incorporates not only an
extremely appropriate color scheme,
but also an elegant form in the
shape of a water drop. Color and
form combine to reinforce product
branding and identification.

New England Cranberry
Studio: Bohoy Design
Art Director /Designer/Illustrator:
Johanna Bohoy

Associative Color Response:
· high-chroma red: brilliant, intense,
  energizing, joy, fun, aggressive
· dark-red family: rich, elegant, earthy,
  refined, taste, expensive, mature
· high-chroma green: ebbing of life,
  springtime, infancy
· dark green: natural, mature growth

Appetite Rating:
· high-chroma red: excellent
· high-chroma green: excellent
· dark green: good

Associative Taste:
· high-chroma red: very sweet

Color Scheme: complementary
primaries with shading

A logo redesign for this line resulted
in a new identity for placement in
higher-end specialty food markets.
The client wanted a clean, simple,
contemporary style, distinct from
the "country" look of most cranberry
products. The graduated sage-green
label gives it a sophisticated look.

The Fine Cheese Co. English Fruits
Studio: Irving
Designer/Illustrator: Julian Roberts

Associative Color Response:
· high-chroma red: brilliant,
  intense, energizing
· earth tone: delicious, deep,
  rich, warm
· high-chroma blue: relaxed,
  mature, classy, expensive
· high-chroma green-yellow: new
  growth, lemony, tart, fruity

Appetite Rating:
· high-chroma red: excellent
· earth tone: excellent
· high-chroma blue: poor to good
· high-chroma green-yellow: excellent

Associative Taste:
· high-chroma red: very sweet

Color Scheme: Lime & Chilli: two
points of a triad; Quince: one hue
plus neutral and tinting

An unusual shape and color
combination for this type of
product, it explodes off the shelf.
This clean and simple design uses
type as image to create a greater
viewing distance for the consumer.

Puria
Art Director/Designer: Chen Wang

Associative Color Response:
· neutral gray: quality, quiet, classic
· black: powerful, elegant,
  spatial, mysterious

Appetite Rating:
· neutral gray: poor to good
· black: excellent

Associative Taste:
· no associative tastes

Color Scheme: achromatic

An achromatic color palette can
be quite powerful. Simplistic in
its construction, this type of color
palette harmonizes well with the
typography and bottle design.

Evian
Studio: Curiosity
Creative Director/Designer:
Gwenazi Nicilas

Associative Color Response:
· dark blue: serene, quiet,
  authoritative, credible, devotion,
  security, service, nautical
· pastel blue: pleasure, peace,
  calm, quiet, hygienic, peaceful,
  refreshing, clean, cool, water

Appetite Rating:
· dark blue: excellent
· pastel blue: excellent

Associative Taste:
· no associative tastes

Color Scheme: monochromatic

When dealing with bottle packaging,
the form of the container should be of
paramount concern. There is no finer
example than the Evian 2004 design,
which is truly a remarkable piece,
both formally and conceptually. Note
how the color scheme and the shape
of the bottle act as one to create a
water droplet.

Opium
Studio: Curiosity
Creative Director/Designer:
Gwenazi Nicilas

Associative Color Response:
· earth-tone red: earthy, warm,
  wholesome, welcome, good,
  healthy, fit, sound
· yellow-orange: enterprise, drive,
  target, goal, luxuriance, cheer, joy,
  fun, excitement, stimulates

Associative Taste:
· yellow-orange: very sweet

Color Scheme: two points of a tetrad

For a successful bottling project
the shape is critical—it helps to
convey the tone and mood. Visual
signifiers carry forth messages, and
these can be broken down into three
categories—form/silhouette, color,
and tone/texture. Form/silhouette
is the most commonly used primary
signifier for any visual message,
and in bottle packaging it is the
most powerful.

Amaral Wines
Studio: Estudio Iuvaro
Art Director: Cecilia Iuvaro
Designers: Mariano Gioia,
Sebastián Yáñez

Associative Color Response:
· black: winter, percussion, spatial, powerful, elegant, mysterious
· mid-green: classic

Appetite Rating:
· black: excellent
· mid-green: excellent

Associative Taste:
· no associative tastes

Color Scheme: one hue plus neutral

Viña MontGras Winery is located near the coast in the Valle de San Antonio, Leyda, in Chile. This unique maritime climate gives the Viña Amaral white wine its unique taste, therefore the simple labeling system references the kinetic movements of the ocean. Note how the blind emboss and foil stamping give the labeling system a more sophisticated, subtle approach.

Chakana Andean Wines
Studio: Zemma & Ruiz Moreno
Designers: Santiago Zemma,
Lucila Marina Ruiz Moreno

Associative Color Response:
· high-chroma red: dramatic, stimulating, brilliant, intense, energizing, sexy
· black: winter, percussion, spatial, powerful, elegant, mysterious
· white: cleanliness, purity, clean, sterling, innocent, perfect balance, zeal, bright, pleasure

Appetite Rating:
· high-chroma red: excellent
· black: excellent
· white: excellent

Associative Taste:
· high-chroma red: very sweet

Color Scheme: one hue plus neutral and white

The jaguar was used on this label to provide intrigue. According to one Mayan myth, the jaguar is "Lord of starry nights," and this largely black label is an excellent choice to reinforce the concept, with red used very selectively in order not to oversweeten the design.

44° North Vodka
Studio: Wallace Church, Inc.
Creative Director: Stan Church
Designer: Camilla Kristiansen

Associative Color Response:
· high-chroma red: brilliant, intense, energizing, sexy, dramatic, active, stimulating, fervid, cheer, joy, fun
· dark blue: serene, quiet, authoritative, credible, devotion, security, service
· neutral gray: quality, quiet, classic, inertia, ashes, passion, practical, timeless, old age

Appetite Rating:
· high-chroma red: excellent
· dark blue: excellent
· neutral gray: poor to good

Associative Taste:
· high-chroma red: very sweet

Color Scheme: two points of a triad

The 44° North Vodka design is clean and tastefully done. The degree of latitude references the state of Idaho in the USA where the spirit is made, and the dark blue references the cool Rocky Mountain waters used in the distilling process.

Aceites Varietales Familia Zuccardi
Studio: Estudio Iuvaro
Art Director: Cecilia Iuvaro
Designers: Mariano Gioia,
Sebastián Yáñez

Associative Color Response:
· dark green: nature, mountains, lakes, natural, mature growth, trustworthy, ingenuity
· mid-green: classic

Appetite Rating:
· dark green: good
· mid-green: excellent

Associative Taste:
· no associative tastes

Color Scheme: monochromatic

A color-coding system for a variety of different blends of olive oils is created through a combination of different ink values of green and colored substrates.

Caves Vidigal
Studio: estudiocrop
Art Director: Dado Queiroz
Designers: Dado Queiroz,
Renan Molin
Photographer: Fabiano Schroden

Associative Color Response:
· dark red: rich, elegant, refined, taste, expensive, mature
· mid-range orange: gentle, entice, good spirits

Appetite Rating:
· mid-range orange: good to excellent

Associative Taste:
· mid-range orange: sweet

Color Scheme: two points of a near complementary with shading and tinting

The Caves Vidigal label is an excellent example of harmony through color and line. This is achieved in the color palette through yellow and magenta; whereas, through line, harmony is achieved by the line vernacular within all parts of the type and graphics.

Etched Turkey
Thanksgiving Wine (2004)
Studio: Wallace Church, Inc.
Creative Director: Stan Church
Designer: Akira Yasuda

Associative Color Response:
· black: powerful, elegant, mysterious, spatial
· white: refreshing, perfect balance, zeal, bright

Appetite Rating:
· black: excellent
· white: excellent

Associative Taste:
· no associative tastes

Color Scheme: direct complementary

The 2004 Thanksgiving wine-bottle design is masterfully executed through harmony and complementary colors. The black is reinforced through the color of the glass and the neck label, whereas white is used to make the mark pop off the bottle.

Valle Escondido Winery
Studio: Estudio Iuvaro
Art Director: Cecilia Iuvaro
Designers: Mariano Gioia,
Sebastián Yáñez

Associative Color Response:
· dark gray: cultured, professional, expensive, sophisticated, wise, classic,
· pastel blue: pleasure, peace, calm, quiet, clean, cool, water, hygienic, peaceful, refreshing, heavenly

Appetite Rating:
· dark gray: excellent
· pastel blue: excellent

Associative Taste:
· no associative tastes

Color Scheme: one hue with tinting and shading

Color is used in a twofold manner within this labeling system. Each variety of wine has a distinctive color palette to differentiate itself from the other wines under the same label, and to distinguish which wine is best for which season. A blind emboss is used to help create kinetic energy and continuity within the illustration across the system.

Las Perdices Range
Studio: Estudio Iuvaro
Art Director: Cecilia Iuvaro
Designers: Mariano Gioia,
Sebastián Yáñez

Associative Color Response:
· dark orange: exhilarating, inspiring, stirring, stimulating, moving, provoking, most exciting
· earth-tone red: warmhearted, welcome, good, healthy, fit, sound
· high-chroma pink: stimulates, aggressive, genial, exciting, happy, high, fun, excitement, sensual, cheer, joy

Appetite Rating:
· high-chroma pink: excellent

Associative Taste:
· high-chroma pink: very sweet

Color Scheme: one hue plus neutral

The use of color as a branding vehicle differentiates the variety of wines under the same label. Copper-foil stamping and a blind emboss create further visual separation within a labeling system that creates its own vernacular.

Séptima Rosé Wine
Studio: Zemma & Ruiz Moreno
Designers: Santiago Zemma,
Lucila Marina Ruiz Moreno

Associative Color Response:
· dark orange: exhilarating, inspiring, stirring, stimulating, moving, provoking
· mid-range pink-red: restrained, toned down, soft, subdued, quiet
· black: elegant, classic

Appetite Rating:
· mid-range pink-red: good
· black: excellent

Associative Taste:
· mid-range pink-red: sweet

Color Scheme: one hue plus neutral with shading

The color of the wine plays the dominant role in establishing the color palette here, and each hue in the label works in concert with it. The white labels suggest purity and freshness and function well on a clear bottle that does not alter the natural hue of the wine.

Pazzo
Creative Director: David Schwemann

Associative Color Response:
· high-chroma red: brilliant, intense, energizing, sexy, dramatic, stimulating
· high-chroma yellow: agreeable, pleasant, welcome, vigorous, noble, youthful energy
· black: powerful, elegant, mysterious, spatial

Appetite Rating:
· high-chroma red: excellent
· high-chroma yellow: good
· black: excellent

Associative Taste:
· high-chroma red: very sweet
· high-chroma yellow: very sweet

Color Scheme: two points of a tetrad plus neutral

This unusual labeling system is highly kinetic through its use of color, form, and line. Superbly done, the Pazzo graphics are a visual feast.

Red Rover 2004 Merlot
Creative Director: David Schwemann

Associative Color Response:
· high-chroma red: brilliant, intense, energizing, sexy, dramatic, stimulating
· high-chroma orange: cleanliness, producing, healing, tasty, growing
· black: powerful, elegant, mysterious, spatial

Appetite Rating:
· high-chroma red: excellent
· high-chroma orange: excellent
· black: excellent

Associative Taste:
· high-chroma red: very sweet
· high-chroma orange: very sweet

Color Scheme: two points of a split complementary plus neutral

The simplistic color palette in combination with the typography and illustration create a unique labeling system. The symmetrical arrangement of type and image creates a strong focal point in conjunction with the bold-red neck label and high-chroma orange label, making this design explode visually off the shelf.

The Fine Cheese Co.

Studio: Irving
Designer: Julian Roberts
Illustrators: Karen Murray, Julian Roberts

This beautiful packaging series harks back to the time of woodblock illustrations and letterpress technology. Although printed using modern methods, this design approach serves the client well. By using or emulating older techniques, the physicality of the design immediately imbues it with a classic and timeless appearance. In using such historical perspective, the Fine Cheese Cracker Series becomes a masterfully executed strategy that ultimately connotes quality.

History is a great teacher, and, as seen here, can be used to create a conceptual strategy. It is a retro piece—retro being

where historical movements and styles are referenced as a formal and conceptual strategy to help connote a tailored message. In this case, the act of referencing requires a thorough understanding of the technological advancements of the day, including all of the processes, methodology, and the overall philosophy found within particular movements and styles. Armed with this knowledge, history can be used as an effective tool to create compelling design such as this.

A two-color job was specified for the Natural, Wholemeal, and Charcoal Crackers packaging; however, the white of the paper was utilized to create an additional third color. All three containers used the strategy of four-side bleeding. (A bleed is where ink is printed beyond the borders of the format, allowing the paper to be cut or chopped to size giving

the appearance, in this case, that the original paper color is pink, turquoise-green, or gray.) This technique allows the white of the paper to appear as though it is ink being used in the printing process, thus stretching the color palette. The Mustard and Black Pepper: For Mature Cheddar Crackers is also a two-color job; however, by using screen tinting six distinctive hues are created. With that said, the screen tints are constrained masterfully to keep the continuity of the packaging series intact. In this case, the raw paper color is used in the same manner as the bleeding inks found in the Natural, Wholemeal, and Charcoal Cracker boxes. The same could be said for the Caraway and Walnut Cracker boxes—these packages use three and four inks, but the color palette is constrained, and the raw paper color is skillfully used to achieve continuity.

Note: With any package-design work the physicality of the project can be broken down into seven categories: concept, type, image/illustration, grid, composition, three-dimensional form, and, most importantly, color. When dealing with a package design or a package-design series, how well the seven categories are braided with each other will create continuity or not. For example, if all seven categories are treated in the same manner, the packaging will be inherently boring. If all are different, continuity is nonexistent and chaos will ensue. The trick to any successful, visually stimulating design is to create a balancing act between the seven categories.

Sandy's Sweets

Art Director: John T. Drew
Designer: Dean Ethington

The tin design for Sandy's Sweets cookies and brownies was developed with a low budget in mind. The client specified a two-color job along with the tin size and make. To further lower the cost of printing, the design team created a package design that could not only be put together by a commercial printing plant, but could also be easily pieced together by the client. Ultimately this would reduce the amount of tins that needed to be ordered at a given time.

The exterior labeling consists of two, two-color crack-and-peel labels, one large on the top of the tin, and one small to hold the paper band on the side. To further reduce costs, the paper band had no printing on it, and the colored paper could be used with any of the cookie or brownie flavors—the color was part of the overall color scheme. In other words, there is only one color change per flavor, and no die cutting is required for the paper band—it is a straight guillotine cut. Color choice was based on an indexical reference of the ingredients used to create the product—in this case, brown for chocolate and magenta for raspberry.

All forms of metal are great conductors of condensation, therefore, if no liner is designed for the inside of a tin, there is a risk that the product inside will get wet and stick to the packaging. In this case, to minimize the cost of the inside liners, there was virtually no printing. The exceptions were the order form and the horizontal liners that divided the stacks. Furthermore, the order form could be substituted for the horizontal liners. Both the horizontal liner and order form could be printed either commercially or through desktop publishing, such as an inkjet printer. The job was designed this way to further reduce printing cost while at the same time giving the consumer multiple chances to order directly from Sandy's Sweets. The interior liners were sealed with a single crack-and-peel label, minimizing piecemeal work. All liners were designed with straight die cuts in mind for ease of production.

Modeled after Japanese packaging, the multiple layers of paper inside need to be unfolded or removed before reaching a single cookie or brownie. This ritual has a psychological effect on the consumer, making the cookie or brownie seem semiprecious and therefore more valuable. Unlike Western packaging (immediate and common), this allows the manufacturer to charge more for their product simply because it is perceived to have a greater value.

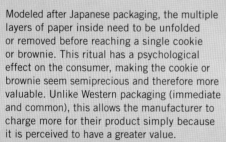

Three Colors

Three-color package design is a rare category of work. It is true that three-color work is less expensive than four-color process; however, the cost benefit these days is negligible, so why is three-color work still undertaken? Three-color package design falls in line with one- and two-color jobs. A mastering of color, shape, imagery, typography, concept, and composition need to work uniquely in tandem to create high-end design. Without this concert of parts the package design would appear cheap and inexpensive.

Any three-color job—be it a logo, annual report, brochure, T-shirt design, or package design—creates a high level of hue flexibility. For example, cyan, magenta, and yellow create all the different high-chroma hues found within the 12-step color wheel. With the added technique of overprinting, a solid understanding of color theory, and a pragmatic understanding of ink opacity and hue mixing, three-color package design can create a striking impact. Couple hue flexibility with the psychological and learned behavioral effects of color, and the most powerful tool available to designers is created. Make no doubt about it, color sells your product.

Paddywax Destinations
Studio: Principle
Art Director: Pamela Zuccker
Designer: Jennifer Sukis
Photographer: Kara Brennan © 2007

Associative Color Response:
· brown: calm, pleasing, rich, thought-provoking, serenity
· orange: warm, cleanliness, joy, happy

Color Scheme: simple analogous with shading

This wonderfully executed package design uses color to convey a cohesive whole across the overall system and uses hue to signify the individual fragrances within it. Sparing no expense, the materials used coupled with the overall design strategy signifies quality and imbues consumer confidence.

Paddywax Jolie
Studio: Principle
Art Director: Pamela Zuccker
Designer: Ally Gerson
Photographer: Kara Brennan © 2007

Associative Color Response:
· pastel green: completely, calm, quiet, smoothing, natural
· green-yellow: new growth
· high-chroma pink: stimulates, aggressive, genial, exciting, happy

Color Scheme: complementary with tinting

Color sells your product. There is no finer example than this package design. Complementary color schemes with tinting are used for each individual packaging, creating a highly kinetic design. Pattern is used to create stability and continuity within the system.

Babu
Art Director/Designer: Chris Walden

Associative Color Response:
· mid-range pink-red: restrained, toned down, soft
· mid-green: classic
· high-chroma blue: spaciousness, dignity, cool, electric, energetic

Appetite Rating:
· mid-range pink-red: good
· mid-green: excellent
· high-chroma blue: poor to good

Associative Taste:
· mid-range pink-red: sweet

Color Scheme: analogous with tinting, shading, and black

This is an excellent example of a simple analogous color palette with tinting and shading. Black is used to give the color palette density and visual separation. White, in this case, is the color of the substrate and would be considered a hue within the color palette, but would create no additional cost when printing. The design is an excellent color study for examining the legibility of type when reversed out to the substrate.

Rasta Mind International
Studio: estudiocrop
Art Director/Designer: Dado Queiroz
Photographer: Fabiano Schroden

Associative Color Response:
· high-chroma red: brilliant, sexy, intense, energizing, dramatic, stimulating
· black: powerful, elegant, mysterious, heavy, basic
· white: cleanliness, purity, clean, sterling

Color Scheme: one hue with white and black

This package is a simple, elegant, and clean design, in which texture is used as a visual magnet within the typography. The anatomical structure of the typography is well chosen, the width-to-height ratio is proportionate to the format of the box, thus creating harmony.

AromaFloria
Art Director: Tanya Quick
Designer: Fernando Munoz

Associative Color Response:
· mid-range pink-red: restrained, toned down, soft, subdued, quiet
· high-chroma orange: healing, tasty, growing, fire, warm, cleanliness, cheerfulness
· high-chroma green: life, use, springtime, infancy, motion, ebbing of life

Color Scheme: Analogous with tinting, shading, and black

The AromaFloria package design series is wonderfully executed, using a multitude of substrates, including plastic, glass, tin, paper, and wood. The color scheme unifies the design and the different substrates, while also color coding all the components. Note: A die cut is used so that the wooden stick can act as a lock for the paper packaging.

King Delight: Grilled Chicken Wrap
Creative Director: Micha Goes
Designer: Andi Friedl

Associative Color Response:
· high-chroma orange: healing, tasty, warm, cleanliness, cheerfulness
· high-chroma green-yellow: new growth, lemony, tart, fruity

Appetite Rating:
· high-chroma orange: excellent
· high-chroma green-yellow: excellent

Associative Taste:
· high-chroma orange: very sweet

Color Scheme: two points of a triad

Going against color conventions, the King Delight package design won the 2004 Food Service Award, despite using a high-chroma greenish-yellow hue that is not generally considered appropriate for meat products. However, the color is not juxtaposed with the product, therefore no unwanted psychological effects occur—a brilliant strategy to use the psychological and learned behavioral properties of the hue without incurring any of the negatives associated with it.

Choklad Platts
Studio: dododesign.se
Art Director/Designer: Dejan Mauzer

Associative Color Response:
· dark red: rich, elegant, refined, taste, expensive, mature, earthy
· high-chroma yellow-orange: fun, enterprise, drive, target, goal, luxuriance, cheer, joy, excitement
· high-chroma red: brilliant, intense, energizing

Appetite Rating:
· dark red: poor
· high-chroma yellow-orange: excellent
· high-chroma red: excellent

Associative Taste:
· high-chroma yellow-orange: very sweet
· high-chroma red: very sweet

Color Scheme: analogous with tinting and shading

The playful use of the typography coupled with the vibrant colors creates a highly dynamic composition. The muted dark red allows the high-chroma yellow and orange to pop on the box, creating a three-dimensional illusion on a two-dimensional plane. The swirls and the background converge underneath the focal point of the composition to lift the name off the page.

Arla Maelk
Designer: Jens Dreier

Associative Color Response:
· black: basic, neutral, cold, classic, strong
· white: light, cool, snow, cleanliness, purity, clean, sterling, innocent
· high-chroma green-yellow: new growth
· high-chroma bluish-purple: classic, powerful
· earth tone: delicious, deep, rich, warm, folksy
· high-chroma yellow-orange: cheer, joy, fun, excitement, stimulates

Appetite Rating:
· black: excellent
· white: excellent
· high-chroma green-yellow: excellent
· high-chroma bluish-purple: excellent
· earth tone: excellent
· high-chroma yellow-orange: excellent

Associative Taste:
· high-chroma yellow-orange: very sweet

Color Scheme: incongruous

Simple and classic color combinations are used in conjunction with a highly kinetic illustration to create impact on the shelf. White is used for whole milk, brown for chocolate milk, and a bluish-purple for low-fat milk.

Love Glove
Art Director/Designer: Chapman Tse

Associative Color Response:
· high-chroma red: surging,
  brilliant, intense, energizing, sexy,
  dramatic, stimulating, active,
  cheer, joy, fun
· high-chroma orange: producing,
  healing, tasty, growing, fire, warm,
  cleanliness, cheerfulness
· earth tone: rustics, delicious, deep,
  rich, warm, folksy, rooted, life

Color Scheme: analogous with
shading

An excellent example of a simple
analogous color palette with shading,
the Love Glove package design is
beautifully executed. The shutter
top with die-cut sides allows the
consumer to preview the product.
With an inner box (shown top),
the rigidity for crush resistance
is improved during shipping.

See's Candy
Art Director: John T. Drew
Designer: Sachi Ito

Associative Color Response:
· high-chroma yellow-orange: fun,
  enterprise, drive, target, goal,
  luxuriance, cheer, joy, excitement
· high-chroma red: brilliant,
  intense, energizing, sexy,
  dramatic, stimulating
· black: powerful, elegant,
  mysterious, heavy, basic, neutral

Appetite Rating:
· high-chroma yellow-orange:
  excellent
· high-chroma red: excellent
· black: excellent

Associative Taste:
· high-chroma yellow-orange:
  very sweet
· high-chroma red: very sweet

Color Scheme: two points of a tetrad
plus neutral

By adding a thread to the exterior
of the package design, a tactile
experience is created. The more
senses involved in opening
a package design, the more
memorable the design will be.

How To Make You Own Candle
Art Director: Mary Ann McLaughlin
Designer: Mashael Al Sulaiti

Associative Color Response:
· high-chroma red: brilliant,
  intense, energizing, sexy,
  dramatic, stimulating
· black: powerful, elegant,
  mysterious, heavy, basic, neutral
· high-chroma orange: producing,
  healing, tasty, growing, fire, warm,
  cleanliness, cheerfulness, masculine
· blue-green: pristine, cleanliness,
  pure, serious

Color Scheme: one hue plus neutral

The substrate is primarily an orange
hue that has been tinted and shaded
to an earth-tone red, creating a near
analogous color palette with the
red and orange hues with which it
harmonizes well. The turquoise is
a near complementary color palette
with the substrate.

Droobles Bubble Gum
Art Director: John T. Drew
Designer: Rachel Pearson

Associative Color Response:
· pastel blue: refreshing, clean,
  cool, water
· dark blue: basic, confident,
  classic, strong
· high-chroma blue: height, lively,
  pleasing, rich

Appetite Rating:
· pastel blue: good
· dark blue: excellent
· high-chroma blue: poor to good

Associative Taste:
· no associative tastes

Color Scheme: monochromatic

This simple, but eloquently
conceived monochromatic study
is refreshingly reinforced through
the typographic specimen chosen,
texture, and line work.

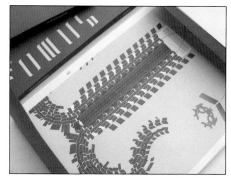

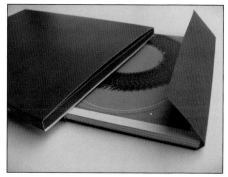

Focus
Studio: Mostardesign Studio
Art Director/Designer: Olivier Gourvat

Associative Color Response:
· high-chroma red: surging,
  brilliant, intense, energizing, sexy,
  dramatic, stimulating
· white: purity, clean, sterling,
  innocent, silent, inexplicable,
  normality, life, work, school
· bluish-purple: powerful,
  regal, classic

Color Scheme: two points of a tetrad
with white

Intensely beautiful, the Mostardesign
Focus packaging consists of 15
illustrations generated by the
studio as a self-promotional piece.
A plastic red Mylar, duplex, and a
high-chroma white cover-weight
paper is used to help expand the
color palette and to frame the work.

The Possum Trot Orchestra
Harbor Road
Studio: One Lucky Guitar, Inc.
Art Directors: Matt Kelley, John Minton

Associative Color Response:
· pastel blue: pleasure, calm, quiet,
  hygienic, peaceful, refreshing
· white: purity, clean, sterling,
  innocent, silent, inexplicable,
  normality, life, work, school
· dark orange: exhilarating, passive,
  inspiring, stirring, stimulating,
  moving, provoking, most exciting,

Color Scheme: near complementary
with shading

This near complementary palette is
a wonderful example of a push-pull
technique when expanding unique
color palettes. The pastel blue is
shaded to darken the hue slightly
and, in this case, pull it forward.
The red-orange has a large amount
of shading combined with tinting
to push the hue back. Generally, cool
colors recede and warm colors come
forward. However, the effect of colors
depends on their context, and in this
unusual color combination, the norm
is reversed.

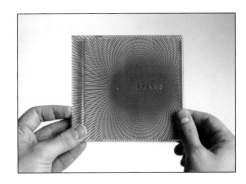

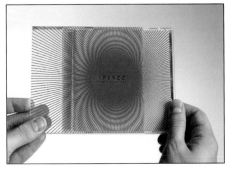

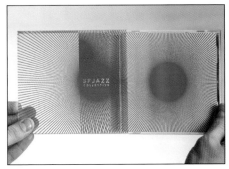

Pophaus Type Foundry
Art Director: John T. Drew
Designer: Lydia Adi

Associative Color Response:
· high-chroma red: excitability, solid, aggression, provocative, strength
· high-chroma yellow: agreeable, pleasant, welcome, vigorous, noble, youthful energy, speed, movement
· high-chroma blue: sobriety, calm, height, lively, pleasing, rich, levels, vertical, honesty, strength, work

Color Scheme: primaries

A self-promotional piece, the Pophaus Type Foundry buttons and the companion palm brochure—a nonfolding brochure that fits in the hand—are wonderfully conceived. Here, the information on the brochure is printed on the back, and the buttons are held in place by inserting the needle through the palm brochure.

Avon Planet Spa
Art Director: Tanya Quick
Designer: Fernando Munoz

Associative Color Response:
· earth-tone orange: earthy, warm, wholesome, welcome, good, healthy, fit, sound
· black: winter, percussion, spatial, powerful, elegant, mysterious

Color Scheme: monochromatic plus neutral

This series is an interesting example of both a monochromatic study and a simple analogous color palette. A white varnish is applied to the bottles and tubes to give it a sand-blasted-glass feel. A monochromatic and simple analogous color palette will always harmonize, making for a restful experience.

**SF Jazz Collective for
Nonesuch Records**
Studio: Doyle Partners

Associative Color Response:
· high-chroma pink: stimulates, aggressive, genial, exciting, happy, high, fun, excitement, attention-getting
· high-chroma yellow-green: lemony, tart, fruity, acidic, sharp, bold, trendy, strength, sunlight, biology
· high-chroma bluish-purple: regal, classic, expensive, powerful, tender, longing, elegant, mystical, spiritual

Color Scheme: primary and two secondaries (incongruous)

The SF Jazz Collective is directed by Joshua Redman and features legendary vibes-player Bobby Hutcherson. For this live recording, the goal was to package the excitement of the performance without appearing to be a traditional jazz album. Two hundred straight lines are arranged in a spiral and printed on a translucent cover and then again on the booklet inside. By sliding the jewel case out of the cover, a lively psychedelic effect is created.

Right Guard (The Dial Corporation)
Studio: Wallace Church, Inc.
Creative Director: Stan Church
Designer: John Bruno

Associative Color Response:
· dark blue: serene, quiet, authoritative, credible, devotion, security, service
· high-chroma yellow: agreeable, pleasant, welcome, vigorous, noble, youthful energy, speed, movement
· high-chroma yellow-green: lemony, tart, fruity, acidic, sharp, bold, trendy, strength, sunlight, biology
· high-chroma blue: dignity, spaciousness, sobriety, calm, height, lively, pleasing, rich
· high-chroma reddish-purple: sweet taste, subtle, restlessness, prolongs life, feminine elegance, tender longing, romanticism

Color Scheme: Incongruous

Gillette enlisted Wallace Church to help refresh the brand's True Blue essence and more effectively target both core brand users and the new Xtreme consumer. The communication hierarchy and composition was optimized to better promote the energized Right Guard brandmark. Textured backgrounds and updated icons were incorporated to communicate a contemporary masculine image, while Xtreme's glowing X was amplified to signal a more youthful experience.

Epona
Studio: Alian Design
Art Director/Designer: Ian Shimkoviak

Associative Color Response:
· high-chroma orange: producing, healing, tasty, growing, fire, warm, cleanliness, cheerfulness, masculine
· high-chroma yellow-orange: enterprise, drive, target, goal, luxuriance, cheer, joy, fun, excitement, stimulates, aggressive, powerful, energy
· high-chroma blue: dignity, spaciousness, sobriety, calm, height, lively, pleasing, rich

Color Scheme: direct complementary

This is an awesome example of understanding how to use color for shelf recognition. The direct color complementary color palette utilizes a warm and cool color scheme making the labeling system explode off the bottle. The analogous color palettes in a number of the labels are tinted less than 40 percent of their opacity to create a dramatic contrast differential from the bottle.

Key Underwear Packs
Studio: Deser
Art Director/Designer: M. Piotrowski

Associative Color Response:
· high-chroma blue: dignity, spaciousness, sobriety, calm, height, lively, pleasing, rich
· silver: futuristic, cool, expensive, money, valuable, classic
· high-chroma yellow: friendly, hot, luminous, energy, magnanimity, intuition, intellect, loudest, brightest, young

Color Scheme: primaries plus neutral

This package is a great example of using two different types of substrate to achieve the visual impact desired. Printed graphics on paper are inserted into a clear plastic tube to achieve high-quality graphics and to emulate a third type of substrate—a metal container.

Deep Herbal
Studio: Fuelhaus
Art Director: Kellie Schroeder
Designer: Ty Webb

Associative Color Response:
· dark red: rich, elegant, refined, taste, expensive, mature, earthy, strong
· dark green: nature, mountains, lakes, natural, mature growth, versatility, traditional
· white: inexplicable, normality, work

Color Scheme: direct complementary with shading

This design is a great example of how to use the same hues in different arrangements to create multiple color studies. By using different proportions of colors and placement, the same hue palette can potentially be used for a range of products, branding the product through color, but achieving diversity through proportion and placement.

Franck Coffee, Zagreb
Studio: Design B
Art Director/Designer: Boris Ljubicic
Photographers/Illustrators:
Boris Ljubicic, Igor Masnjak

Associative Color Response:
· high-chroma red: surging,
  brilliant, intense, energizing,
  sexy, dramatic, stimulating,
  fervid, active, cheer, joy, fun
· dark green: nature, mountains,
  lakes, natural, mature growth,
  versatility, traditional, money,
  trustworthy, refreshing
· gold: warm, opulent, expensive,
  radiant, valuable, prestigious

Appetite Rating:
· high-chroma red: excellent
· dark green: good
· gold: excellent

Associative Taste:
· high-chroma red: very sweet

Color Scheme: direct complementary
with shading plus white

The Franck coffee package design
is a wonderful example of a direct
complementary color palette being
used to create diversity within a
product line. Three hues (dark green,
red, and gold) are proportionately
changed to create brand recognition
for each product within the line.

wasp
Studio: design@qirk.com
Designer: Daryl Geary

Associative Color Response:
· high-chroma orange: cheerful, lively, exciting, bright, luminous, tasty, growing, fire, warm, cleanliness, cheerfulness
· high-chroma yellow-green: lemony, tart, fruity, acidic, sharp, bold, trendy, strength, sunlight, biology
· high-chroma reddish-purple: subtle, sweet taste, exciting, sensual
· high-chroma blue: height, lively, pleasing, rich, cold, wet

Appetite Rating:
· high-chroma orange: excellent
· high-chroma yellow-green: excellent
· high-chroma reddish-purple: excellent
· high-chroma blue: good

Associative Taste:
· high-chroma orange: very sweet
· high-chroma yellow-green: very sweet, lemony

Color Scheme: tetrad

A true high-chroma tetrad, the Wasp Energy Drink utilizes brand recognition through color in a masterful way. Note how the hues are even injected into the drink itself, branding the product without the need for graphics or typography.

Briannas
Studio: The Hively Agency
Art Director/Designer: Sarah Munt

Associative Color Response:
· black: powerful, elegant, mysterious, classic
· earth tone: rustics, delicious, deep, rich, warm, folksy, rooted, life, work, wholesome
· high-chroma orange: healing, tasty, growing, fire, warm, cleanliness, cheerfulness
· dark red: rich, elegant, refined, taste, expensive, mature, earthy, strong, warm, ripe
· high-chroma reddish-purple: sweet taste, subtle, tender longing, romanticism, exciting, sensual
· mid-green: nature, mountains, lakes, natural, mature growth, versatility, traditional

Appetite Rating:
· black: excellent
· earth tone: good
· high-chroma orange: excellent
· high-chroma reddish-purple: excellent
· mid-green: good

Associative Taste:
· high-chroma orange: very sweet

Color Scheme: two points of a split complementary with shading

The symmetrical balance, typographic arrangement, and color scheme stays consistent with the typographical arrangement, allowing for greater flexibility within the illustrations. Each illustration creates a strong focal point to promote shelf recognition.

Perla Beer
Studio: DESer
Art Director/Designer: M. Piotrowski

Associative Color Response:
· high-chroma red: surging, sexy, brilliant, intense, energizing, dramatic, stimulating
· high-chroma green: life, use, motion, ebbing of life, springtime, infancy, wilderness, fresh
· gold: warm, opulent, expensive, radiant, valuable, prestigious

Appetite Rating:
· high-chroma red: excellent
· high-chroma green: excellent
· gold: excellent

Associative Taste:
· high-chroma red: very sweet

Color Scheme: direct complementary with gold

The direct complementary color palette used here conveys an organic feel, and the line work found within the graphics is reminiscent of farm fields. The red shield and band pop off the cooler green background allowing for ease of readability and brand recognition.

Mossback
Studio: CF NAPA
Creative Director: David Schwemann

Associative Color Response:
· gold: warm, opulent, expensive, radiant, valuable, prestigious
· high-chroma red: surging, brilliant, intense, energizing, sexy, dramatic, stimulating
· high-chroma yellow-orange: enterprise, drive, target, goal, luxuriance, cheer, joy, fun, excitement, stimulates
· high-chroma orange: producing, healing, tasty, growing, fire, warm, cleanliness, cheerfulness, masculine, fearlessness, curiosity

Appetite Rating:
· gold: excellent
· high-chroma red: excellent
· high-chroma yellow-orange: excellent
· high-chroma orange: excellent

Associative Taste:
· high-chroma red: very sweet
· high-chroma yellow-orange: very sweet
· high-chroma orange: very sweet

Color Scheme: complex analogous with shading plus neutral

UV ink is used on the label to create texture and depth. The natural color of the wine combined with the dark-green bottle creates the hue black that harmonizes perfectly with the labeling system.

Vagabond
Studio: CF NAPA
Creative Director: David Schwemann

Associative Color Response:
· high-chroma red: surging,
  brilliant, intense, energizing, sexy,
  dramatic, stimulating, fervid,
  active, cheer, joy, fun, aggressive
· high-chroma orange: producing,
  healing, tasty, growing, fire, warm,
  cleanliness, cheerfulness, masculine
· high-chroma yellow-orange: fun,
  joy, enterprise, drive, target, goal,
  luxuriance, cheer, excitement,
  stimulates, aggressive, powerful
· black: percussion, spatial,
  powerful, elegant, mysterious

Appetite Rating:
· high-chroma red: excellent
· high-chroma orange: excellent
· high-chroma yellow-orange:
  excellent
· black: excellent

Associative Taste:
· high-chroma red: very sweet
· high-chroma orange: very sweet
· high-chroma yellow-orange:
  very sweet

Color Scheme: analogous plus black

The warm analogous color palette
pops off the black glass. Note
how the black outlines within the
illustration tie into the color of the
bottle and neck label.

Be Friends
Studio: Zemma & Ruiz Moreno

Associative Color Response:
· gold: warm, opulent, expensive,
  radiant, valuable, prestigious
· earth tone: deep, rich, warm
· black: winter, percussion, spatial,
  powerful, elegant, mysterious

Appetite Rating:
· gold: excellent
· earth tone: good
· black: excellent

Associative Taste:
· no associative tastes

Color Scheme: simple analogous
plus black

The labeling system is sophisticated
and elegant, conveyed through
a bronze-and-gold hue. The gold
honeybee is foil stamped to convey
the same connotations as a crescent
shield, whereas the typographic
composition and font structure
is clean.

Captain Morgan Private Stock
Studio: SandorMax
Designer: Zoltan Csillag

Associative Color Response:
· high-chroma yellow-orange:
  enterprise, drive, target, goal,
  luxuriance, cheer, joy, fun,
  excitement, stimulates
· high-chroma red: brilliant,
  intense, energizing, sexy,
  dramatic, stimulating
· black: winter, percussion, spatial,
  powerful, elegant, mysterious

Appetite Rating:
· high-chroma yellow-orange:
  excellent
· high-chroma red: excellent
· black: excellent

Associative Taste:
· high-chroma yellow-orange:
  very sweet
· high-chroma red: very sweet

Color Scheme: analogous with
shading plus a black hue

Concept designs for the launch of
Captain Morgan's Premium Rum,
Private Stock. Note how sampling
the color of the rum creates the
foundation of the color palette.

Turning Leaves Thanksgiving Wine
Studio: Wallace Church, Inc.
Creative Director: Stan Church
Designer: Nin Glaister

Associative Color Response:
· high-chroma yellow-orange:
  enterprise, drive, target, goal,
  luxuriance, cheer, joy, fun,
  excitement, stimulates
· high-chroma orange: producing,
  healing, tasty, growing, fire, warm,
  cleanliness, cheerfulness
· dark-red family: rich, elegant,
  refined, taste, expensive, mature
· high-chroma red: surging, sexy,
  brilliant, intense, energizing,
  dramatic, stimulating

Appetite Rating:
· high-chroma yellow-orange:
  excellent
· high-chroma orange: excellent
· high-chroma red: excellent

Associative Taste:
· high-chroma yellow-orange:
  very sweet
· high-chroma orange: very sweet
· high-chroma red: very sweet

Color Scheme: analogous plus black

This complex analogous color
scheme is beautifully executed on
black glass to create an incredible
design. Note how the label wraps
around each bottle, working on
a micro level, and when placed
together the label works on a
macro level by creating a much
larger labeling system for viewing
at a distance.

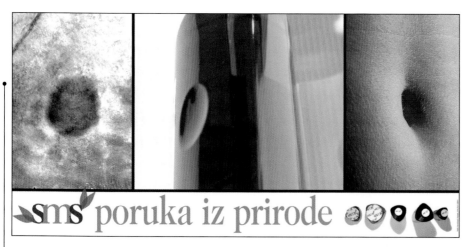

sms poruka iz prirode

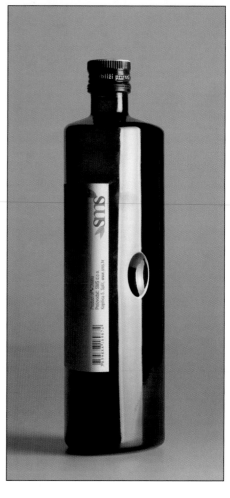

SMS
Studio: International
Art Director/Designer/Photographer:
Boris Ljubicic

Associative Color Response:
· high-chroma red: surging, sexy,
  brilliant, intense, energizing,
  dramatic, stimulating
· high-chroma orange: producing,
  healing, tasty, growing, fire, warm,
  cleanliness, cheerfulness
· dark green: nature, mountains,
  lakes, natural, mature growth,
  versatility, traditional, money,
  trustworthy, refreshing
· silver: futuristic, cool, expensive,
  money, valuable, classic

Appetite Rating:
· high-chroma red: excellent
· high-chroma orange: excellent
· dark green: good
· silver: excellent

Associative Taste:
· high-chroma red: very sweet
· high-chroma orange: very sweet

Color Scheme: near analogous with
a complementary green and blue

The design of the SMS olive oil
bottle is rooted in the legend of
how the St. Peter's Fish got its name.
When St. Peter was baptizing people,
he rolled up his pant legs to let some
fish swim through. As they passed
he noticed an unusual looking one. He
reached down, grabbed the fish, and
said, "You will be called the same as
I." This is why the fish has one black
stain on its left side and four lines on
its right side—the marks of a thumb
and four fingers. To represent this,
the bottle has a concave imprint
that operates as a unique ergonomic
design. This beautifully conceived
design relates culturally to the
product's branding.

U'luvka Vodka
Studio: Aloof Design
Art Director: Sam Aloof
Designer: Andrew Scrase,
Jon Hodkinson

Associative Color Response:
· silver: futuristic, cool, expensive,
  money, valuable, classic
· black: winter, percussion, spatial,
  powerful, elegant, mysterious,
  heavy, basic
· earth tone: deep, rich, warm,
  durable, secure

Appetite Rating:
· black: excellent
· silver: excellent
· earth tone: excellent

Associative Taste:
· no associative tastes

Color Scheme: near achromatic

U'luvka Vodka is an exceptional
package system for the luxury
market. Black, brown, silver, and
a spot varnish create a unique color
scheme that is delicately executed.
The unique bottle designs and
custom packaging create an air of
quality that is unsurpassed within
this marketplace, making U'luvka
Vodka an extremely successful
branding strategy.

Echoes of Summer
Studio: Bohoy Design
Creative Director/Designer:
Johnanna Bohoy

Associative Color Response:
· gold: warm, opulent, expensive,
  radiant, valuable, prestigious
· high-chroma red: surging, hope,
  brilliant, intense, energizing, sexy,
  dramatic, stimulating, fervid,
  active, cheer, joy, fun, aggressive
· high-chroma yellow: anticipation,
  agreeable, pleasant, welcome,
  vigorous, noble, youthful energy

Appetite Rating:
· gold: excellent
· high-chroma red: excellent
· high-chroma yellow: good

Associative Taste:
· high-chroma red: very sweet
· high-chroma yellow: very sweet

Color Scheme: warm incongruous

A color palette that conveys the taste
of summer; the Echoes of Summer
fruit jams, chutneys, and fruit
butters have a glowing sun behind
the single fruit with a gold cap, gold
bottom border, and gold type that
complement yellow and red.

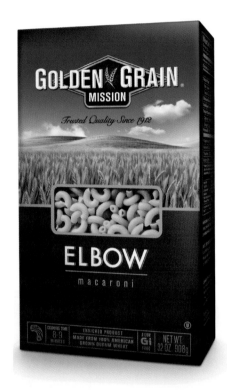

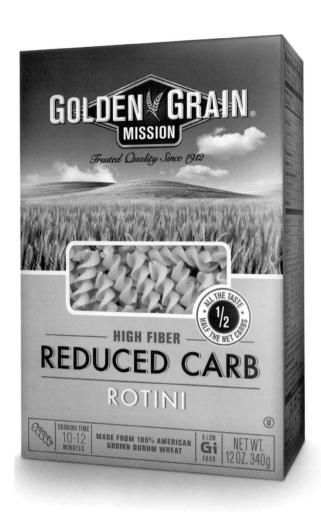

Golden Grain Mission Pasta

Wallace Church: Golden Grain Mission
and Mueller's pasta
Project: Mueller's Pasta
Studio: Wallace Church
Creative Director: Stan Church
Designer: Jeremy Creighton
Project: Golden Grain Mission Pasta
Studio: Wallace Church
Creative Director: Stan Church
Designer: Clare Reece-Raybould

Both Golden Grain Mission and Mueller's
pasta by Wallace Church use a classic triadic
color scheme of red, blue, and yellow. Although
strictly speaking this is a four-color job, it is
an interesting study because it exemplifies the
diversity that can be achieved with the same
three primary colors. Given that three-color

printing is no longer significantly cheaper
than four color, the designers used this triadic
simply to reinforce the brand recognition of
each product. Thus, when presented with the
packages a consumer will quickly identify
the products as pasta, but have very diverse
brand associations tied to each package. This
is accomplished through many methodological
steps, but three steps are most often credited
with significantly impacting and establishing
a brand: value of color, relative quantity of
color, and assignment of color.

When confronted with the use of similar
colors, the first step is to subtly change the
relative value of each color. Shades (made
by the addition of black to a color), tints (the
addition of white to a color), and secondary
colors (the mixing of two primary colors) will
dramatically change the perception.

For example, in both packages red and
yellow are mixed to create a secondary warm
yellow. A shade is added to create a brown
that adds depth through tone (the addition
of gray). The secondary colors and the
shades create a warm yellow-brown that
suggests a rustic quality to the wheat
grain—this is an excellent choice of color
based on a knowledge of learned behavioral
and/or psychological effects of color. This
color also has an excellent appetite rating
for baked goods, and a good-to-excellent
rating for food. For that matter, white also has
an excellent appetite rating (see Chapter 10).

Tints are used more selectively. For
example, Mueller's package does not tint
the blue. Instead, a high-chroma blue is
used together with a light tint of yellow to
signify golden shafts of wheat in the field.

In contrast, the Golden Grain package uses tints of blue and yellow to create depth in the fields of grain and the glow of a sky-blue summer's day. This use of color conceptually reinforces the product's name and image as a high-quality grain grown in a pristine pastoral environment.

The second step to differentiate further similar color schemes should be to vary the quantities of each color used within the overall packaging scheme. Mueller's pasta creates an emblematic US flag with its broad band of white, gray-toned star, and clean stripes of blue and red. Of the primary colors, yellow is used selectively as an accent color on the Mueller packaging, whereas on the Golden Grain Mission Pasta package, yellow or red nearly covers two-thirds of the design. The predominant use of white on the Mueller's

packaging is clean and crisp—almost al dente— and the warm reds and yellows of the Golden Grain Mission Pasta package are welcoming, rather like an idyllic farm.

The third step is to assign different colors to the foreground, middle ground, and background on each design. Again, Mueller's packaging consistently uses white dramatically to cover two-thirds of the background on each package within the series. When viewed in a row, the alternating middle-ground colors of red and blue will appear to undulate like a waving flag. Golden Grain Mission Pasta uses an image that references a line from the patriotic hymn "America the Beautiful"—"amber waves of grain"—to define the background setting. With a number of packages placed side by side on a supermarket shelf, the image will reference the big blue sky and seemingly endless fields of

grain one witnesses while traveling through the American "heartland" or "bread basket." Its middle ground fades into the expansive landscape, while subtly differentiating the pasta varieties offered. Both packages reference "all-American" qualities in uniquely defined methods that compound the identifying characteristics of each brand, while using golden-yellow and white to highlight the foreground and accent the type.

Red Ambrosia:
Collection Sensual de Corps

Studio: Arcadia Studio SF
Designer/Creative Director: Isabelle Guérin-Groelz

Strictly speaking, the Collection Sensual de Corps' package series is a two-color job, however, the techniques of tinting, overprinting, and shading create three distinct hues for every individual box and its associated labeling. Each box, together with its companion pieces, create a unique color palette that is distinctive. Continuity is brought about through the form of the box, its interior presentation, and overall styling. This elegant box construction is designed and fashioned to emulate the handcrafted sensibilities of the Ukiyo-e and Art Nouveau movements, and a timeless package-design series is created that not only communicates quality, but also becomes a desirable and collectible object itself.

When a designer is attempting to emulate a particular style or movement, understanding the principles of that movement—the technology of the day and how that technology influenced outcome, the rules and postulations employed by the designers, as well as contemporary philosophy—will yield incredible insight into how and why a design or a movement took hold, and it is worth investigating all these elements to get the best result from any modern design that references the past. The designer of this masterful series, having researched the chosen movements, reflected this in the materials, construction methods, number of colors chosen, printing techniques applied, and illustration style seen here.

Note: Observe how this package series is not a simple reproduction of older pieces but is, rather, a skillful conceptual and formal approach that uniquely solves the problem, while, by the association of its references, at the same time elevating the qualitative value of the product.

SIDE BACK

TOP

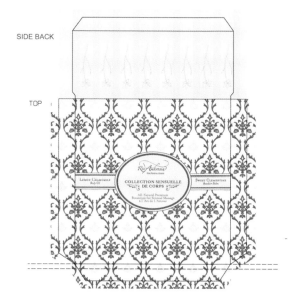

INSIDE BOX TOP FACING FRONT

designed by   a arcadia STUDIO

BOTTOM

SIDE BACK

TOP

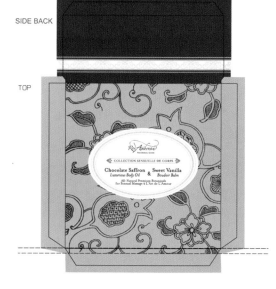

INSIDE BOX TOP FACING FRONT

Four Colors

Rarely is a package design solely printed with four colors. Most often there is at least a flood varnish, making the job five colors. In many cases, a four-color process job will contain a flood varnish, spot varnish, and one or two spot hues—a Pantone, Toyo, or Trumatch hue, for example. In these cases, different color effects are used to create different levels of subtlety or visual impact, and they can create a level of sophistication unsurpassed by any other technique found within print-based graphics.

With the globalization of the marketplace and advancements in new technology, the amount of four-color package design being printed today has skyrocketed. This relatively new phenomenon has changed the way consumers view the qualitative level of the products they buy. As a designer, it has never been more important to understand fully color in all its forms. This includes an appreciation of the many substrates that are available to enhance the perceived value of a product and its delivery system: packaging.

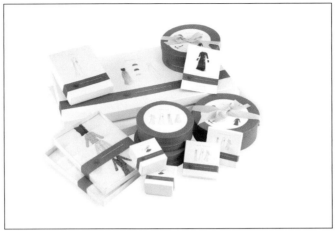

Andrew's Ties
Art Director/Designer: Inyoung Choi

Associative Color Response:
· high-chroma red: brilliant, intense, energizing, sexy, dramatic, stimulating
· black: percussion, spatial, powerful, elegant, mysterious
· dark green: traditional, money, trustworthy, refreshing

Color Scheme: direct complementary plus neutral

The bags and tie boxes are classified as iconic packaging, and the visual communication is direct and immediate (hard sale). The other boxes and bags use color symbolism to create a soft-sale approach. Note: The hard-sale components are placed on the shelf and used as store-display items for consumer recognition; the soft-sale items are used after the merchandise has been bought to pack for safe travel.

Flora
Art Director: Kelly Bryant
Designer: Kat McCluskey

Associative Color Response:
· high-chroma red: surging, sexy, brilliant, intense, energizing, dramatic, stimulating
· earth-tone red: warm, wholesome, welcome, good, healthy, fit, sound
· high-chroma blue: dignity, spaciousness, sobriety, calm, height, lively, pleasing, rich
· high-chroma yellow-orange: enterprise, drive, target, goal, luxuriance, cheer, joy, fun, excitement, stimulates
· dark orange: exhilarating, inspiring, stirring, stimulating, moving, provoking
· hearth-tone red: warm, wholesome, welcome, good, healthy, fit, sound

Color Scheme: incongruous

The Flora package has a beautifully executed, near complementary color palette. The striped exterior helps to create an exaggerated verticality.

Jacqueline Kennedy: The White House Years
Studio: Nita B. Creative
Art Director: Renita Breitenbucher
Designers: Andrea Egbert, Kimberly Welter, Renita Breitenbucher
Illustration: Virginia Johnson

Associative Color Response:
· high-chroma pink: stimulates, aggressive, genial, exciting, happy, high, fun, excitement, attention-getting, promising
· pastel pink: soft, sweet, tender, cute, comfortable, snug, rarefied, delicate, female babies, delicate, cozy, subtle
· black: spatial, powerful, elegant, mysterious, heavy, basic, neutral
· high-chroma green: life, use, motion, ebbing of life, springtime, infancy, wilderness, hope, peace

Color Scheme: direct complementary plus yellow and neutral

Marshall Field's, sponsor of "Jacqueline Kennedy: The White House Years" at the Field Museum in Chicago, wanted to capture Jackie Kennedy's sense of style for the product packaging to accompany the exhibit. From collector's plates, to fine porcelain pillboxes, to an elegant, almost aristocratic stationery set, the range is graced with classic images of the white gloves, dresses, coats, and pillbox hats that she made famous. The timeless, elegant packaging—a work of art in its own right—was designed in "Jackie pink," with cloth-covered button detailing capturing the spirit, style, and grace that she embodied. Special care was taken when considering "Jackie pink," as it was the color that would tie the branding together on the store shelves. The watercolor illustrations by Virginia Johnson incorporate a perfect array of colors to reflect the texture and style of each item of clothing.

Belle Hop Travel Accessories
Studio: SGDP
Creative Director: Marcus Norman
Designers: Marcus Norman, Augusta Toppins
Illustrators: Robyn Neild, Augusta Toppins

Associative Color Response:
· black: spatial, powerful, elegant, mysterious, heavy, basic, neutral
· high-chroma red: surging, brilliant, intense, energizing, sexy, dramatic, stimulating
· high-chroma blue: dignity, spaciousness, sobriety, calm, height, lively, pleasing, rich
· earth-tone red: warm, wholesome, welcome, good, healthy, fit, sound
· high-chroma reddish-purple: sweet taste, subtle, restlessness, prolongs life, feminine elegance, tender longing

Color Scheme: two points of a triad plus neutral

This packaging was developed to appeal to women in a very personal and romantic way. With travel as the central concept, the idea was embellished by using a contemporary, unique illustration to create a persona, an array of "passport-inspired" graphic elements, and a soft, neutral, feminine color palette that allowed the various bright colors of the product to speak clearly. All packages were designed to have a consistent color palette in order to create a unified system, and the substrate used allowed the vivid colors to be clearly visible.

Ganesh and Krishna Kits
Studio: Alian Design
Art Director/Designer: Ian Shimkoviak

Associative Color Response:
- dark gray: wise, cultured, mature, professional, classic, expensive, sophisticated, solid, enduring
- neutral gray: quality, quiet, classic, inertia, ashes, passion, practical, timeless, old age, cunning, cool
- high-chroma yellow-orange: enterprise, drive, target, goal, luxuriance, cheer, joy, fun, excitement, stimulates
- dark orange: exhilarating, inspiring, stirring, stimulating, moving, provoking
- high-chroma orange: producing, healing, tasty, growing, fire, warm, cleanliness, cheerfulness
- high-chroma blue: dignity, spaciousness, sobriety, calm, height, lively, pleasing, rich
- mid-green: safari, warlike, forces, military, camouflaged, classic

Color Scheme:
Ganesh Kit: analogous with complementary
Krishna Kit: achromatic with complementary

The high quality of the materials used in the Ganesh and Krishna boxes is evident when picked up. This sense of quality is conveyed through the materials used both inside and out—a branding strategy that ultimately yields an increase in profit margin.

Rock Street Journal
Studio: The Grafiosi
Art Director/Designer: Pushkar Thakur

Associative Color Response:
- black: spatial, powerful, elegant, mysterious, heavy, basic, neutral
- high-chroma blue: dignity, spaciousness, sobriety, calm, height, lively, pleasing, rich
- high-chroma green: life, use, motion, ebbing of life, springtime, infancy, wilderness, hope, peace
- high-chroma yellow-orange: enterprise, drive, target, goal, luxuriance, cheer, joy, fun, excitement, stimulates
- mid-range pink-red: restrained, toned down, soft, subdued, quiet, sentimental, sober, tame, domestic

Color Scheme: incongruous

Reminiscent of 1960s psychedelic designs, this CD cover uses a modular system (copying and pasting) to create an illustrative pattern made from the individual band members.

The Private Press
Designer: Gabriela Lopez De Dennis

Associative Color Response:
- high-chroma orange: producing, healing, tasty, growing, fire, warm, cleanliness, cheerfulness
- high-chroma blue: dignity, spaciousness, sobriety, calm, height, lively, pleasing, rich
- earth-tone red: warm, wholesome, welcome, good, healthy, fit, sound
- high-chroma yellow-orange: enterprise, drive, target, goal, luxuriance, cheer, joy, fun, excitement, stimulates
- black: spatial, powerful, elegant, mysterious, heavy, basic, neutral

Color Scheme: near complementary with shading plus neutral

This CD package design fuses a multitude of illustration styles into a superb collage. The detail found in the composite front-cover image is fascinating when juxtaposed with its counterpart on the back. The opposition of form found between the front and back is what makes this package design so interesting to look at.

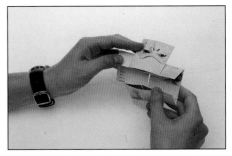

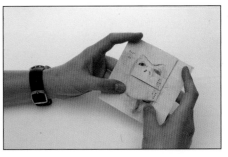

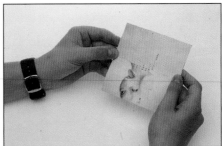

L.A. Salgado
Studio: estudiocrop and L.A. Salgado
Art Directors: Beto Janz, Dado Queiroz
Designer: Dado Queiroz
Illustrator: Beto Janz Oswaldo S. Lima
Photographer: Fabiano Schroden

Associative Color Response:
· black: spatial, powerful, elegant,
  mysterious, heavy, basic, neutral
· white: light, cool, snow,
  cleanliness, purity, clean, sterling,
  innocent, silent, inexplicable,
  normality, life
· neutral gray: quality, quiet, classic,
  inertia, ashes, passion, practical,
  timeless, old age, cunning, cool
· earth-tone red: warm, wholesome,
  welcome, good, healthy, fit, sound
· mid-range pink-red: restrained,
  toned down, soft, subdued, quiet,
  sentimental, sober, tame, domestic
· dark red: rich, elegant, refined,
  taste, expensive, mature
· pastel green: empathy, innate,
  completely, calm, quiet, smoothing,
  natural, sympathy, compassion

Color Scheme: direct complementary
with shading plus neutrals

Incredible in its design and concept,
this CD package becomes an
interactive toy, creating a multitude
of metamorphosing images.
Destined to be a collector's item, this
design is truly a masterpiece.

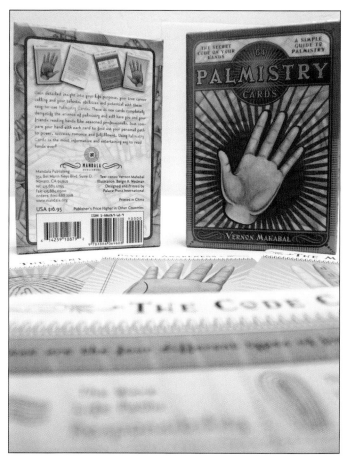

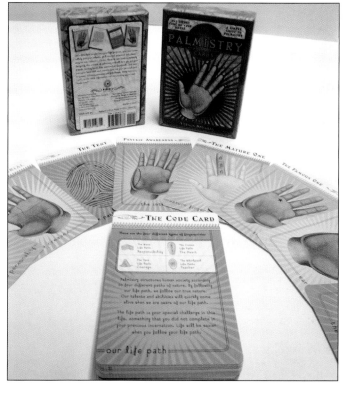

Palmistry

Studio: Alian Design
Art Director/Designer: Ian Shimkoviak

Associative Color Response:

· high-chroma red: surging, sexy, brilliant, intense, energizing, dramatic, stimulating
· mid-range pink-red: restrained, toned down, soft, subdued, quiet, sentimental, sober, tame, domestic
· mid-range orange: gentle, entice, good spirits, glad, nurturing, soft, fuzzy, delicious, fruity, sweet, inviting
· high-chroma orange: producing, healing, tasty, growing, fire, warm, cleanliness, cheerfulness
· high-chroma yellow-orange: enterprise, drive, target, goal, luxuriance, cheer, joy, fun, excitement, stimulates
· high-chroma blue: dignity, spaciousness, sobriety, calm, height, lively, pleasing, rich

Color Scheme: near complementary

The near complementary color combination with high-chroma hues creates a truly dynamic box design. The color palette coupled with the graphics not only make this design stand out from its competitors, but also make the product explode off the shelf.

Mocafe

Studio: Mary Hutchison Design LLC
Art Director/Designer:
Mary Chin Hutchison

Associative Color Response:
· earth-tone red: warm, wholesome, welcome, good, healthy, fit, sound
· high-chroma orange: producing, healing, tasty, growing, fire, warm, cleanliness, cheerfulness
· high-chroma yellow-orange: enterprise, drive, target, goal, luxuriance, cheer, joy, fun, excitement, stimulates
· high-chroma yellow-green: lemony, tart, fruity, acidic, sharp, bold, trendy, strength, sunlight, biology
· high-chroma green: life, use, motion, ebbing of life, springtime, infancy, wilderness, hope, peace
· pastel blue: pleasure, calm, quiet, hygienic, peaceful, refreshing, clean, cool, water, heavenly

Appetite Rating:
· high-chroma orange: excellent
· high-chroma yellow-orange: excellent
· high-chroma yellow-green: excellent
· high-chroma green: excellent
· pastel blue: excellent

Associative Taste:
· high-chroma orange: producing, healing, tasty, growing, fire, warm, cleanliness, cheerfulness
· high-chroma orange: very sweet
· high-chroma yellow-orange: very sweet
· high-chroma yellow-green: very sweet, lemony

Color Scheme: near complementary

This package design series is a great example of color-coding. Note how the graphics and typography are basically the same, and only the lower color bar changes from vessel to vessel.

I Am Imagination

Studio: Gouthier Design
a brand collective
Creative Director: Jonathan Gouthier
Designers: Gouthier Design
Creative Team

Associative Color Response:
· black: spatial, powerful, elegant, mysterious, heavy, basic, neutral
· earth-tone red: warm, wholesome, welcome, good, healthy, fit, sound
· high-chroma orange: producing, healing, tasty, growing, fire, warm, cleanliness, cheerfulness
· high-chroma green-yellow: new growth, lemony, tart, fruity, acidic
· high-chroma green: life, use, motion, ebbing of life, springtime, infancy, wilderness, hope, peace
· dark green: nature, mountains, lakes, natural, mature growth, versatility, traditional, money, trustworthy, refreshing

Color Scheme: near complementary plus black

Fifteen local ad. agencies were asked to put their ideas on a foam head, which was then photographed and used for marketing.

Charlie & the Chocolate Factory

Studio: Nita B. Creative
Art Director: Renita Breitenbucher
Designers: Renita Breitenbucher, Kimberly Welter
Illustrator: Quentin Blake

Associative Color Response:
· high-chroma green: life, use, motion, ebbing of life, springtime, infancy, wilderness, hope, peace
· high-chroma reddish-purple: sweet taste, subtle, restlessness, prolongs life, feminine elegance, tender longing
· high-chroma blue: dignity, spaciousness, sobriety, calm, height, lively, pleasing, rich
· high-chroma yellow: anticipation, agreeable, pleasant, welcome, vigorous, noble, youthful energy
· high-chroma orange: producing, healing, tasty, growing, fire, warm, cleanliness, cheerfulness
· mid-range orange: gentle, entice, good spirits, glad, nurturing, soft, fuzzy, delicious, fruity, sweet, inviting

Color Scheme: incongruous

Each holiday season, Marshall Field's creates a themed display in its stores in downtown Chicago and Minneapolis, and these have become an annual destination for thousands of families and tourists. Field's wanted to create a product line to sell in conjunction with their 2003 holiday theme, "Charlie and the Chocolate Factory." A bright, energetic color palette and original illustrations by Quentin Blake, of confections and Chocolate Factory characters, were used to bring the "Charlie" product line to life. As this line was varied, careful attention was made to the production of each piece and how color was applied. Because of Quentin Blake's vibrant and intricate watercolor illustrations, most of the product and packaging was printed in 4-color process. Other applications that required individual PMS colors were thoughtfully chosen, such as threads for the apron and caps, or inks on the erasers and soap-on-a-rope.

Marshall Field's
Art Director/Designer/Illustrator:
Renita Breitenbucher
Studio: Nita B. Creative

Associative Color Response:
· high-chroma red: surging, brilliant, intense, energizing, sexy, dramatic, stimulating
· high-chroma reddish-purple: sweet taste, subtle, restlessness, prolongs life, feminine elegance, tender longing
· high-chroma purple: celibacy, rage, deep, nostalgia, memories, power, spirituality, infinity, dignified
· dark green: nature, mountains, lakes, natural, mature growth, versatility, traditional, money, trustworthy, refreshing
· pastel green: empathy, innate, completely, calm, quiet, smoothing, natural, sympathy, compassion

Appetite Rating:
· high-chroma red: excellent
· high-chroma reddish-purple: excellent
· high-chroma purple: excellent
· dark green: good
· pastel green: excellent

Associative Taste:
· high-chroma red: very sweet

Color Scheme: direct complementary

Candy canes, sugar plums, gingerbread houses: candy and confections are a part of the Christmas season, so Marshall Field's developed a line of candies and gifts not only to grace the holidays, but also to satisfy the palates of those who had just toured the store's 2003 "Charlie & the Chocolate Factory" holiday exhibit. The packaging was given playful colors and candy shapes that coordinated perfectly with the merchandise, while maintaining Marshall Field's unmistakable brand.

Vivil, Sugar-Free
Studio: Solutions
Creative Director: Micha Goes
Designer: Andi Friedl

Associative Color Response:
· high-chroma red: surging, sexy, brilliant, intense, energizing, dramatic, stimulating
· high-chroma yellow-orange: enterprise, drive, target, goal, luxuriance, cheer, joy, fun, excitement, stimulates
· pastel pink: soft, sweet, tender, cute, comfortable, snug, rarefied, delicate, female babies, delicate, cozy, subtle
· high-chroma green-yellow: new growth, lemony, tart, fruity, acidic
· high-chroma green: life, use, motion, ebbing of life, springtime, infancy, wilderness, hope, peace
· dark green: nature, mountains, lakes, natural, mature growth, versatility, traditional, money, trustworthy, refreshing

Appetite Rating:
· high-chroma red: excellent
· high-chroma yellow-orange: excellent
· pastel pink: excellent
· high-chroma green-yellow: excellent
· high-chroma green: excellent
· dark green: good

Associative Taste:
· high-chroma red: very sweet
· high-chroma yellow-orange: very sweet
· pastel pink: sweet

Color Scheme: direct complementary with tinting

This Vivil package design takes advantage of intense high-chroma hues to increase the consumer's emotive response.

Self-promotional: Imageódesign
Studio: Twointandem
Art Directors/Designers: Sanver Kanidinc, Elena Ruano Kanidinc

Associative Color Response:
· high-chroma green-yellow: new growth, lemony, tart, fruity, acidic
· high-chroma yellow-green: lemony, tart, fruity, acidic, sharp, bold, trendy, strength, sunlight, biology
· high-chroma purple: celibacy, rage, deep, nostalgia, memories, power, spirituality, infinity, dignified
· high-chroma reddish-purple: sweet taste, subtle, restlessness, prolongs life, feminine elegance, tender longing

Color Scheme: direct complementary/ near complementary

A conceptual piece, with this neat, clean kit Twointandem introduced their new Imageódesign. The business card lists their services, inviting clients to freshen up their look while reinforcing the promotional message. Inspired by bath products (a daisy-shaped bar of soap and a shower cap are found inside), they played off the opposite—stinky, old, tired, and stale. Numerous empirical tests were conducted to find the most refreshing combinations of scents, colors, and shapes.

Zummer
Studio: Midnite Oil
Art Director/Designer:
Mongkolsri Janjarasskul

Associative Color Response:
· high-chroma red: surging, brilliant, intense, energizing, sexy, dramatic
· pastel pink: soft, sweet, tender, cute, comfortable, snug, rarefied, delicate, female babies, delicate, cozy, subtle
· high-chroma green-yellow: new growth, lemony, tart, fruity, acidic
· high-chroma green: life, use, motion, ebbing of life, springtime, infancy, wilderness, hope, peace
· black: spatial, powerful, elegant, mysterious, heavy, basic, neutral

Appetite Rating:
· high-chroma red: excellent
· pastel pink: excellent
· high-chroma green-yellow: excellent
· high-chroma green: excellent
· black: excellent

Associative Taste:
· high-chroma red: very sweet
· pastel pink: sweet

Color Scheme: direct complementary plus neutral

The original Zummer logo and motif utilized traditional Chinese brushwork. This design incorporates an Oriental watercolor approach to portray a fresh look while maintaining brand recognition.

Nestlé (Thai) Ltd.
Designer: FiF DESIGN House Team

Associative Color Response:
· high-chroma yellow-orange: enterprise, drive, target, goal, luxuriance, cheer, joy, fun, excitement, stimulates
· pastel yellow: pleasant, sunshine, glad, compassionate, tender, kindhearted, cheerful
· golden-yellow/beige: dignified, pleasant, autumn, flowers, harvest, rich, sun
· high-chroma red: surging, sexy, brilliant, intense, energizing, dramatic, stimulating
· high-chroma green-yellow: new growth, lemony, tart, fruity, acidic
· high-chroma blue: poor to good

Appetite Rating:
· high-chroma yellow-orange: excellent
· pastel yellow: poor to good
· golden-yellow/beige: good to excellent
· high-chroma red: excellent
· high-chroma green-yellow: excellent
· high-chroma blue: poor to good

Associative Taste:
· high-chroma yellow-orange: very sweet
· pastel yellow: sweet
· high-chroma red: very sweet

Color Scheme: analogous plus primary hues

As seen here, ergonomics plays an important role in package design. The design of the tin can ergonomically fits within the palm of the hand.

Godiva Chocolatier
Art Director: John T. Drew
Designer: Lydia Adi

Associative Color Response:
· earth-tone red: warm, wholesome, welcome, good, healthy, fit, sound
· earth tone: delicious, deep, rich, warm, life, work, wholesome
· dark orange: exhilarating, inspiring, stirring, stimulating, moving, provoking
· mid-range orange: gentle, entice, good spirits, glad, nurturing, soft, fuzzy, delicious, fruity, sweet, inviting
· high-chroma green-yellow: new growth, lemony, tart, fruity, acidic

Appetite Rating:
· earth tone: good
· mid-range orange: good to excellent
· high-chroma green-yellow: excellent

Associative Taste:
· mid-range orange: sweet

Color Scheme: near complementary

The conceptual strategy for this design was based on the multitude of flavors well-crafted chocolates can provide. A visual metaphorical representation of this phenomenon is layered graphically on the cover of the tin.

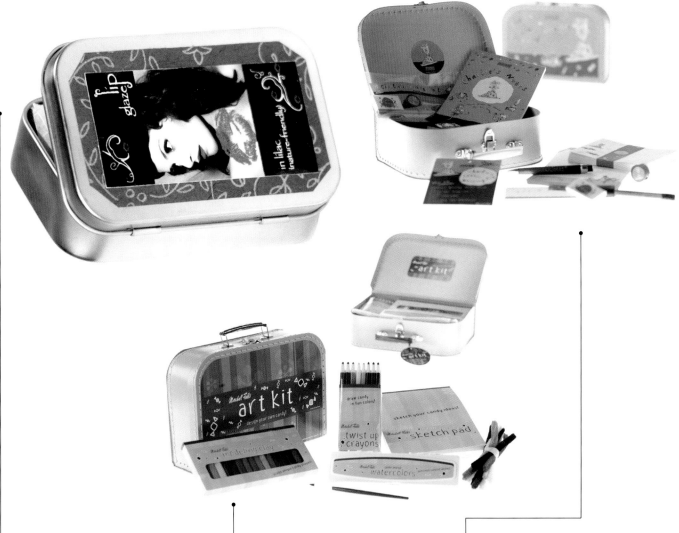

Lip Glaze

Art Director: John T. Drew
Designer: Sara Abdi

Associative Color Response:

· black: spatial, powerful, elegant, mysterious, heavy, basic, neutral
· high-chroma blue: dignity, spaciousness, sobriety, calm, height, lively, pleasing, rich
· mid-range pink-red: restrained, toned down, soft, subdued, quiet, sentimental, sober, tame, domestic
· high-chroma yellow-orange: enterprise, drive, target, goal, luxuriance, cheer, joy, fun, excitement, stimulates
· pastel blue: pleasure, calm, quiet, hygienic, peaceful, refreshing, clean, cool, water, heavenly

Color Scheme: two points of a tetrad

A high-contrast, pushed image is used to visually separate the lip glaze from the female model. An indexical reference of the glaze is used repeatedly in different sizes to reinforce the content.

Art Kit

Art Director/Designer/Illustrator:
Renita Breitenbucher
Studio: Nita B. Creative

Associative Color Response:

· high-chroma blue: dignity, spaciousness, sobriety, calm, height, lively, pleasing, rich
· high-chroma reddish-purple: sweet taste, subtle, restlessness, prolongs life, feminine elegance, tender longing
· pastel green: empathy, innate, completely, calm, quiet, smoothing, natural, sympathy, compassion
· high-chroma green: life, use, motion, ebbing of life, springtime, infancy, wilderness, hope, peace
· high-chroma red: surging, brilliant, intense, energizing, sexy, dramatic, stimulating
· mid-range pink-red: restrained, toned down, soft, subdued, quiet, sentimental, sober, tame, domestic

· high-chroma pink: stimulates, aggressive, genial, exciting, happy, high, fun, excitement, attention-getting, promising
· golden-yellow/beige: dignified, pleasant, autumn, flowers, harvest, rich, sun

Color Scheme: direct complementary

For this package a high-chroma direct complementary color palette is used to take advantage of their color associations and/or learned behavioral effects. A crude childlike illustration style and typography complements the color palette.

Charlie's Notes

Studio: Nita B. Creative
Art Director: Renita Breitenbucher
Designers: Renita Breitenbucher, Kimberly Welter
Illustrator: Quentin Blake

Associative Color Response:

· golden-yellow/beige: dignified, pleasant, autumn, flowers, harvest, rich, sun
· high-chroma orange: producing, healing, tasty, growing, fire, warm, cleanliness, cheerfulness
· high-chroma red: surging, sexy, brilliant, intense, energizing, dramatic, stimulating
· pastel blue: pleasure, calm, quiet, hygienic, peaceful, refreshing, clean, cool, water, heavenly
· high-chroma blue: dignity, spaciousness, sobriety, calm, height, lively, pleasing, rich

Color Scheme: direct complementary

An intense color palette softened with a pastel blue creates a natural backdrop for the childlike illustrations and typography. Packaging this product as a "lunch box"— something young children can associate with—is an excellent marketing strategy.

Paddywax: Journey of The Bee
Studio: Principle
Art Director: Pamela Zuccker
Designer: Ally Gerson
Photographer: Kara Brennan © 2007

Associative Color Response:
· high-chroma green-yellow: new growth, lemony, tart, fruity, acidic
· gold: warm, opulent, expensive, radiant, valuable, prestigious
· earth tone: delicious, deep, rich, warm, life, work, wholesome
· high-chroma blue: dignity, spaciousness, sobriety, calm, height, lively, pleasing, rich
· high-chroma red: surging, sexy, brilliant, intense, energizing, dramatic, stimulating
· neutral gray: quality, quiet, classic, inertia, ashes, passion, practical, timeless, old age, cunning, cool
· high-chroma yellow-orange: enterprise, drive, target, goal, luxuriance, cheer, joy, fun, excitement, stimulates

Color Scheme: incongruous

Each fragrance in this line reflects a stop that a bee would make on its journey from the early blossoms of sweet clover to the raw honey in their hive. Each box boasts a modern sensibility, from the crisp black-and-white honeycomb pattern on the lid to the whimsical gold-foiled flight pattern that is revealed on the glossy, colored box when opened. The glass is matte black with a gold-foiled bee, and is hand poured with a honey-colored beeswax blend.

Bols Liqueur
Studio: 1972dg
Art Director/Designer: Carlos Marques

Associative Color Response:
· dark red: rich, elegant, refined, taste, expensive, mature
· high-chroma orange: producing, healing, tasty, growing, fire, warm, cleanliness, cheerfulness
· mid-range orange: gentle, good spirits, glad, nurturing, soft, fuzzy, delicious, fruity, sweet, inviting
· high-chroma yellow-orange: enterprise, drive, target, goal, luxuriance, cheer, joy, fun, excitement, stimulates
· pastel blue: pleasure, calm, quiet, hygienic, peaceful, refreshing, clean, cool, water, heavenly
· black: spatial, powerful, elegant, mysterious, heavy, basic, neutral

Appetite Rating:
· high-chroma orange: excellent
· mid-range orange: good to excellent
· high-chroma yellow-orange: excellent
· pastel blue: excellent
· black: excellent

Associative Taste:
· high-chroma orange: very sweet
· mid-range orange: sweet
· high-chroma yellow-orange: very sweet

Color Scheme: direct complementary

An explosion of hue, this package design uses overprinting to achieve a multitude of colors. Typography is employed as image to create a bold flat-pattern illustration.

Anheuser-Busch Lemon Tattoo Beer
Studio: SandorMax
Designer: Zoltan Csillag

Associative Color Response:
· high-chroma yellow: anticipation, agreeable, pleasant, welcome, vigorous, noble, youthful energy
· mid-range pink-red: restrained, toned down, soft, subdued, quiet, sentimental, sober, tame, domestic
· high-chroma bluish-purple: meditative, restlessness, expensive, regal, classic, powerful, tender, longing, elegant
· high-chroma green-yellow: new growth, lemony, tart, fruity, acidic
· pastel blue: pleasure, calm, quiet, hygienic, peaceful, refreshing, clean, cool, water, heavenly

Appetite Rating:
· high-chroma yellow: good
· mid-range pink-red: good
· high-chroma bluish-purple: excellent
· high-chroma green-yellow: excellent
· pastel blue: excellent

Associative Taste:
· high-chroma yellow: very sweet
· mid-range pink-red: sweet

Color Scheme: Two points of a triad

Texture is a visual magnet, and here Lemon Tattoo uses it to the fullest extent. By employing this technique, an aged appearance is immediately established, promoting longevity within the marketplace.

Heinz Heritage
Studio: Wallace Church
Creative Director: Stan Church

Associative Color Response:
· gold: warm, opulent, expensive, radiant, valuable, prestigious
· high-chroma blue: dignity, spaciousness, sobriety, calm, height, lively, pleasing, rich
· high-chroma red: surging, sexy, brilliant, intense, energizing, dramatic, stimulating
· high-chroma green: life, use, motion, ebbing of life, springtime, infancy, wilderness, hope, peace
· black: spatial, powerful, elegant, mysterious, heavy, basic, neutral

Appetite Rating:
· gold: excellent
· high-chroma blue: poor to good
· high-chroma red: excellent
· high-chroma green: excellent
· black: excellent

Associative Taste:
· high-chroma red: very sweet

Color Scheme: primaries plus neutral

H.J. Heinz Company, the king of ketchup, has marketed dozens of products under the Heinz brand for over 100 years. These used inconsistent and dated expressions of the Heinz identity and, as a result, they were getting lost on shelf and denigrating overall brand perception. Heinz consulted with Wallace Church to revive its "heritage" brands. A visual position was created around the brand's "tried-and-true" essence. Leveraging the brand's unique authenticity and recasting the message in a contemporary context was required.

A more prominent logo and enhanced "keystone" shape highlight the Heinz brand, while consistent form and flavor "staging areas" enable consumers to quickly identify products. This architecture is consistently applied across the entire brand franchise, helping to elevate these products to the "icon" status that its ketchup enjoys.

The Vines of Ilok
Studio: International
Art Director/Designer: Boris Ljubicic

Associative Color Response:
· black: spatial, powerful, elegant, mysterious, heavy, basic, neutral
· high-chroma yellow-orange: enterprise, drive, target, goal, luxuriance, cheer, joy, fun, excitement, stimulates
· high-chroma orange: producing, healing, tasty, growing, fire, warm, cleanliness, cheerfulness
· pastel yellow: pleasant, sunshine, glad, compassionate, tender, kindhearted, cheerful
· dark red: rich, elegant, refined, taste, expensive, mature
· pastel blue: pleasure, calm, quiet, hygienic, peaceful, refreshing, clean, cool, water, heavenly
· black: spatial, powerful, elegant, mysterious, heavy, basic, neutral

Appetite Rating:
· black: excellent
· high-chroma yellow-orange: excellent
· high-chroma orange: excellent
· pastel yellow: poor to good
· pastel blue: excellent
· black: excellent

Associative Taste:
· high-chroma yellow-orange: very sweet
· high-chroma orange: very sweet
· pastel yellow: sweet

Color Scheme: analogous plus neutral

The mountains of Ilok with their beautiful vineyards were the inspiration for this package design. Color coding was used to establish different product lines while the same typography and imagery work consistently throughout.

California Sunshine
Studio: REFLECTUR.COM
Art Director/Designer: Gwendolyn Hicks

Associative Color Response:
· high-chroma red: surging, brilliant, intense, energizing, sexy, dramatic, stimulating
· earth-tone red: warm, wholesome, welcome, good, healthy, fit, sound
· high-chroma orange: producing, healing, tasty, growing, fire, warm, cleanliness, cheerfulness
· high-chroma green-yellow: new growth, lemony, tart, fruity, acidic
· mid-range red-purple: charming, elegant, select, refined, subtle, nostalgic, delicate, sweet scented, floral, sweet taste
· pastel blue: pleasure, calm, quiet, hygienic, peaceful, refreshing, clean, cool, water, heavenly
· black: spatial, powerful, elegant, mysterious, heavy, basic, neutral

Appetite Rating:
· high-chroma red: excellent
· high-chroma orange: excellent
· high-chroma green-yellow: excellent
· mid-range red-purple: good
· pastel blue: excellent
· black: excellent

Associative Taste:
· high-chroma red: very sweet
· high-chroma orange: very sweet
· mid-range red-purple: sweet

Color Scheme: incongruous

These beautiful rural illustrations are majestic in their execution, reminiscent of the orange-crate labels from southern California in the 1920s.

5 California Blossoms
Art Director: John T. Drew
Designer: Michael Stapleton

Associative Color Response:
· mid-range pink-red: restrained, toned down, soft, subdued, quiet, sentimental, sober, tame, domestic
· pastel pink: soft, sweet, tender, cute, comfortable, snug, rarefied, delicate, female babies, delicate, cozy, subtle
· high-chroma reddish-purple: sweet taste, subtle, restlessness, prolongs life, feminine elegance, tender longing
· high-chroma orange: producing, healing, tasty, growing, fire, warm, cleanliness, cheerfulness
· high-chroma yellow-orange: enterprise, drive, target, goal, luxuriance, cheer, joy, fun, excitement, stimulates
· high-chroma yellow: anticipation, agreeable, pleasant, welcome, vigorous, noble, youthful energy
· high-chroma purple: celibacy, rage,

deep, nostalgia, memories, power, spirituality, infinity, dignified
· high-chroma bluish-purple: meditative, restlessness, expensive, regal, classic, powerful, tender, longing, elegant
· high-chroma blue: dignity, spaciousness, sobriety, calm, height, lively, pleasing, rich
· black: spatial, powerful, elegant, mysterious, heavy, basic, neutral

Color Scheme: analogous

The modular illustrations—each illustration is made from one or two parts, copied, pasted, and scaled up or down—are beautifully executed with high-chroma colors and flat patterns. The die cut for the exterior package is cleverly conceived by indexically referencing a bee, helping to place the package design in context.

Pure & Natural:
Revitalising Moisturiser
Studio: Midnite Oil
Art Director/Designer:
Mongkolsri Janjarasskul

Associative Color Response:
· pastel green: empathy, innate, completely, calm, quiet, smoothing, natural, sympathy, compassion
· neutral gray: quality, quiet, classic, inertia, ashes, passion, practical, timeless, old age, cunning, cool
· dark gray: wise, cultured, mature, professional, classic, expensive, sophisticated, solid, enduring,
· high-chroma red: surging, sexy, brilliant, intense, energizing, dramatic, stimulating
· high-chroma orange: producing, healing, tasty, growing, fire, warm, cleanliness, cheerfulness

Color Scheme: near complementary plus neutrals

Pure & Natural is a series of cosmetics from in2it, which contain ingredients including fruit and vegetable extracts. Transparent packaging substrates were used so that the consumer could see the slices of different fruits suspended within the product.

Expect

Art Director/Designer: Chapman Tse

Associative Color Response:
· black: spatial, powerful, elegant, mysterious, heavy, basic, neutral
· gold: warm, opulent, expensive, radiant, valuable, prestigious
· high-chroma green: life, use, motion, ebbing of life, springtime, infancy, wilderness, hope, peace
· high-chroma yellow-orange: joy, fun, enterprise, drive, target, goal, luxuriance, excitement, stimulates
· dark orange: exhilarating, inspiring, stirring, stimulating, moving, provoking
· high-chroma orange: producing, healing, tasty, growing, fire, warm, cleanliness, cheerfulness

Appetite Rating:
· black: excellent
· gold: excellent
· high-chroma green: excellent
· high-chroma yellow-orange: excellent
· high-chroma orange: excellent

Associative Taste:
· high-chroma yellow-orange: very sweet
· high-chroma orange: very sweet

Color Scheme: incongruous/ achromatic

This near achromatic color scheme uses warm accent hues to separate the tea leaves and product name.

Vida Orgánica

Studio: Estudio Iuvaro
Art Director: Cecilia Iuvaro
Designers: Mariano Gioia, Sebastián Yáñez

Associative Color Response:
· black: spatial, powerful, elegant, mysterious, heavy, basic, neutral
· mid-range red-purple: charming, elegant, select, refined, subtle, nostalgic, delicate, sweet scented, floral, sweet taste
· high-chroma orange: producing, healing, tasty, growing, fire, warm, cleanliness, cheerfulness
· high-chroma green-yellow: new growth, lemony, tart, fruity, acidic
· dark green: nature, mountains, lakes, natural, mature growth, versatility, traditional, money, trustworthy, refreshing
· dark orange: exhilarating, inspiring, stirring, stimulating, moving, provoking

Appetite Rating:
· black: excellent
· mid-range red-purple: good
· high-chroma orange: excellent
· high-chroma green-yellow: excellent
· dark green: good
· dark orange: poor

Associative Taste:
· mid-range red-purple: sweet
· high-chroma orange: very sweet

Color Scheme: Near triad plus neutral

Vida Orgánica is the only wine belonging to the Familia Zuccardi Vineyard that is made from organically cultivated grapevines. The packaging has been redesigned while paying homage to the original design by Estudio Iuvaro. The redesign objective was to incorporate a wider use of color in order to differentiate the varietals from one another and to produce a greater impact in the market place.

Paddywax Classic

Studio: Principle
Art Director/Designer: Pamela Zuccker
Photographer: David Lefler © 2007

Associative Color Response:
· high-chroma blue: dignity, spaciousness, sobriety, calm, height, lively, pleasing, rich
· high-chroma red: surging, sexy, brilliant, intense, energizing, dramatic, stimulating
· high-chroma yellow-green: lemony, tart, fruity, acidic, sharp, bold, trendy, strength, sunlight, biology
· black: spatial, powerful, elegant, mysterious, heavy, basic, neutral
· earth-tone red: warm, wholesome, welcome, good, healthy, fit, sound
· dark green: nature, mountains, lakes, natural, mature growth, versatility, traditional, money, trustworthy, refreshing

Color Scheme: near triad

Paddywax needed to reestablish a bold presence in their core product line, and Principle was brought in to develop new packaging and point-of-sale materials. The old packaging left them susceptible to being perceived as "country." To address this, the designer came up with a preppy-chic identity system that combined classic black-and-white stitched ribbon with colorful stripes and solids to reflect the intense color palette of the wax. Tubular packaging was updated with a sophisticated, rigid box that, when separated, exposes the signature stripe pattern. The result was a whole new look and feel that will drive future design and communications decisions.

Martha Stewart Everyday
Studio: Doyle Partners

Associative Color Response:

· blue-green: pristine, pure, serious, cleanliness, incorruptible, pensive, tranquillity, lively
· high-chroma red: surging, sexy, brilliant, intense, energizing, dramatic, stimulating
· neutral gray: quality, quiet, classic, inertia, ashes, passion, practical, timeless, old age, cunning, cool
· high-chroma orange: producing, healing, tasty, growing, fire, warm, cleanliness, cheerfulness
· golden-yellow/beige: dignified, pleasant, autumn, flowers, harvest, rich, sun
· black: spatial, powerful, elegant, mysterious, heavy, basic, neutral
· high-chroma blue: dignity, spaciousness, sobriety, calm, height, lively, pleasing, rich

Color Scheme: analogous plus neutral, near complementary plus neutral with shading and tinting, and incongruous plus neutral with shading and tinting

The Martha Stewart Everyday system is designed with a simple logo and an overall clarity that is synonymous with the brand, delivered in a wide assortment of bold colors and accessible type. This crisp, colorful packaging provides a cohesive, unifying effect for products in many different categories.

Packaging was constructed to highlight the product attributes, allowing light to shine through the glassware packages, letting customers feel the weight of flatware, or even presenting uninterrupted surfaces of plates in a subtle range of colors—all conceived to give customers a better understanding of the design properties of the products.

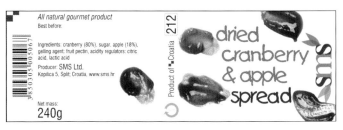

SMS Jam
Studio: International
Art Director/Designer/Photography/
Illustrator: Boris Ljubicic

Associative Color Response:
· neutral gray: quality, quiet, classic, inertia, ashes, passion, practical, timeless, old age, cunning, cool
· high-chroma red: surging, sexy, brilliant, intense, energizing, dramatic, stimulating
· dark red: rich, elegant, refined, taste, expensive, mature
· high-chroma orange: producing, healing, tasty, growing, fire, warm, cleanliness, cheerfulness
· mid-green: warlike, forces, safari, military, camouflaged, classic

Appetite Rating:
· neutral gray: poor to good
· high-chroma red: excellent
· high-chroma orange: excellent
· mid-green: excellent

Associative Taste:
· high-chroma red: very sweet
· high-chroma orange: very sweet

Color Scheme: analogous plus neutral and tinting

Surely no one has ever eaten jam without getting his or her hands sticky? The conceptual strategy for this piece is based on that assumption. SMS Jams are high-quality delicatessen products that are "so tasty that we couldn't hide the evidence."

Matches

Studio: Irving
Art Directors: Julian Roberts, Mark Brown
Designer: Dan Adams
Marbling Pattern Designer: Ann Muir
Client: Tom Chapman, Matches

This line of boxes and bags for the international fashion boutique Matches makes use of the traditional art of marbleized paper. As Matches expanded from a local fashion retailer to a respected and recognized brand throughout Europe, the Middle East, and the USA, the packaging had to take on the demands of global retailers. This is a particularly tough market: the packaging design must not only reflect the retailer's intent, but also the individual consumer's desires and particular tastes. This can be regional and site specific, so marbling

was chosen as an international representation of quality that would not override the savvy tastes of the consumer.

Marbling is an ancient art that uses diverse techniques to float color onto paper or other substrates and create a pattern reminiscent of marble. Ann Muir, a paper-marbling specialist, was asked to create a selection of designs incorporating traditional marbleizing methods, patterns, and colors. Eight patterns were chosen for their distinctive designs and corresponding colors, and these patterns were then used to create the foundational structure for a line of boxes and bags. In order to accommodate the diversity of products—ranging from men's to women's clothing, shoes, and accessories—three primary and secondary packages were designed. These initial structures were of varying sizes and included accessory

envelopes, bags, and boxes. The branding bar and logotype was incorporated into each of the structures, and they pulled colors from the seasons—fall, spring, summer, winter—as well as the primary and secondary colors of the marbled paper. Each is dramatically accented with a dark, receding color and bright accent color that subtly pulls the eye and reinforces the brand recognition. These colors are again found in the interior of the package, pulling the eye to the product and framing it as if it was a work of art. Fabric handles were dyed to match both the accent colors and marbling. Like the marbleized paper, this fabric imparts a sense of quality and craftsmanship. The boxes were designed to pack flat—ideal for large volume storage. They close seamlessly with integral magnetic strips, which creates a refined touch.

The packaging line holds up both individually and as a whole. Like old hat boxes stacked on top of the wardrobe, they have become collectors' items for those who appreciate fine design. There is an association with the marbled endpapers of a classic novel—the motif communicates a sense of quality and timelessness. In the fashion industry this can be likened to the perennial "little black dress" or well-placed accessories. As a perfect mode of communication for a fashion innovator, both the package and the product it contains becomes part of the consumer's permanent collection, a sign of their good taste, and it will refresh the Matches brand each time it is unveiled.

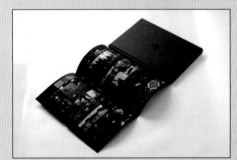

Levi's Flu Sports Clothing and Apparel

Art Director: Shun Kawakami
Designers: Shun Kawakami, Yu-Ki Sakurai
Photographer: Ikuma Yamada
Styling: Sakae Soeda
Artwork: Tadashi Ura, Yoza, Ko-Zou

This unique design series encapsulates the Levi's FLU clothing line from Japan through a combination of photographs and graphic elements which creates a highly kinetic composition that resonates with its intended audience. A dichotomy is created between two contrasting styles that are fused together through the use of photography, typography, and color—which also create continuity between the multiple components. (For print-production purposes, black and white are considered hues— white being created by the substrate adding to the array of colors within this composition.)

The indexical and iconic signifiers are used to create, control, and broadcast a message to its target audience. Here the most noteworthy indexical signifiers are the paintball splatters applied to the work in a two-dimensional format to make it appear as though the design has been hung on the wall and shot at, which also suggests a graffiti'd environment. The fine swirling lines and floral filigree connote the ornate and exotic tattoos and T-shirt designs popular today. The combination of this indexical information juxtaposed with an iconic figure makes the overall composition quite kinetic. The black-and-white photographs found within a few of the components are also used to convey an urban environment, so giving context.

To further enhance the visual dichotomy within this series, the iconic four-color photos are used by themselves to create a more conservative/corporate look. By doing so, a high-end, quality appearance is achieved that not only appeals to the original target audience, but also is well suited for the more mature market that may be purchasing the clothing line for others. The blending of the indexical and iconic information coupled with the duality found within this work ultimately connotes quality, a commodity that can only be brought about through a careful analysis of the target audience(s) and executed through a sound conceptual strategy.

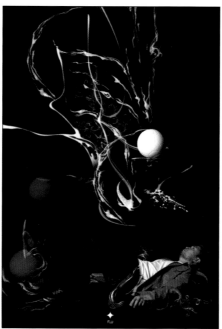

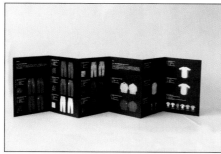

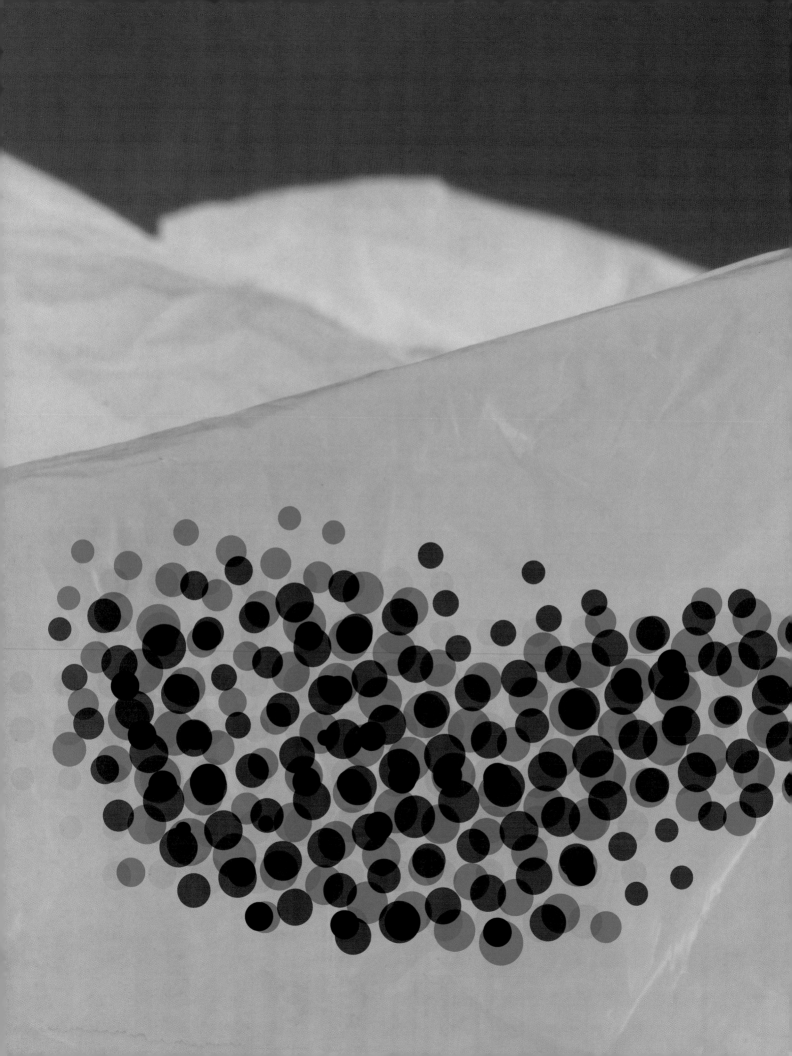

Spot Colors

The management of color is a very complex issue, with many facets that can make or break a design. Since the 1980s color-management issues have shifted increasingly to the designer. In the past, these responsibilities lay with photographers, special-effects houses, prepress houses, and printers, but today it is the designer's responsibility to make sure that most, if not all color issues are addressed prior to print production. Printing no longer takes place next door; oftentimes it is done halfway across the world. Therefore, understanding the complexity of color-management issues is critical for a successful outcome.

With the globalization of the marketplace, numerous ink-matching systems are becoming more commonplace. Understanding how to specify, use, and combine different ink-matching systems will help to create a unique outcome. Learning how to control and anticipate this visual outcome requires not only an understanding of these systems, but also a deeper understanding of how, why, and when to use them. This applies not only to the substrate in which these ink systems will be utilized, but also, ultimately, to the applications that will be used to create the mechanicals.

Figure 1

Figure 2

Different Ink Systems

Within our industry there are many different standard ink-matching systems for print production. Each provides a range of colors that are created through their primaries. For example, four-color process primaries—cyan, magenta, yellow, and black—provide a full spectrum of colors for print-production purposes. However, because of the amount of primaries and their chroma, the color spectrum, or gamma, is quite small when compared with other standardized systems.

The print industry uses these systems so that the appearance of color can remain uniform throughout the process—from client, to designer, to prepress house, to printer, and, finally, to consumer. Without such systems, there would be a drift in color appearance; the color originally specified would vary throughout the process, including on the final product.

For designers, standardized ink-matching systems can be broken down into five categories: four- and six-color process ink systems for offset sheet-fed lithography or web-fed lithography; standardized spot-color systems offered by PANTONE, Toyo, and Trumatch (these are specified hues often unattainable by traditional four-color process systems for lithography printing); silkscreen inks; flexography inks; and home/desktop-printer inks (including ink-jet printers and plotter printers). When dealing with the process of flexography or silkscreen ink, many of the same manufacturers (PANTONE, Toyo, Trumatch) offer a color system for these media. There are many other manufacturers of ink-matching systems, but these three are the most widely used or specified within the industry.

Within these five categories, three are most often used in the day-to-day operations of a design studio: four- and six-color process ink systems; spot-color systems; and home/desktop-printer ink systems. These three categories tend to intersect with one another because they incorporate the most common production processes from A to Z—designer comprehensive to final printed product. This intersection of different ink-matching systems often creates havoc in color appearance within the design process. In other words, uniform color appearance from system to system breaks down, and often color drifting creeps into the process. (To understand how to color manage your work-flow environment, so guarding against this eventuality, see "Color Work Flow" in Chapter 8.)

Figure 1
Art Director/Designer: Art Chantry

Coarse line art overprinted in red, green, yellow, and black instead of the traditional four-color-process primaries destabilizes the image and emphasizes the "psycho" qualities.

Figure 2
Art Director/Designer: Art Chantry

The bright magenta background, as well as a distinctive, lacelike pattern created from interlocking "Ms," is provocative, feminine, and nontraditional, like the performers and the eclectic collection of old and new songs they sing.

Diagram 1
This diagram demonstrates how images would color drift if standardized matching systems did not exist.

For package design, flexography and silkscreen ink systems are, more often than not, part of the process—although, depending upon the type of job, lithography printing can be substituted for these. Each printing system has its strengths, and which is to be used is most often down to the substrate specified. For each printing method—lithography, flexography, and silkscreen as well as those for home/desktop printers—the inks are formulated differently. These ink systems can be arranged on a scale from very translucent to semiopaque. All inks are designed to be translucent, as during the printing process one hue is laid on top of another to create additional colors, but some are more translucent than others. Flexography has the most translucent inks, while silkscreen inks are the most opaque. Four- and six-color process, including lithography and home/desktop printers, fall somewhere in the middle.

Figure 4

Figure 3

Figure 5

Figure 3
Art Director: John T. Drew
Designer: Valeria Pena

The wooden crates, sewn closures, and corrugated paper of this seed packaging and point-of-purchase display creates an earth-friendly message that beckons the consumer to engage in a tactile manner.

Figure 4
Studio: Bright Strategic Design
Art Director: Glenn Sakamoto

Because the flexographic process is able to print solids, it is used here to unify this brand, while color distinguishes each flavor. Once the package is torn open, the ears of the kitty align with the top of the resealable pouch causing the darker color to recede further into the frame.

Figure 5
Studio: Exhibit A: Design Group
Art Director: Cory Ripley
Designers: Cory Ripley,
Robert Spofforth

Fay's Gourmet Jamaican Rumba Cake captures the richness of the cake's taste and references the Jamaican heritage of the recipe. The package is designed to visually articulate both gourmet and contemporary. A dominant bright yellow was selected for several reasons—it's very approachable, it's one of the colors in the Jamaican flag, and demands attention in a retail environment. The packaging creates a wall of sunshine that stops consumers in their tracks.

Figure 6

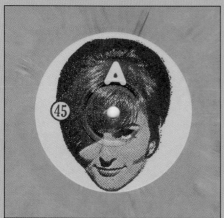

Figure 7

Figure 8

Home/desktop ink systems are not standardized from one manufacturer to another, and with a multitude of companies making desktop color printers, color drifting of the specified hue or image is more likely to happen from device to device. However, this is slowly changing. Pantone offers standardized lines of inks for printer devices. Nonetheless, matching colors from one process to another or from one device to another can sometimes create havoc and delay. As a general rule, a hard-copy color proof should be pulled from a machine or device that has a greater color spectrum, or gamma, than the document you have created. For example, if you print a CMYK color document to a Creo Digital Matchprint, the Matchprint has a greater color gamma and will match any of the CMYK colors. (See more about color management in the Color Work Flow section of Chapter 8.)

All commercial ink manufacturers offer color swatch books that show their complete range of colors as well as different color techniques, including overprinting, tinting, and shading of spot hues. Pantone offers a world-renowned color-communication system, and the company offers a complete line of swatch books and color-communication tools for plastics, textiles, the Hexachrome® Color System (a patented six-color process system made for print), metallics, pastels, four-color process, and coated and uncoated solid colors for inks and the graphic arts industries. These swatch books identify the available hues and builds (the percentage of primaries used within the system to create an individual hue). For example, Pantone, Inc.'s solid Basic Colors/Primaries are PANTONE Yellow, PANTONE Yellow 012, PANTONE

Figure 6
Art Director/Designer: Art Chantry

The construction of this image is easily adaptable to both silkscreen and offset printing. The white type and black counterform could easily be silkscreened with opaque inks on brown-toned paper or card stock, leaving the image to be constructed by the exposed substrate. Likewise, the type could be knocked out of the black to expose white stock when offset printing.

Figure 7
Art Director/Designer: Art Chantry

The duotone image for the A and B side of this record make use of a flat tint of one color in combination with the full tonal range of black expressed through a coarse-dot screen. The hole is perfectly positioned to insinuate an empty head or brain.

Figure 8
Studio: Articulate Solutions® Inc.
Creative Director/Logo and Package Designers: Katherine Filice
Graphic Designers: Bryce Hendry, Camilla Saufley

The ubiquity of PANTONE color allows the designer to specify everything from paper and ink to wax and thread colors. This is particularly important and effective in packaging that uses metallic colors.

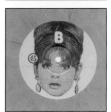

Diagram 2
This is a facsimile of the same images printed out on four different color printers.

Orange 021, PANTONE Warm Red, PANTONE Red 032, PANTONE Rubine Red, PANTONE Rhodamine Red, PANTONE Purple, PANTONE Violet, PANTONE Blue 072, PANTONE Reflex Blue, PANTONE Green, and PANTONE Black, and these are the color primaries that make up the PANTONE formula guide solid colors. Toyo and Trumatch also offer similar guides. Unfortunately these color swatch books are quite expensive, but they are absolutely essential for a graphic designer to communicate with clients and printers because it helps maintain color uniformity.

Different color swatch books or color systems can be used with different systems from the same manufacturer—for example, PANTONE solid uncoated hues used with PANTONE metallic hues, PANTONE pastel hues, or both. Color systems from different manufacturers can be used in combination to create a color experience that is not only unique, but also communicates the message. In some cases, using hues from different manufacturers adds a level of subtlety that cannot be achieved through a single manufacturer. However, this is recommended only with commercial printing and should not be tried with an ink-jet or plotter printer.

Figure 9

Overprinting:
100% cyan over 100% magenta

Diagram 3
This diagram demonstrates
overprinting, tinting, and shading.

Tinting:
left: 100% cyan
right: 70% cyan

Shading:
left: 100% cyan
right: 100% cyan + 10% black

Figure 9
Studio: Irving
Designer: Julian Roberts

Warm gold tones in the typography
are referenced in the high shine of
the foil that individually wraps these
chocolate liqueurs.

Alternative Inks for Overprinting

A number of alternative ink systems can be used for overprinting, and when used with more conventional spot-color systems can create truly unique color outcomes. Four such ink systems are thermochromic, photochromic, metallic, and glow-in-the-dark (Day-Glo).

Thermochromic inks are heat sensitive and change their color appearance when exposed to different temperatures. These inks are designed to interact with low temperatures such as beverages that are refrigerated, body temperature by holding or rubbing an object, and high temperatures that can warn an individual of danger. Consequently, they are great for food and beverage packaging. For example, when a beverage is placed in the refrigerator, once it cools down to optimum drinking temperature the design changes to indicate it is ready for consumption; or changes in the appearance of the ink in the presence of high temperatures can warn an individual of danger. This type of ink has been formulated to work with standard printing equipment, including offset litho presses.

Photochromic inks are invisible until they are exposed to certain types of light—daylight or UV light, for example. Thus, a package can appear to have a simple design in artificial light, but when exposed to daylight it blossoms into a colorful array. In this way a two-part message can be created, allowing the consumer to interact with the design longer for greater brand recognition.

Metallic inks are typically created using silver, gold, or copper colors in different shades and quantities, and mixed with other pigments to create a wide variety of hues. Pantone offers a line of metallic colors that, when used with conventional inks for overprinting, create an interesting viewing experience. Metallic inks are typically more opaque than traditional ones, and experimentation is recommended. Doing this with commercial printing is an expensive proposition, one where mistakes can be costly, so a cheap way of experimenting with metallic overprinting is to create a color bar of the ink(s) you wish to use that can be positioned on the waste paper—beyond the trim—of another job. Many printers will allow you to do this (in small amounts) at no additional cost.

Glow-in-the-dark (e.g., Day-Glo) inks have been around for a long time, and they offer a much higher chroma level than traditional spot colors. These inks can create visual separation unlike any other ink system, and when overprinted with traditional systems create striking results. Pantone offers a line of fluorescent (glow-in-the-dark) colors that can be printed using silkscreen, lithography, and flexography. However, they do fade in sunlight quite quickly.

Figure 10

Figure 10
Studio: Domot Antistudio

The opacity of the metallic ink seems to shine on this wine label when contrasted with the rich black and brilliant pink. In this capacity the label fades into the sheen of the bottle, making it appear as if the print is directly applied to the bottle.

| 20% cyan over 100% yellow | 40% cyan over 100% yellow | 60% cyan over 100% yellow | 80% cyan over 100% yellow | 100% cyan over 100% yellow |

Diagram 4
Creating a color bar that is 1 x 5in so that it can be positioned on the waste paper is a good way to conduct empirical studies. The bar should be set up so that screen percentages are overprinted on top of another hue.

Figure 11

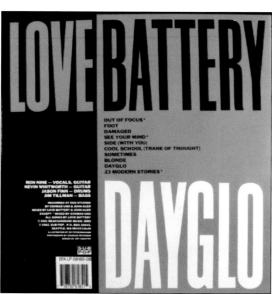

Figure 12

Overprinting

Many clients have budgetary constraints in the development of their package design, and color printing is most often one of them. If used correctly, overprinting can be an excellent way of expanding the color palette by selecting the appropriate hues for the right color effect with no additional cost. Choosing the right colors for the right effect is an easy task so long as the designer understands the basic principles.

·   Pure hues will create the greatest variety of color range, both in additional hues and in the amounts of chroma. In print-based graphics, a pure hue is made from one ink.

·   Pure hues overprinted with semipure hues will create a large variety of color range, both in additional hues and in the amounts of chroma. However, the chroma value will not be as great as mixing pure hues. In print-based graphics, semipure ink is considered to be a hue with no more than three inks (one of which is a small percentage of one of the hues) and with no portion of black or white.

·   Semipure hues when overprinting will create a wide variety of colors in additional hues, but the chroma of the colors will be reduced. When overprinting two semipure hues, typically a wide variety of semipure hues to earth tones are created.

·   Muddy/dirty hues overprinted with muddy/dirty colors create a spectrum of muddy colors. Muddy/dirty hues are colors made up of three or more inks, one of which is black.

·   Pure hues overprinted with muddy/dirty colors create a broad color spectrum that ranges from light to dark, but such hues typically do not create a wide variety of stand-alone hues. These colors tend to have a muddy/dirty shade running throughout.

·   Semipure hues overprinted with muddy/dirty colors create a color spectrum from light to dark, but they typically create a spectrum of only muddy/dirty hues.

·   In print-based graphics, white can be an ink that is applied to an individual hue or it can be applied as a stand-alone color. When white ink is mixed or overprinted using any of the above scenarios, low-chroma (pastel) colors will be created.

Figure 13
Art Director/Designer: Akio Okumura

For overprinting, pure and semi-pure colors will create the widest spectrum of hues, including light to dark.

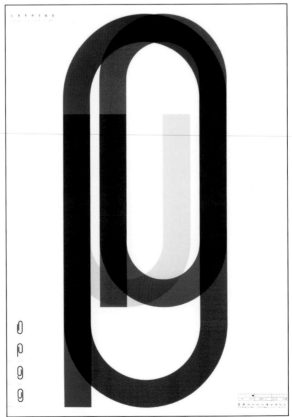

Figure 13

Building Spot-Color Matrices for Overprinting

To generate overprinting spot colors and their tints, simply create a color matrix of each spot hue with 5 percent increments, from 0 to 100 percent. This can be created in Adobe Photoshop, InDesign, or Illustrator. (QuarkXPress 7 and later has overprinting capabilities, but not with two hues at 100 percent of color.)

This method can also be used to create a press proof for monotones, duotones, tritones, and four-color process images. To create the press proof all you need to know is where and on which printer the color proof will be pulled. Always print the color matrix and images on the same paper intended for the final proof. If you are using duotones and tritones, include a sample strip from each on the document as well. The strip should be from an area on the image that shows full color and tonal range. It is a good idea to have examples of one image set up three or four times with different color densities; in this way you are assured that one of the sample strips will be correct.

For this demonstration, Photoshop will be used to create the document. However, Illustrator or InDesign can also be used.

1. In Photoshop, set up a document at 72dpi. If monotones, duotones, tritones, and four-color process images are used within this document, make sure to set the dpi at 300.

2. Use the guidelines to create vertical and horizontal strips, 1in x 10in (2.54cm x 25.4cm), on two layers.

3. Using the rectangular Marquee tool and the Fill setting under Edit in the main menu, fill the vertical strips with the spot color. Each time you create and fill one of the vertical strips, change the opacity setting within the Fill dialog box. Start with 5 percent and move up in 5 percent increments to 100 percent.

4. Repeat the process for the other color on another layer, making sure you change the direction of the strips from vertical to horizontal.

5. Once you have completed the hues and tints, use the Multiply feature in the Layers dialog box and delete any unnecessary layers. (Sometimes it is helpful to create three or four layers of spot colors to determine, for example, which two hues will be used in the final document.) Within the Layers dialog box you can turn the Multiply feature quickly on and off to see different color effects. (Do not use the Multiply feature in the Fill dialog box.)

6. Flatten the document by selecting Flatten Image within the Layer dialog box and print it out.

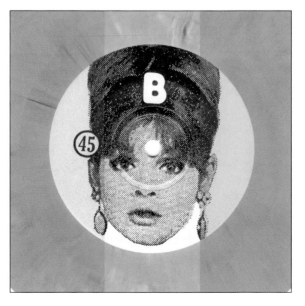

Diagram 5
It is prudent when pulling a high-end color proof or press proof to create vertical image strips that capture the most continuous tone. Make sure to set the curve settings three different ways. Ultimately this will give you more options in making sure that the color balance is correct.

These diagrams demonstrate spot color matrixes of hues that can be reproduced in CMYK color space.

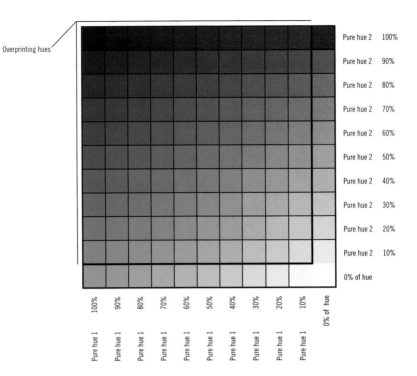

Overprinting hues

Pure hue 2   100%
Pure hue 2   90%
Pure hue 2   80%
Pure hue 2   70%
Pure hue 2   60%
Pure hue 2   50%
Pure hue 2   40%
Pure hue 2   30%
Pure hue 2   20%
Pure hue 2   10%
0% of hue

100% 90% 80% 70% 60% 50% 40% 30% 20% 10% 0% of hue

Pure hue 1 (×10)

Diagram 6 This is a composite two-color matrix that demonstrates a monochromatic study of both hue one and two, and the additional overprinted colors created by these screen percentages.

Diagram 7 (a and b) This diagram demonstrates how to create each layer in Photoshop. Once the two layers are created use the Multiply feature to verify overprinted hues.

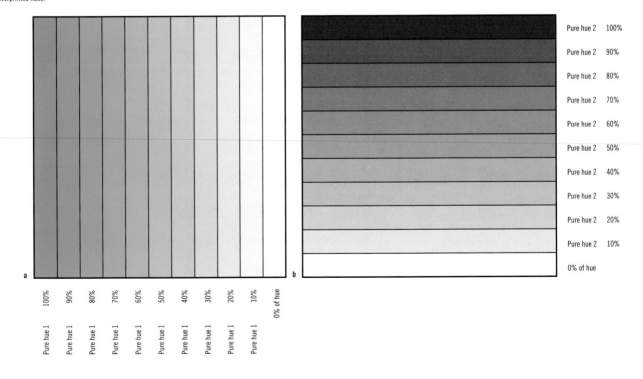

a

100% 90% 80% 70% 60% 50% 40% 30% 20% 10% 0% of hue

Pure hue 1 (×10)

b

Pure hue 2   100%
Pure hue 2   90%
Pure hue 2   80%
Pure hue 2   70%
Pure hue 2   60%
Pure hue 2   50%
Pure hue 2   40%
Pure hue 2   30%
Pure hue 2   20%
Pure hue 2   10%
0% of hue

Diagram 8 (a–i) This nine-part diagram shows the effects of different hues in screen percentages and overprinting percentages.

a
Pure hue 1

b
Pure hue 2

c
Pure hue 1 overprinting pure hue 2

d
Semipure hue 1

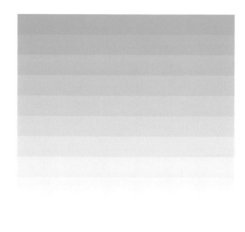

e
Pure hue 1

f
Semipure hue 1 overprinting pure hue 1

g
Semipure hue 1

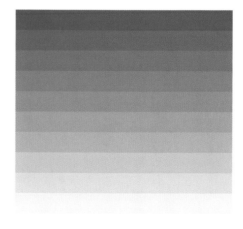

h
Semipure hue 2

i
Semipure hue 1 overprinting semipure hue 2

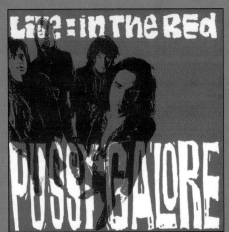

Figure 14

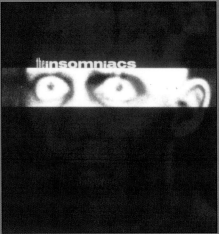

Figure 15

Setting up Proofs and Mechanicals for Overprinting

A client proof should not be taken to press. It should be used only to show the client accurate color appearance. For those graphic designers educated precomputer, the process of producing a client proof and an electronic mechanical for press will be much easier to comprehend. It is very similar to the way in which proofs and traditional mechanicals were produced for press in the past. The concept is basically the same—only the tools have changed.

Often with programs used for press purposes, overprinting or the simulation of overprinting is not available. (This is not the case with Adobe Illustrator, InDesign, Photoshop, and QuarkXPress 7 or later.) Being able to see what you are designing is critical. The system outlined below allows you to preview what these colors will look like when overprinting in applications that do not have overprinting capability, and to set up a separate electronic mechanical for press. More importantly, it allows you to show your clients what the printed sample will look like.

Figure 14
Art Director/Designer: Art Chantry
Photographer: Michael Levine

Overprinting green on red creates a relative black. Only the solid green within the knocked-out white type hints at the true nature of the color build. This is an excellent way to achieve the appearance of four colors (red, green, black, and white) within a two-color printing process.

Figure 15
Art Director/Designer: Art Chantry

As two parts of the primary triad, yellow and blue create excellent contrast.

Diagram 9
The Acuity Color System is an extensive four-color process library. The matrices found within this system allow the designer to color calibrate their printer with ease.

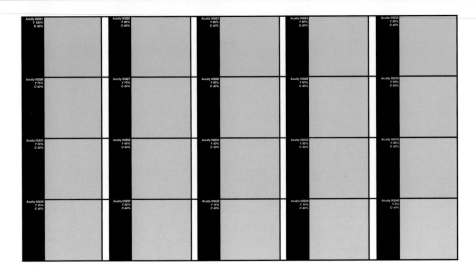

Several simple rules guide the effective creation of a client proof and an electronic mechanical for press:

Rule 1:
The electronic client proof should never be taken to a service bureau or printing firm when film is going to be produced for the job. This will add confusion.

Rule 2:
A color printout of the client proof should be provided to the service bureau or printing firm along with the electronic file for press.

Rule 3:
To show accurate overprinting of spot colors, the individual spot hues must be within the CMYK color spectrum if using a low-end ink-jet or plotter printer. Use the PANTONE® COLOR BRIDGE® to verify which PANTONE colors can be reproduced using CMYK primaries.

Rule 4:
If the spot hues fall outside of the CMYK color spectrum, a hard copy must be pulled from a printer that has a greater color gamma than the spot hues. Chromix offers a line of software called ColorThink Pro and ColorThink v2 that will show the color gammas of different systems, including ink and printers. In other words, the software will demonstrate if a printer is capable of printing a particular color gamma or not.

Rule 5:
Keep the written instructions to the printer or service bureau simple and clear. In this case, less is more.

Figure 16

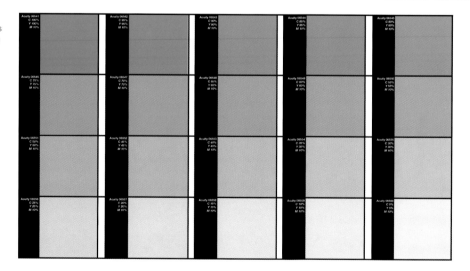

Diagram 10
The Acuity color matrix demonstrates some of the green hues found within the system.

Figure 16
Art Director/Designer: Art Chantry

A bright pink contains the additive primary red, or the subtractive primary magenta. When overprinted with green, a third color is created. In this album cover, overprinting is used selectively to highlight visually and semantically the word "double."

Figure 17

Figure 18

Setting up Client Proofs for Overprinting

This process allows you to create a document that simulates two overprinting spot colors for client approval only. If this document were taken to press (in QuarkXPress 6.5 and earlier), four pieces of film would be RIPed (Raster Image Processor), and the job would no longer be considered two color. (This does not apply to Adobe InDesign, Illustrator, Photoshop, or QuarkXPress 7 and later.) Follow the same steps to produce a client proof using three and four spot-color builds.

1. Choose the spot colors desired.

2. Create the spot-color matrix as described above. Apply the Multiply feature in the Layers dialog box in Photoshop once the matrix is created. This allows you to verify visually how the colors will overprint. If you omit this, Photoshop will not accurately simulate the overprinting of two spot colors. (Make sure that this is a separate document for color study purposes only. If the spot color(s) fall outside of the CMYK color spectrum, set the document up in RGB mode. In this way, the file will be able to emulate the spot color(s) gamma. It is also important to print the document out to a device that will capture this color gamma.)

3. Print out the color matrix and select the colors you desire from the printed spot-color matrix, making sure you skip at least two or three squares between the colors to be used. Do not pick colors that are side by side as their color-value differential will not be sufficient for hue difference to be

Figure 17
Art Director/Designer: Art Chantry
Photographer: Isabeile Soulier

The CD insert to the left exemplifies the relative color differences between overprinting complementary colors—red and green in the splash marks, for example—to create black or using a solid process black as in the title bar. The difference is clearly visible when the two "blacks" are adjacent.

Figure 18
Art Director/Designer: Art Chantry

When printed using four-color process, this album cover effectively demonstrates how the subtractive primaries of cyan, magenta, and yellow can create the additive colors of red and green. The third additive primary, blue, could be implied if yellow was not printed as a solid throughout the background layer.

Diagram 11 (a–e)
Examples of spot color (SC) matrices using tints and overprinting are shown in a–c.

1. SC 1 20%
2. SC 1 80%
3. SC 2 20%
4. SC 2 100%
5. SC 1 20%; SC 2 60%
6. SC 1 80%; SC 2 60%
7. SC 1 40%; SC 2 100%
8. SC 1 80%; SC 2 100%

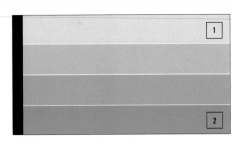

a

detected. If the design calls for a pie chart, choose colors that are three or four squares apart in any direction. Remember, Chromix offers a line of software called ColorThink Pro and ColorThink v2 that will show the color gammas of different systems, including ink and printers. ColorThink will show you if the PANTONE colors chosen fall outside of the printer's color gamma. If the PANTONE color(s) falls outside the printer's color spectrum, a higher-end proofing system is required for a hard-copy proof.

4. In Photoshop use the Eyedrop tool to click on each color chosen. Write down the CMYK percentages. (This is required only for QuarkXPress 6.5 documents and earlier.) If using InDesign, Illustrator, Photoshop, or QuarkXPress 7 or later versions, simply write down the percentage of color for each overprinted hue—for example, PANTONE 123 C 80 percent and PANTONE 381 C 20 percent. (QuarkXPress 7 will not construct a document that has two overprinting colors at 100 percent.)

5. Choose the software application desired for the print job.

6. Under the color feature found within QuarkXPress 6.5 and earlier, plug in the CMYK percentages for each color. For InDesign, Illustrator, Photoshop, or QuarkXPress 7 and later load the spot colors and create their overprinting percentages in the document. (QuarkXPress 7 will not construct a document that has two overprinting colors at 100 percent.)

7. In QuarkXPress 6.5 and earlier use these percentages to name each new color—for example, C 20 M 80 Y 5 K 3—and type in the color builds to create the new color. (This does not apply to InDesign, Illustrator, Photoshop, or QuarkXPress 7 and later.)

8. In QuarkXPress 6.5 and earlier create the design using only the colors that are derived from the spot-color matrix to allow the client proof to simulate the overprinting of two spot colors. (This does not apply to InDesign, Illustrator, Photoshop, or QuarkXPress 7 and later. In these software applications, simply create the document using these specified spot colors.)

9. For monotones and duotones produce photographs with one or both spot colors at 100 percent.

10. After the monotones and duotones have been created, in QuarkXPress 6.5 and earlier copy these files in duplicate and save them as CMYK documents. Place these duplicate CMYK documents in the above QuarkXPress file for position only (FPO). For InDesign, Illustrator, and QuarkXPress 7 and later, place the monotone or duotone files into the document.

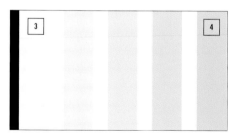

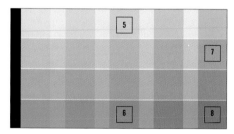

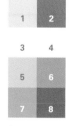

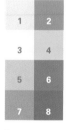

b
The spot color opacity is stepped down in 20% increments, creating tinted hues.

c
The spot colors found in a and b are overprinted, creating additional hues.

d
Electronic mechanical made from yellow and magenta. To create an overprinting mechanical, two of the three four-color primaries should be used. This will allow for up to three spot hues.

e
Printed result and client proof.

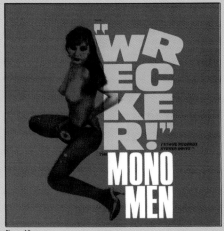

Figure 19

Overprinting Spot Colors for Press

Until the mid-1980s it was usual to create traditional mechanicals for press. These were constructed with illustration board, photo stats, typesetting stats, and rubylith and/or amberlith overlays. The black base plate was always placed on the illustration board, and the consecutive color plates laid over. All written indication was placed on a tissue overlay instructing the strippers (the individuals who create film composites by cutting them apart and stripping them together prior to platemaking) on the types of colors being utilized, percentages of color, screen frequency, and any other information that needed to be communicated.

Today, most of this information is automatically composed and specified. Up to the end of the 1980s the overprinting of two spot colors was commonplace. Today, this lost art is being revitalized through Adobe Photoshop, Illustrator, InDesign, and QuarkXPress 7 and later, or through the creation of an electronic file specifically as a mechanical for press via QuarkXPress 6.5 or earlier.

With Adobe products, the overprinting feature is called Multiply. In Illustrator and InDesign, the overprinting feature can be found under Window in the main menu—scroll down to Transparency and release the mouse. Within the Transparency dialog box click on the scroll-down menu. The default setting is Normal. Scroll over Multiply and release the mouse. This creates an overprinting document with as many colors/spot colors as desired. Note that an overprinting document has elements (type, flat graphics, images, and the like) that are built on top or partially on top of one another. This is typically achieved by layering elements in the Layer dialog box. In Photoshop the Multiply feature is found in the Layer dialog box and operates the same way.

In QuarkXPress 7 overprinting can be achieved through the Colors dialog box. First load the spot hues desired under Edit in the main menu by scrolling down to Colors. Once the hues are loaded into the Colors dialog box, overprinting can be achieved through the opacity setting within the Colors dialog box. Remember, QuarkXPress 7 cannot overprint two or more hues at 100 percent of color.

Figure 20

Figure 19
Art Director/Designer: Art Chantry
Photographer: Susan McKeever

Black is printed over the solid background of red and yellow-orange, creating an effective fake duotone.

Figure 20
Art Director/Designer: Art Chantry
Photographer: Charles Peterson

The psychedelic effect of the type is cleanly executed through the overlapping of subtractive primaries. In contrast, narrowing the subtractive gamma blends the photography into the red-purple of the typography.

a

b

c   d

Diagram 12 (a–d)
These four diagrams illustrate how documents built in the four-color process primaries can be altered to print in any spot hues. Three spot hues are shown in a–c; in d, all three spot hues from a–c are overprinted to create a new color palette.

For QuarkXPress 6.5 and earlier, the procedure to create an overprinting document is quite different. Using either the magenta and yellow or the cyan and yellow plates, QuarkXPress can create overprinting documents. For that matter, any software application can create the desired overprinting mechanical using this method. Cyan and yellow offer the greatest difference in color appearance; greens indicate where the two spot colors will overprint. By using only two of the four process colors, the job will RIP on two pieces of film. To set up a two-color overprinting mechanical for press, follow the steps below.

1. Create the client proof as indicated in Setting Up Client Proofs for Overprinting. This proof needs to be complete and signed off by the client before you can start the electronic mechanical.

2. Using the spot-color matrix created, indicate the screen percentages of each color build. These percentages should give only the amount used from each spot color. For example, PANTONE 185 C 10 percent and PANTONE 259 C 85 percent make up one overprinting color. Do not write down the CMYK builds of each color.

3. Once you have written down the overprinting colors and their corresponding screen percentages (PANTONE 185 C 10 percent and PANTONE 259 C 85 percent), open up the client proof.

4. Save the client proof as a duplicate copy and save the file. Make sure you mark the file clearly for press.

5. Working with the duplicate copy, open up the Color dialog box. Some programs may require you to go through the main menu to edit and create new or edited colors; these will appear in the Color dialog box once you have saved them.

6. On a piece of paper indicate which spot color is to be substituted with yellow and which with cyan. (It does not matter which is replaced with which.)

7. Replace each color that was created within the client proof to simulate spot-color overprinting with cyan, yellow, and combinations of the two with the correct screen percentages for the spot-color builds. The electronic mechanical should now have a color palette made only from cyan and its tints, yellow and its tints, and screen percentages of the two, creating different values of green.

8. Print out the electronic mechanical, with crop marks, for viewing. A low-end ink-jet printer is sufficient for this task.

9. At the bottom of the printout write, as appropriate, "Yellow prints as PANTONE 185 C and cyan prints as PANTONE 259 C." The stripper will scratch out the yellow and cyan names on the film work and replace them with PANTONE 185 C and PANTONE 259 C.

10. Write down any other indication to be communicated to the printer, and the file is ready to go to press.

11. Take the printouts of both the client proof and the electronic mechanical to press. Mark the client proof to indicate that it is a facsimile of what the printed job should look like.

Figure 21

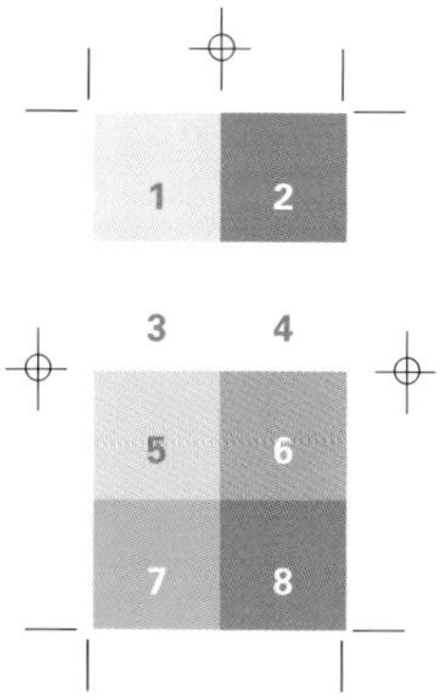

Diagram 13
Electronic mechanical made from yellow and magenta. With this type of mechanical any spot color can be substituted from any color-matching system.

Printer, yellow prints as PANTONE 123 and magenta prints as PANTONE 226

Figure 21
Art Director/Designer: Art Chantry

This one-color piece activates white space through coarse-dot screens that are repeated at the same size throughout the fish and the water. The screen is referenced on both the front and back of the album cover with a smaller dot in the typography.

Figure 22

Manual Color Syncing and Overprinting

Setting up a document to color sync the hues on screen to a printout is easy. The document will simulate overprinting for client proofs and setting up an electronic file for press to allow overprinting.

1. Open the document and make a duplicate copy so that both documents are on the screen together.

2. Choose the color matrices that are color appropriate for the document from the Acuity Color System, and open the color-matrix document. (The Acuity Color System can be found with the book *Color Management: A Comprehensive Guide for Graphic Designers* by Sarah A. Meyer and John T. Drew and published by RotoVision.) If you are using two spot colors, create a color matrix (see step 2 under Building Spot-Color Matrices for Overprinting).

3. Print out the color matrices appropriate to the working document.

4. From the printout, choose the hues that represent the colors on screen.

5. Make the necessary color adjustments on the duplicate document by plugging in the new CMYK color builds or spot-color percentages. If the spot color(s) fall outside of the CMYK color spectrum, set the document up in RGB mode. In this way,

Figure 22
Art Director/Designer: Art Chantry
Photography: Rhawn York

Overprinting is used to its fullest in this CD packaging. However, the knock out on the CD is of particular note where the metallic sheen of the CD becomes an interesting part of the design.

Diagram 14 (a–e)
Follow these steps for building a spot-color matrix for overprinting.

a

Image before adjustment on computer screen (step 1).

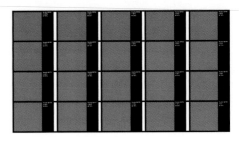

b

Open or create a color matrix (step 2).

the file will be able to emulate the gamma of the spot color(s). It is also important to print the document out to a device that will capture this color gamma. (The color builds in the original will no longer match the color builds in the duplicate document—they will look very different.)

6. Print out the duplicate document. It should closely match the original working file on screen. (Note: Repeat this process every time the original document is printed to another device or different paper is used. Changing the printing device from an inkjet printer to an Iris, or changing the paper stock from uncoated to coated, will alter the color appearance. Remember, Chromix offers a line of software called ColorThink Pro and ColorThink v2 that will show the color gammas of different systems, including ink and printers. Calibrate your devices—computer screen, scanner, printer, and digital camera. This will help in the process of matching colors. See Color Work Flow in Chapter 8 for more details.)

Figure 23

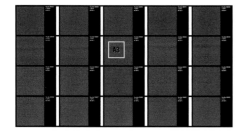

c

Print out color matrix (step 3), then choose hues from matrix (step 4).

d

Adjusted image on screen (step 5).

e

Color printout after making adjustment to document (step 6).

Figure 23
Art Director/Designer: Art Chantry

Ordinarily a fake duotone utilizes a solid field of color. In this case, white rectangles are knocked out of the red field to highlight the individual band members, forcing the duotone further into the background.

Specials and Finishing Techniques

The goal of a package design is not only to attract the eye and build brand recognition, but also to protect the contents, and create a container that opens easily and can be shipped readily. Upon first perusing an aisle of products, it is the packaging that attracts our eye. Whether the product arrives safely and the package opens easily for the client to consume is dependent on the forethought of the designer. Time tested, successful packaging that meets these measures of quality will result in consumer demand and increased shelf space in the hyper competitive market. There is no finer way to meet these objects than through the use of specialized finishing techniques.

Special coatings and finishing techniques provide protection and visual appeal to a package. These techniques can be bold and aggressive, or bring an air of class and sophistication. Tactile finishing techniques, such as foil stamping, embossing, engraving, and thermography, can create a sense of handcrafted quality. Die cuts and varnishes can further this layer of complexity, or simply provide a protective barrier for the product inside. In many cases, only the use of these techniques will make the package stand out from the plethora of choices.

Figure 1

Foil Stamping

The traditional art of gold leafing, or gilding, is commonly simulated through inks that suspend metal flakes in the resin of the ink. These metallic inks are generally categorized as leafing and nonleafing. During the drying process the metal particles of a leafing ink rise to the surface while the resin is absorbed by the substrate; when nonleafing ink dries the metal flakes soak into the resin. Varnishes are strongly recommended for leafing inks where the metal particles sit on top and are exposed to the environment. Although a varnish is not required for nonleafing metallic, it is recommended in order to prevent fingerprints, chipping, scuff marks, and tarnishing. For example, copper alloy, the most common ink additive used to simulate gold, is highly susceptible to tarnishing—in fact, all metals except gold will tarnish with prolonged exposure to air, but gold is much more expensive than varnished copper alloy. However, varnishes tend to decrease the overall shine of metallic ink, creating an unburnished or shell-gold effect. As a result, foil stamping is often preferred. Other names for foil stamping are hot stamping, dry stamping, flat stamping, leaf stamping, foil imprinting, leafing, and blocking.

Foil stamping is the process whereby a thin layer of foil is adhered to the surface through the use of a heated plate or die that is stamped onto the surface of the substrate. Foil stamping can more accurately reflect the highly burnished or polished look of gilding and will not tarnish under normal conditions. In addition, it may be more cost effective than ink. Ink would require multiple passes, opaque undercoats, and varnishes to get the same result.

Figure 1
Studio: CF NAPA
Creative Director: David Schuemann

Metallic inks and embossing create an air of subtle sophistication and modernity to this wine label.

Diagram 1
This illustration demonstrates two basic plate techniques. A more highly specialized technique, the second is most commonly used for recessed surfaces such as some embossing/debossing and engraving.

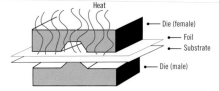

Foil stamping with a female and male die (basics of engraving and embossing)

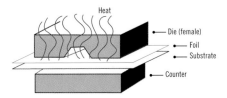

Conventional foil stamping

Ink can be applied over a foil if a foil formulated to accept ink is specified. By contrast, foil stamping should never be applied over a varnish or coating without consultation with the vendor. When foil stamping over a preprinted area, the ink should be wax free and dry to prevent pick, where the foil inconsistently adheres to the substrate, so causing ragged edges to the design. Inks that include Teflon or silicon and lacquers or UV coatings are also problematic. To get the best result it is often advisable to knock out areas where a varnish will be placed. However, knock outs should be used only with advice of the printer because registration must be considered. In general, kiss fit or butte registering is often used over trapping, so it is unwise to proceed without consultation.

Foils come in a multitude of colors, with satin, matte, pearlescent, opalescent, or glossy finishes. Some replicate the patina of age, banding, and mottling, like an old statue exposed to the elements. Most commonly the colors are categorized as metallic, pigment, effect, holographic, and scratch-off. Metallic comes in a full range of colors, but silver and gold are the most common and consist of a thin layer of colored aluminum that provides sheen. Pigmented foils are typically flat and are often used on the signature portion of credit cards. Effect foils come in a wide range of screen patterns, stripes, light diffractions, snake skin, stone, wood grains, and holograms. Holographic foils are often used for visual effects or security seals and can be specially designed with an inlaid image. Holograms consist of two sub-categories: random and registered. Random holographic images are repeated or wallpapered

Figure 2

Figure 3

Diagram 2
The typical composition of foil is defined in the three layers to the left. More complex foils that carry metallic, diffraction, holographic, and magnetic materials or printed grains are illustrated on the right.

Figure 2
Studio: Dustin Edward Arnold/DL&Co.
Creative Director: Douglas Little
Designer: Dustin E. Arnold

The box for Modern Alchemy fragranced candles imparts a metallic elegance, but it is standardized. Only the ribbon on top of the box states the fragrance name, cutting production costs and allowing the product line to grow easily.

Figure 3
Studio: Midnite Oil
Art Director/Designer:
Mongkolsri Janjarasskul

As packaging for a high-quality pearl-extract health-and-beauty product imported from China, the product pricing is on the high end. Thus, the packaging imparts a look and feel of a luxurious and precious gift through the use of metallic inks and foil.

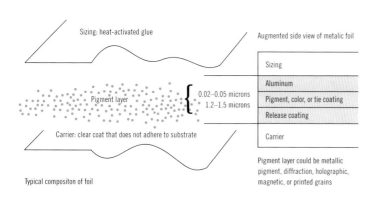

Sizing: heat-activated glue

Augmented side view of metalic foil

Pigment layer

{ 0.02–0.05 microns
1.2–1.5 microns

| Sizing |
| Aluminum |
| Pigment, color, or tie coating |
| Release coating |
| Carrier |

Carrier: clear coat that does not adhere to substrate

Pigment layer could be metallic pigment, diffraction, holographic, magnetic, or printed grains

Typical composition of foil

Figure 4

Figure 5

patterns that are randomly applied. Registered holograms have a holographic image and registration marks within the foil. The foiled image is then applied with a stamping machine that tightly registers each layer. There are four basic types of holographic images: holographic pattern, multiple plane, three-dimensional, and stereogram. Scratch-off foils lack a hardening agent that permanently adheres the pigment to the substrate, and they are commonly used for lottery scratch cards and similar. All of these foils can be applied in flat patterns or in coarse dot screens and patterns. In each case the designer should consult with the vendor.

Foils have a tendency to spread or fill in thin spaces. Therefore, type with loose kerning and well-defined thick and thin strokes is suggested. A rule of thumb is to lay out the design so that the typographic thins or the space between areas is no less than half the thickness of the substrate. Designs that include large areas of foil with thin type, intricate details, or fine lines may require two passes to maintain quality. In addition, textured paper may prevent large solids or large type from adhering consistently. This can be aggravated by parchment and recycled stocks that lack tensile strength or surface tension. The surface tension of paper is measured by the dyne count, and this should be higher than 40. Because of the short grain structures or dry, flaky qualities of a substrate, the foil will find it difficult to adhere to a sheet of less than 40 dyne count and the results may be dull, or the foil may crack, peel, or flake off. This is of particular importance to a design that will undergo heat extremes, such as a letterhead

Figure 4
Studio: Gouthier Design
a brand collective
Creative Director: Jonathan Gouthier
Designers: Gouthier Design
Creative Team

The property-brand launch announcement for an ultraluxury real-estate development had to have a sense of craft. Utilizing limited colors and unique printing techniques—such as blind embossing and foil—a true sense of the Italian Tuscan countryside came out.

Figures 5 and 6
Studio: Gouthier Design
a brand collective
Creative Director: Jonathan Gouthier
Designers: Gouthier Design
Creative Team

The luxury brochure for the Domani property comes in a box that was shrink-wrapped and ribbon tied. Receiving a package that imparts quality execution at every level of printing and finishing invites clients to peruse more intently.

that may be used in a laser printer. The opacity of a foil should also be tested before using it on a dark stock.

The design to be foiled should not be placed too close to the edge of the paper or a puckering effect will occur. This is particularly important in a package design where humidity and condensation are concerns. Some humidity issues can be addressed by the choice of the substrate. For example, a heavier stock with a longer grain structure will be less likely to curl under conditions of extreme moisture. In general, for consistent high quality, heavy paper with a cast coating, thick plastic, or book cloth is the default. Other materials could include vinyl, leather, wood, and textiles. Foil stamping is particularly effective with embossing because the emboss will stretch the foil over the relief image, creating seemingly cleaner and more defined lines.

Figure 6

Diagram 3
These three illustrations define the most common applications for foil on an embossed or debossed substrate. This is of particular importance when dealing with the counters of type or any delicate illustration.

Bevel in with foil

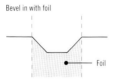

Foil

Bevel in with foil split

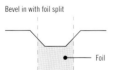

Foil

Bevel out with foil

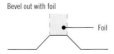

Foil

Examples of different foil applications on a bevel

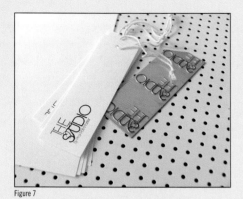

Figure 7

Embossing and Debossing

Embossing is the process whereby a metal die containing a relief image presses into the paper, creating a raised image. Debossing creates a lowered image through the same process. Embossing and debossing are equally effective in conjunction with foil, ink, varnish, or plain paper. When plain paper is embossed without registering it to a printed image, it is called a blind emboss. When using embossing or debossing the design must abide by the same principles to create a result that is appealing visually as well as to the touch.

Embosses come in single or multiple levels depending on the design indicated. Each level may conform to a specified embossing effect, such as round lift, beveled flat lift, raised faceted, or sculptured. Beveled dies create sharp details and edges that will not tear the paper on deep embosses. Sculptured dies are hand-engraved and utilize a variety of edge angles and fields of depth to simulate complex detail. The designer can specify different effects for each level of an emboss on a layered comprehensive that indicates the levels and the amount of detail. The paper stock should be relatively soft and accepting of dies so that it will not crack or pucker, and should be embossed with the grain. If multiple levels are specified, the weight and caliper should be communicated so that the depth of the die will correspond to the thickness of the paper. In most cases, complicated designs such as a multilevel or sculptural engraving will require

the use of a brass die that will hold up to pressure on long runs and stamp with detail. Often brass dies are photoetched or machine tooled with the aid of a computer. The benefit is that computerized machine tooling creates an extremely precise die, which is better for complex designs. Other more cost-effective alternatives to brass include magnesium and copper. Magnesium is most often used for short runs of single-level designs with minimum detail and even distribution of foils on coated or smooth stock. Copper is a great heat conductor, and it is preferred for medium runs of single-level emboss that have large areas of foil on textured or recycled stock.

Line art is most compatible with embossing. Detailed line art should be saved at 100 percent of size and 600dpi or greater. Proofing of a die can occur only after the die is constructed, so it is wise to keep in mind that the results will appear smaller than the original because of the rounded, beveled, or faceted edge of the emboss. This can be an advantage to a designer trying to imply fine detail; however, if thin forms or counters are not thickened on the original, they will be completely lost or filled in on the final design.

Figure 7
Studio: milkxhake
Art Director/Designer: milkxhake

The Studio by Pro Wolf Master is a New York street-fashion store based in Hong Kong, for which a new identity was imparted to all packaging including T-shirt envelopes and bags. The debossing die seen here stamps a filigreed "T" on brilliant-white stock to create an elegant hangtag.

Diagram 4
As seen from the side, a slight raising (emboss) or lowering (deboss) of the surface of the substrate will occur.

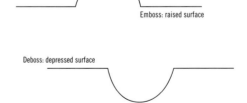

Emboss: raised surface

Deboss: depressed surface

Embossing tends to flatten or smooth out the texture of paper while raising the surface. Again, designers can use this to their advantage by specifying a blind emboss on a roughly textured paper. The contrast of the burnished blind emboss to the textured paper is called glazing. Glazing requires more pressure and heat, but creates outstanding contrast on dark stock. If a lighter stock is required, gloss emboss is suggested. A gloss emboss uses a clear foil with the blind emboss to create a highly varnished effect.

Many other effects can be achieved with foil stamping and embossing. These include refractive engraving, tint leaf combination, and textured emboss. Typically, refractive engraving applies metallic foil with a crosshatched embossing die. The crosshatch adds texture and emphasizes the spectral reflections of the foil. Tint leaf combination is similar to a gloss emboss with the difference that a pastel tint is used. Textured embosses add dimensionality and can be used over large surfaces. They come in a variety of standardized textures, such as orange peel, pebble, or wood grain.

Figure 8

Figure 9

Figures 8 and 9
Studio: ICAN DESIGN
Art Director/Designer: Daniel Rodgers

Loose-leaf white Pai Mu Tan tea is luxuriously marketed with a subdued color palette that is made tactile through a blind-embossed logo mark. The historic typefaces—Dutch 766 and Dutch 801—echo the long history of importing tea to the UK.

Diagram 5
Engraver's symbols: these are a few of the symbols used by engravers for differentiating die effects.

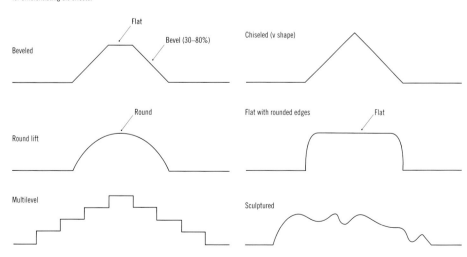

Beveled — Flat — Bevel (30–80%)

Chiseled (v shape)

Round lift — Round

Flat with rounded edges — Flat

Multilevel

Sculptured

Figure 10

Figure 11

Engraving and Thermography

Engraving is a highly specialized technique used to create plates and dies for foil stamping or the intaglio and gravure printing processes. Traditionally, an engraver used a burin to mechanically scratch the surface of a metal plate made from copper or steel. Today, dies can be created mechanically by hand, chemically etched, or laser burned, and often come in limited plate sizes so check with the printer that they have the right size before creating the design. When engraving is used as a printing process, the recessed areas, or wells, carry ink that is then transferred to the paper under pressure. The depth and diameter of the recess dictates the density of the ink, and thereby its relative darkness or lightness. Images are created through a series of these engraved wells. The wells produce images that are inherently sharp with fine details. It is best to use recipe, spot, or match colors with engraving rather than simulate the four-color continuous tone of offset lithography. The sharp quality of engraving does not lend itself to continuous-tone images that require some dot gain to create a pleasing result; it is much better for detailed work, so screen tints and outlines reproduce more accurately than large areas of color that may mottle.

Engraving will greatly enhance long runs of packaging by raising the surface of the image slightly, causing an effect similar to a shallow emboss. However, the ink is slightly raised, as is the surface of the paper, because the printing technique forces the paper against a recessed surface. The ink must dry very fast and cannot be viscous, so it tends to hold the form of the engraved recess. Specially formulated inks with

Figure 10
Studio: Dustin Edward Arnold/DL&Co.
Creative Director: Douglas Little
Designer: Dustin E. Arnold

Fostered with a well-crafted die, the front of Douglas Little & Co. Parlour Collection Candles packaging shows the quality that can be attained through gold leafing and engraving.

Figure 11
Studio: Dustin Edward Arnold/DL&Co.
Creative Director: Douglas Little
Designer: Dustin E. Arnold

Complex levels of depth and fine detail can be seen in this close-up.

Diagram 6
Engraving wells: this diagram is equally well suited for the gravure process.

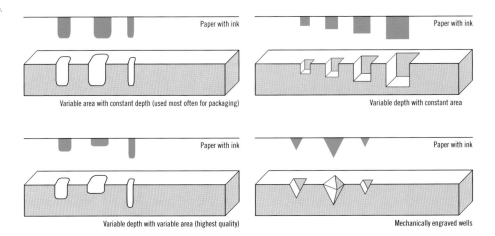

Paper with ink

Variable area with constant depth (used most often for packaging)

Paper with ink

Variable depth with constant area

Paper with ink

Variable depth with variable area (highest quality)

Paper with ink

Mechanically engraved wells

a high opacity are used. These inks are good for printing light colors on dark papers, but, as in most printing, they reproduce best on high-quality paper. Woven stock tends to hold the detail of an engraving best; laid paper may feather the ink, and coated paper will often crack under the pressure of printing. Since engraving is a highly specialized technique, it is suggested that your printer be consulted before designing any job for this process.

Overall, the effect of engraving is desirable, but it can be prohibitive for small jobs because of the costs inherent in this specialty process. Thermography is an economical option that simulates the effects of engraving without a die and in a shorter time. A heat-sensitive or UV resin is mixed into the ink. When the ink is printed and exposed to heat or UV light, the resin reacts, giving the image a raised surface similar to engraving. The quality of thermography is dependent upon the size of the grains in the resin powder, how well the powder adheres, and the consistency of the ink and heat. Small grains of resin are better for details, whereas larger grains of resin fill solid areas more consistently—although large solids are not recommended because they have a tendency to cause blistering. In addition, large areas should not be folded or scored because the ink may crack, and bleeds must be die cut because a guillotine cutter can also crack the resin. Thermography is not recommended for packages that will be handled excessively or exposed to extreme heat because the surface is susceptible to dulling and scratches.

Thermography will never be as crisp as engraving, but under the right circumstances the results will be evenly raised and glossy. If the ink, heat/UV, and resin are not accurately controlled, the result will be a stippled and inconsistently raised or bumpy surface. To ensure accuracy, use thermography on small areas of line art rather than screen tints or half-tones, and select type that is 7pt. or greater. The stock should be a fairly rigid cover stock of 20lb. or more and untextured. Textures tend to attract resin in nonimage areas, and glossy stocks do not contrast as well as matte with the thermographic process.

Figure 12

Diagram 7
Identifying thermography vs. engraving. These two vantages illustrate the differences in distribution of ink and effects on the substrate of engraving and thermography, and will help the designer to differentiate between the two.

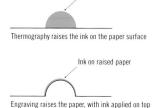

Ink

Thermography raises the ink on the paper surface

Ink on raised paper

Engraving raises the paper, with ink applied on top

Figure 12
Studio: Dustin Edward Arnold
Art Director/Designer:
Dustin E. Arnold

This limited-edition engraved carrier-box for stationery imparts elegance and makes a timeless gift.

Coatings and Varnishes

Four basic types of coatings are applied to packaging: varnish, aqueous coating, UV coating, and laminates. A varnish is the ink vehicle without pigment. Aqueous coating is, as the name implies, a resin and water-based covering. UV coatings are plastics that dry when exposed to UV light; they can give an extremely high-gloss appearance. Laminates are plastics that are glued to the surface, providing the highest level of water resistance. Each comes in gloss, satin, or matte/dull. Next to laminates, gloss varnishes or gloss aqueous coatings provide the best protection and varying levels of shine. Matte is dull in appearance and tends to scratch easily, whereas satin is approximately halfway between gloss and matte. The coating will feel smooth if applied accurately. If the surface feels bumpy or scratchy, similar to sandpaper, then the coating was not regulated.

Packaging design makes use of coatings to protect the surface and visually enhance the product. Some coatings will increase shelf life or protect the inks from UV light. If a coating is applied over a wet ink (wet trapped), it will not increase the gloss of the image or substrate, but it may darken the ink color. This is an excellent way to increase the apparent density of a solid color or depth in an image. If the coating is applied over a dry ink (dry trapped), the color will darken and interesting visual effects may be incorporated. Such effects may be used to suggest more shine on certain parts of an image, reduce glare, or enhance unprinted stock with spot applications. Since some coatings yellow with age or change the brightness rating of a white stock, it is important to talk to the printer about the qualities of the coating, the desired effects, and the shelf life of the package.

There are some general rules to follow in order to get the best results. For example, packages should never be coated where gluing or stamping—such as "born on" dating—will occur, and the stock will determine the type of coating used. Most often varnishes are used for uncoated stock and aqueous coatings are used for coated stock. The high water content of aqueous coating tends to buckle and curl uncoated paper. Aqueous coatings are desirable for sustainable packaging because they are water based and wax free. They yield the most dramatic visual results, but cost significantly more than a traditional varnish. Aqueous coatings increase the brilliance of colors and protect surfaces from scratches, scuffs, and fingerprints. Unfortunately, such coatings will change the structure of the paper, making it difficult to register both sides of a printed

Figure 13

Figure 13
Studio: Irving
Designer: Julian Roberts
Typographer: Heather Darwall-Smith

A flood varnish will keep the folds of this metallic packaging from cracking or becoming scuffed as it is wrapped with a ribbon for handling and gift giving.

Figure 14
Art Director: John T. Drew
Designer: Kyle Goodwin

In this case, the spot varnish adds a layer of subtlety and sophistication unsurpassed by any other finishing technique. As each box is pulled from the consecutive package, the spot varnish acts as a layer of lace or lingerie to reveal more, and to convey a sense of quality. Truly a magnificent piece, this design clearly illustrates the true potential of any finishing technique, and especially a spot varnish.

Figure 14

piece, so, when using an aqueous coating for packaging, it is often recommended that the reverse side utilize loose registration or flood varnishes and colors. Of particular importance to packaging is the ability to diminish cracking at folds with aqueous coating. Dry trapping a spot-aqueous coating can dramatically enhance the visual appeal of a package.

Varnishes are a more economical method of protecting paper against scuffing and rubbing during handling or bulk processing, especially when flooded across the whole surface (flood varnish). Nontoxic varnishes provide a barrier for food packaging, but dull varnishes will scuff and should be used only to prevent fingerprint marks. Pigments, tints, and pearling particles can be incorporated into the vehicle of a varnish, but in most instances varnishes have no visual effects and are not recommended for such. For example, a high-gloss varnish on an uncoated sheet may be completely absorbed and invisible to the naked eye. If any noticeable visual effect is desired, it is imperative that a spot varnish be dry trapped on a coated sheet. For example, a photo that is dry trapped with a gloss varnish on glossy paper may take on the qualities of a photographic print. However, this should be attempted only with the consultation of the printer, because the same results may be accomplished more cost effectively by dull varnishing the background on a glossy paper or with an aqueous coating.

Figure 15

Figure 15
Studio: Irving
Designer: Julian Roberts
Illustrator: Stuart Thompson

The embossing dramatically high-lights the subtle shift in red, and complements the gold band as well as the yellow interior of the folds. These folds are created by a complex die and score, and are unified by the red string that ensures its closure.

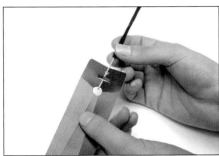

Figure 16

Die Cuts and Laser Cuts

Packaging often involves paper engineering, that is the art of folding, scoring, and cutting paper to create three-dimensional shapes and structures. The discipline involves a complex understanding of paper structure, including tensile strength and grain direction. The qualities of paper—whether it can hold up to temperature extremes, humidity, or pressure—is determined by the paper structure. Some of the key qualities a package designer looks for in a substrate are the ability to accept ink well and to remain intact at the core and the surface of the package. The grain of the paper often helps to determine these issues. Paper is made of pulp composed of long fibers. During the process of making paper the pulp will align. The grain is the direction the majority of the fiber or pulp runs. In general terms, this

includes but is not limited to three-dimensional plastic extrusions, polypropylene, glass, paper, and cardboard. Packaging design requires considerable forethought and research into the strength of any stock used.

Folds that fall against the grain—across the fibers—have inherently less tensile strength. They will often crack or fail under pressure. This is of considerable importance when designing packages that will be stacked or that will house fragile materials. So prominent folds should always run parallel to the grain. Scoring is an appropriate method of creating a fold. There are two types of scoring: blade and blunt, or rounded. Blade scores slightly cut the fibers, whereas blunt scores simply deboss the paper. As the paper is folded, the ridge of the score is bent into the fold. For example, on a box the ridge will be on the interior of the structure and the deboss will be stretched across the exterior. Although scoring at a fold will maximize the results, some cracking may occur where a large amount of ink is used, particularly with double hits and varnishes. Coated stock will exaggerate any cracking.

Die cutting is one of the most common methods of engineering a score, perforation, or specialized cut for package design. Like a cookie cutter, dull and/or sharp steel rules

Figure 17

Figure 16
Designer: Piero Quintiliani
Photographer: Marco Cavallo

Although inexpensive to create, the ease and elegance of "Incènse" assembly promotes the use of the unique kit.

Figure 17
Designer: Piero Quintiliani
Photographer: Marco Cavallo

Created from the dieing and scoring of thin cardboard, "Incènse" is both a package and a holder. Taking inspiration from the art of minimalism, this package is easily manufactured, flat packed, and distributed.

Diagram 8
Grain direction is important in the engineering of paper. In particular, folds against the grain are weaker and subject to cracking.

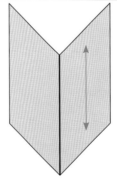

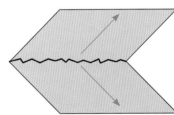

A fold with the grain is
less likely to crack

A fold against the grain
is more likley to crack

are bent to the desired shape and then pressed into the paper. Labels and stickers with peel-off backing use a form of die cutting called a kiss die cut. Both types of die cutting adhere to the same principles. Preprinted areas that must tightly register to a die cut should incorporate bleeds to accommodate the tolerance of the machinery. This is most common in packages that have a flooded image or color across the surface. This type of bleed should adhere to the norm of 1/8in (3.18mm) to 1/25in (1mm). Images that peek through a die-cut window should bleed approximately 1/16in (1.59mm). Die cuts that have a fine line around the edge should be created with a thick rule so that the die can be stamped within the width. In all cases the thickness of the stock and the slight compression of the stock at the cut or fold will alter the construction of the bleed and the die. It is important to keep in mind that approximately 1/32in (0.79mm) will be lost on either side of a fold or cut. The printing-and-finishing house should be consulted in advance, and the design should accommodate the loss of space.

Highly complex shapes are not suitable for die cutting—they are more accurately reproduced through laser cutting. A laser can cut to an astounding level of intricacy. The biggest disadvantage, however, is that laser cutting will slightly singe the edge. This can be made less apparent by using dark-colored stocks or hiding the singe on the reverse side or interior of the package.

Figure 18

Diagram 9
The fold is often defined as a mountain or valley fold. In either case, the indentation of a score should always fall on the inside of a fold.

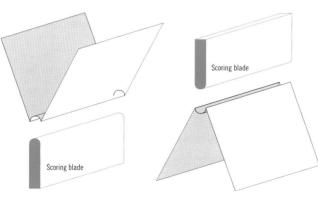

Scoring blade

Scoring blade

Valley fold

Mountain fold

Diagram 10
These are a few of the symbols used by die manufacturers for the construction of a die and its package design.

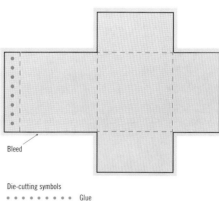

Bleed

Die-cutting symbols
·········· Glue
– – – – – – Score and fold
—————— Cut

Figure 18
Art Director: John T. Drew
Designer: Gaylord Somera

When assembled, the laser-cut snowflake on the lid of this white chocolate creates a tone-on-tone effect and hints at the form inside. Once opened, a traditional die cut, score, and emboss house the white chocolate. Turning down the corners allows the receiver to share and reveal a four-point snowflake that can be used as an ornament.

Packaging Materials and Printing Stocks

6

Packaging utilizes a wider variety of substrates than many other disciplines within graphic design. Not only does it deal with different types of paper, more often than not it also utilizes plastics, glass, wood, metals, and their various combinations. Within each category of substrate there are typically different production techniques used to achieve an array of packaging products. For innovative design, we must have a knowledge base of what is available and achievable. With all materials, the management of color is critical to the success of the final outcome. Understanding how to predict outcome, in terms of practical application, appearance, and manipulation of different substrates, can and will lead to innovative color work.

All material in three-dimensional space has color that is brought about by the sun or by artificial light. By altering material on a molecular/structural basis, color can be modified through the absorption or reflection of light, and this can prolong or shorten the shelf life of a product. Understanding why and how to manipulate a particular substrate will lead to cost-effective measures, better ergonomics, a prolonged shelf life, and ultimately, better package design.

Figure 1

Paper

With paper, many factors determine the outcome of color appearance, such as the brightness, opacity, coating, finish, use of materials in the papermaking process—cotton, pulp, fibers/particles, glue, postconsumer fibers, calcium carbonates, and the like—dyes and colorants, fillers, and many more. There are thousands of choices on the market today, each having the ability to affect the outcome of color/ink appearance. For designers, the most critical factor is the brightness rating of the paper specified. The brightness rating is determined by the percentage of light that is being reflected off the paper. For example, if 2 percent of the light is being absorbed and 98 percent is reflected, the paper has a 98 percent brightness rating, meaning 2 percent of color chroma is lost.

When using dyes, colorants, and specialty fibers, the loss of brightness can be quite severe. For print-based graphics, it is quite common to use paper that is not white. In these cases, printing to the actual substrate is critical for accurate color appearance. Most color-management devices and software applications can achieve relative color accuracy when using white paper, but this is an all but impossible task when using papers that are not. If specifying paper that is not white, scan in the paper sample and place it, on its own layer, in Illustrator or Photoshop. In this way a designer can see exactly the effect that a specified paper has on color appearance. Make sure to

---

Figure 1
Studio: Dustin Edward Arnold/
DL&Co.
Creative Director: Douglas Little
Designer: Dustin E. Arnold

Tone-on-tone black is accented by
the diversity of packaging materials
and offset by delicate silver for these
Douglas Little & Co. Fleurs du Noir
fragranced candles.

Diagram 1
This diagram shows the effects
that colored substrates have
on final outcome.

Fox River Confetti: Yellow

Benefit Vertical Lines: In the Buff

Fraser Papers Genesis: Snow

Fraser Papers Passport: Straw

use the Multiply feature in these programs to simulate the color outcome when printed. (This document should be created as a color-study file and not used for press—either that or delete the paper layer before going to press. When printing to ink-jet or plotter printers, turn the paper layer off and print the document using the specified paper.)

When using translucent or metallic papers, the same procedure should be undertaken. This will ensure that expectations are met and that there are no hidden surprises further down the line. With translucent papers, the majority of brightness is lost when light passes through the paper instead of reflecting off it. In addition, the opacity settings on the hues specified may need to be lower to simulate final outcome. Again, this document should be created as a color-study file only. Metallic papers create a different phenomenon that is hard to duplicate on the screen. Materials used in the making of this paper reflect light at a much higher percentage than its nonmetallic counterpart. That said, most metallic papers also include dyes or colorants that increase the reflectance disparity, making it hard to duplicate on screen.

Figure 2

Figure 3

Figure 2
Studio: Irving
Designer: Julian Roberts

This heavyweight box guards its interior from exposure and damage, yet, rather than looking like a fortress, it opens like a gift by removing the delicate gold sticker.

Figure 3
Studio: One Lucky Guitar, Inc.
Art Director: Matt Kelley

Although untraditional, Vorderman Photography business cards create an interesting package in and of themselves. As the card is "unwrapped" via the perforated die, the proportions of a 4 x 4in (10 x 10cm) format are revealed as well as traditional cropping angles used in photographic composition.

Figure 4

Card Stock and Text Stock

There are four categories of paper: bond, text, cover/card, and bristol. Each has its place within the field of graphic design. For print-based graphics, text- and cover-weight papers are the two most commonly used for press purposes. For package design, cover or card stock is used to create most high-end graphics. There are many ways to create package design, but, because of its thickness and rigidity, cover-weight paper is ideal for external purposes. In package design, text-weight paper is most often used in the interior of a package. There is no better example of this than high-end Japanese package design. This works in three layers: an exterior (cover-weight paper) and two interior layers of different text-weight papers. This method of working gives the impression that the consumer is holding a semiprecious object. In the West, packaging is usually created using one or two layers—an exterior cover paper or an exterior and one interior text-weight paper.

Bond paper is used primarily for comprehensive purposes, and is ideal for laser, ink-jet printers, and copying machines. Typical bond paper weights are 20lb, 24lb, 28lb, 32lb, and 40lb. In North America paper weight is determined by one ream of paper in its standard size. For example, 500 sheets of 17 x 22in (432 x 508mm, a standard size for bond paper) equals 24lb. The typical weights of text paper are 50lb, 60lb, 70lb, 80lb, 90lb, 100lb, and 120lb. Text-weight paper is ideal both for comprehensive purposes and press production. Typical weights of cover paper are 55lb, 65lb, 80lb, and 100lb. Cover-weight paper is also thicker and has more rigidity,

Figure 5

Figure 4
Studio: Typework Studio
Designer/Photographer: Jason Feltz

The warm hues of this analogous two-color palette on recycled stock create an inviting tone for the promotional CD of St. Paul's Cathedral Choir

Figure 5
Studio: Irving
Art Director: Julian Roberts
Designer: Dan Adams

The stock weight and reinforced wall of this brilliant-red interior package make an excellent protective barrier for shipping as well as a striking display.

making it a stronger paper than its text-weight counterpart. The typical weights for bristol paper are 67lb, 80lb, 100lb, and 120lb, and it is used for illustrations, comprehensive, and press production. Cover and bristol paper should not be run through copiers, lasers, ink-jet printers, or plotter printers unless specified. (If a cover-weight metallic paper is specified, run the text equivalent through the printer. The grippers on these printers will hold up better over time.)

When creating package design, testing cover-weight paper for how well it folds is essential for the final outcome. Some cover-weight papers do not fold well, especially across the grain. (All pulp-based paper has a grain that runs the length of the paper, not the width.) The fibers within the paper can pull apart when folded, visibly cracking the coating or, with translucent papers, creating a white line. In these cases a score fold is recommended. A score fold is created with a rounded, blunt metal bar that is pressed into the paper, helping to create a cleaner fold.

When using paper that has a hue other than white, color studies are recommended. This will help to predict the final outcome, and over time will create a morgue folder of scan paper samples that are easily accessible for color studies. A morgue folder is a hard-copy folder with a collection, in this case, of paper samples that have been tested for outcome. (See the previous section to set up a document using a paper source as well as the Color Work Flow section in Chapter 8.)

Cardboard

There are two different weights of cardboard—single-fluted and double-fluted. Fluting is the accordion-fold paper that is sandwiched between the two exterior pieces. The two flat pieces of paper are cover weight, and they are glued to the fluted interior. Depending upon the desired effect, different types of cover-weight paper stock can be applied to both the interior and exterior of the cardboard. For example, a white glossy paper stock can be applied to the exterior of the cardboard so that it can be silkscreened after construction, or an image can be printed on the white paper prior to gluing. A double-weight cardboard is usually reserved for packing heavier items—computers and refrigerators, for example—and offers superior crush resistance. Single-weight cardboard is used for less heavy products, while still offering a high crush resistance.

Figure 6 Figure 7

Figure 6
Studio: Irving
Designer: Julian Roberts

The balsamic vinegar bottle carries the classic logotype in a clean, modern way. When packaged together—oil and balsamic vinegar—the design is unified with a shocking red cap and framed with a black-and-red box.

Figure 7
Studio: Irving
Designer: Julian Roberts

Seen separately, the oil bottle holds up equally well and appears classically subdued and elegant.

Figure 8

Figure 9

Plastics

More and more plastics are being used to create a higher percentage of all package design. In fact, the diversity offered by plastic materials is quite incredible. No longer is plastic associated with cheap packaging or poorly designed products. Plastics can be molded and colored into almost anything. From blister packaging to flexible plastic packaging (plastic bags that are printable through the use of flexography), or from clamshell vacuum-packed packaging to polypropylene packaging, no other substrate can offer such a diversity of form and usage. The following are the different types of plastic packaging and some of their usages:

1. Blister Packaging is an inexpensive solution to product packaging that is tamper proof, durable, and typically—but by no means always—transparent. It is called blister packaging because of the way in which the product is displayed under a clear bubble or similar. Typically blister packaging is used in conjunction with other, printable substrates. There are several variations: clamshell, vacuum formed, trapped, and heat sealed. Most of these are self-explanatory; however, trapped blister is when the product is enclosed between two layers of plastic.

2. Flexible Plastic Packaging (blown film) is ideal for frozen foods (to seal in freshness), transportation packaging, and medical products. This type of packaging is ideal for flexographic printing.

3. Folding Box Board is a versatile material with a wide range of applications. It can be folded (even score folded), is very adaptable to temperature change, can be made from single or multi-ply, and can be coated or uncoated. This type of material can be printed using lithography or commercial silkscreening. From the healthcare industry to the frozen-foods section, this material is used across all packaging. Folding box board is most typically used for the exterior, and many different finishing techniques can be applied.

4. Litho Lamination is a printed sheet or preprinted roll and corrugated board, and it is used to create a durable, yet attractive solution. The durability or flute of the material is defined by its characteristics. F-flute is very fine, offering excellent crush resistance, rigidity, and a premium printing surface. E-flute is fine, offering excellent crush resistance. It is used most often for smaller containers. B-flute is the most widely specified, and it has compression strength and crush resistance. C-flute is larger than B-flute and has great compression strength, but it lacks crush resistance.

5. Plastic Clamshell is a type of packaging that closes like a book, but usually has male and female parts to secure the packaging shut. Typically, clamshell plastic packaging is used for products and foods, and labels are stuck to the exterior or a printed insert is placed inside the container.

6. Polypropylene Packaging is versatile and has a wide range of applications. It can be folded and used like a hinge. It can be opaque or translucent and color specified. It is semirigid and best used for utilitarian purposes, being useful rather than beautiful. It also has a high resistance to fatigue,

Figure 10

Figure 8
Studio: Irving
Art Director: Julian Roberts
Designer: Dan Adams

Festive holographic foils and plastics shimmer and shine, providing a strong graphic counterpart to the gold stars printed on the outermost paper.

Figure 9
Studio: Wallace Church

Gillette's Mach3 established global recognition by utilizing the aerodynamic possibilities that plastic affords in combination with a well-structured brand defined by glowing substrates, breakthrough graphics, and bold logos. Gillette's Mach3 Turbo built upon the value-added benefits of superior speed and comfort with a package that creates three-dimensionality through a separate piece of plastic that attaches the background speed swash to the razor cover. As the name implies, the checker pattern of the packaging is reminiscent of championship racing flags.

Figure 10
Studio: Wallace Church

The brand recognition is still clear and impeccable, with overtones of other-worldliness implied by the astral lighting effects in the background.

chemicals, and it is not easily affected by heat. Typical packaging applications are conference kits, gifts, binders, hospitality kits, presentation kits, and press kits.

7. Polymorphous Paper is designed to resemble traditional paper, but it offers the benefit of being water resistant. It can be printed using lithography, commercial silkscreen, letterpress, and flexography. Many finishing techniques can also be used on this paper (foil stamping, embossing, and die cutting, for example). Oil-free inks (fully oxidizing minerals) are recommended for this type of paper, and hard drying gets the best results.

8. Rigid Box Board is a plastic that is wrapped with a printable sheet suitable for lithography. Finishing techniques can be applied to this material, such as lamination, embossing, foil stamping, spot varnish, or even fabric. This type of material can be classified as luxurious, and it is typically used on higher-end products.

Figure 11

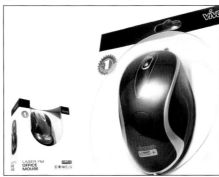

Figure 12

Figure 13

Figure 11
Studio: Midnite Oil
Art Director/Designer:
Mongkolsri Janjarasskul

Designed as a gift box as well as a package, this translucent polypropylene subtly takes on the colors of the handmade resin jewelry inside while urging the recipient to open it for a peek at the product.

Figure 13
Studio: Jefferson Acker
Art Director: Glenn Sakamoto

Inspired by a makeup compact, this technology packaging protects the product from physical force and data destruction.

Figure 12
Studio: SOLUTIONS Branding & Design Companies
Art Director: Pia Grumeth
Designer: Jan Jentsch

The Vivanco Laser Mouse is differentiated by its blister packaging and pure-white display. This, in combination with the clear and matte lacquer, highlights the product's benefits and advertise it as a precision instrument.

Figure 14

Plastic Bottles and Tubes

There are many different processes used to create plastic bottles and tubes, the one used, is dependent on the size, quantity, and quality required. These are the most common:

1. Injection Stretch Blow Molding is a high-quality process that is used to create containers for carbonated drinks, cooking oil, health, medical, oral-hygiene products, and toiletries containers. This type of molding is a four-step process (injection, condition, blow, and discharge) that gives good qualitative control over the end product.

2. Injection Blow Molding is a process designed to produce hollow objects, most commonly bottles, jars, and tubes, in large quantities. This process offers a superior quality than extrusion blow molding.

3. Extrusion Blow Molding is a process designed for making large quantities of containers, but it offers an inferior quality than injection blow molding, because its process usually creates a visible seam. Plastic bottles can be made from this process, but larger objects are more typical—fuel tanks, vent ducts, and water cans, for example.

   The plastic bottles, jars, and tubes created using the methods above can be printed using flexography, silkscreen printing, pressure-sensitive labeling, crack-and-peel labeling (lithography), or heat-shrink labeling. In some cases, colorants can be specified or added to the plastic.

4. Thermoforming is a process designed primarily for the food-packaging industry, and can be used only with thermoplastic sheets. Thermoplastic sheets hold up well to different temperatures, and are commonly used for frozen goods, margarine, snacks, delicatessen tubs, bakery packaging, and cups.

5. Vacuum Forming is a six-step process (clamping, heating, prestretching, vacuuming, cooling and releasing, and finishing). It is one of the oldest forming processes and offers low cost and quality. Typical packages produced are yoghurt pots, sandwich boxes, or anything that needs to be form-to-fit.

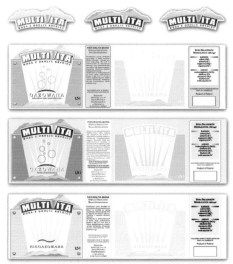

Figure 15

Figure 14
Studio: SOLUTIONS Branding & Design Companies
Creative Director: Martin Weber
Designers: The Complete Team

This product stays up-to-date by focusing the package on special promotions and seasonal highlights.

Figure 15
Studio: DESer
Art Director/Designer: M. Piotrowski

This design utilizes a more graphic stylization, with an implied "V" bringing the background mountains to the foreground in the same way as a glacial stream collects water from a mountain range.

Figure 16
Studio: SOLUTIONS Branding & Design Companies
Art Director: Fanny El Tom Creative Director: Bettina Gabriel

Schwarzkopf's relaunch of its international haircare range, Bonacure, is established through color as an upbeat professional product with a light and pure touch.

Figure 16

Glass

Using glass bottles to preserve foods and beverages is a method that has been around for a very long time—beer bottles can be traced back to the 1500s, and wine bottles to an even earlier date. As glass bottling evolved and trade expanded, new techniques and colorants were exchanged and developed. However, it took until the mid-19th century for companies to become systemized to fully exploit color.

One of the first commercial glass-bottling companies to produce a wide variety of colors was the Hemingray Company, founded in Kentucky in the 1800s, which produced a line of bottles that were shades of yellow, amber, red-amber, brown-amber, electric-blue, peacock-blue, and various shades of cobalt-blue. These colors were chosen for good reason—to varying degrees these hues block or reduce the amount of UV light from penetrating the bottle and spoiling the contents. Blocking UV light is still a concern for manufacturers in the food and beverage and pharmaceutical sectors, and most governments regulate what types of glass can be used for different perishables, particularly pharmaceutical drugs. There is some scientific evidence that Miron violet glass, which blocks about 53 percent of the UV light, preserves some perishables for a longer time. (A study was conducted by the Swiss government in which olive oil placed into an olive-green glass container lasted 18 months on the shelf, whereas the same olive oil lasted 36 months in a container of Miron violet glass.) Olive-green glass has the same/equivalent UV protection as amber—it blocks out UV light to

Figure 18

Figure 19

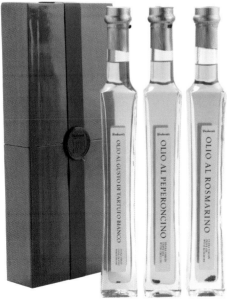

Figure 17

Figure 17
Studio: Irving
Designer: Julian Roberts

The elongated shape of these three bottles emphasizes the subtle contrasting colors of the oil, and unifies with the inside of the brilliant-red box with impact.

Figure 18
Art Director: John T. Drew
Designer: Kyung Jin Cha

The multiple tactile levels of packaging both protect the product and impart traditional appeal, establishing it as highly valued.

Figure 19
Studio: Irving
Designer/Illustrator: Julian Roberts

The shape of this glass bottle imparts an old-world and luxurious feel to the product.

Figure 20

Figure 21

the 400nm (nanometer) wavelength. UV light is in the range of 20 to 380nm, and visible light is from 400 to 700nm.

The most common colors used in mass glass-bottling production are amber, green, olive-green, cobalt-blue, black, violet, and (UV) ray-absorbing clear glass. Black and violet glass cost about twice as much as the other colors. Green glass blocks out 34 to 40 percent of the UV light in the range of 350 to 390nm; cobalt-blue glass blocks about 24 to 28 percent of UV light in the range of 350 to 380nm; and violet glass blocks out 52 to 55 percent of UV light in the range of 330 to 380nm.

Clear glass (called flint) has additives that help to block out UV light. There are five types: an additive with a hint of yellow or amber that blocks about 56 percent of UV light, a green-yellow additive that blocks out 37 percent, a green additive that blocks about 28 percent, a purple additive that blocks about 84 percent, and a dark-green-yellow that offers the poorest UV protection. All of these additives do not effect the overall clearness and can only be noticed upon close inspection.

Other colors commonly produced are dark violet, light gray, amber-brown, neutral gray, novel gray, bronze, brown, gray-green, electric-blue, deep-red-root-beer amber, and turquoise-blue. All of these colors offer some UV protection.

Figure 20
Studio: Design Team One, Inc.
Art Director: Dan Bittman

The total package design for Meier's Wines retains a unified look through type and composition; however, the 50-plus varieties are differentiated through the bottle's shape and color as well as coated and uncoated labels, four-color versus two-color imagery, and metallic inks, embossing, or foil stamping.

Figure 21
Studio: Irving
Designer/Illustrator: Julian Roberts

The squareness of the label is reiterated in the form the bottle. Its gently rounded corners help to prevent breakage and scratches during shipping and display.

The percentages of UV and visible light that are blocked by different glasses are as listed below.

	UV	Visible light
Dark violet	40–45%	40–45%
Violet	52–55%	0–3%
Green	34–40%	32–80%
Gray-green	10%	30%
Brown-amber	0–15%	70%
Novel gray	1–14%	35–55%
Neutral gray	20%	20%
Black	0%	0–5%
Bronze	11%	70%
Cobalt-blue	20–28%	80–90%
Olive-green	0%	0–60%
Turquoise-blue	21%	60–87%

Almost any other color can be created; however, it is likely that it will be far more expensive to produce, and it will offer limited UV protection.

There are four main methods of labeling glass products: a paper label that is glued to the side of the bottle (these types of labels include printed graphics and foil stamping); a clear plastic label that is glued to the side of the bottle with printed graphics; printed graphics directly onto the bottle (typically done by commercial silkscreening or flexography); or some type of container, for example a box, that encloses the bottle. In many cases, labels and enclosures (boxes and/or bags) are created for higher-end products. With Miron violet glass, the company recommends printing directly onto the glass so that as much light as possible can penetrate the bottle.

Figure 22   Figure 23

Figure 22
Studio: Irving
Designer: Julian Roberts

The duotone image of this oil references the history and iconography of the region through the feel of an old sepia-tone photograph, whereas the blue plastic surrounding the cap imparts qualities of the sea.

Figure 23
Studio: Irving
Designer/Illustrator: Julian Roberts

The monotone image in the background of the label adds context, but the four-color image that seals the cap draws the eye upward, beyond the mountains, to the top of this glass bottle.

Figure 24

Tins

Metal tins come in a variety of shapes and sizes (slip covers round, rectangle, square, seamless window top), hinged lids, screw-on lids, deep styles, high-capacity containers, media containers, etc.) that are typically made from tin or aluminum. They come in five standard colors—aluminum, metal, silver, gold, and white—and in many cases interior paper and plastic liners for food products are premanufactured to fit. Metal tins are more expensive to produce than glass products, but from a graphic-design perspective more can be done with them. Unlike a bottle, designers can design both the interior and exterior of a container to suit both the functionality and the aesthetic requirements of the audience. This is often achieved by printing directly onto the exterior of the tin through flexography, or by embossing, using crack-and-peel labels applied directly to the tin, creating paper/plastic banding that goes around the tin and attaches to itself, or any combination of the above. Both the crack-and-peel and banding can have printed graphics on them.

Metal tins are generally used for baked goods (breads, cookies, potato chips, pretzels), candy, bath products (soaps), candles, tea, coffee, hot-chocolate mixes, seasonal food products, and media (CDs, DVDs, film). Most tins are watertight and air sealed, making them ideal for sealing in freshness and storage longevity. Because of their relative expense, however, this type of container is typically used for higher-end products or to give the appearance of such.

Figure 24
Art Director: John T. Drew
Designer: Maki Mori

Upon opening each tin, a layer of
protective paper veils the product
and reiterates the brand. Nutritional
facts are carried on the reverse side
of a "gift card."

Figure 25

Figure 26

Figure 25
Art Director: John T. Drew
Designer: Rodrigo Estacio

Tin provides consistency and imparts
quality to this diverse product line.
Crack-and-peel stickers easily tailor
the look of the tin to the flavor of
the pastry.

Figure 26
Art Director: John T. Drew
Designer: Rodrigo Estacio

This pastry packaging can be
assembled by the baker, thus cutting
costs. The paper choice adapts and
cushions the diverse product line,
reducing the amount of damage
when handled.

Storage, Display, and Aging

Two areas of package design are in play when considering the distribution, storage, and display of a package: packaging and packing. For graphic designers, packaging is what is most readily associated with the product. Packaging refers to the container or material that directly houses the consumer product whereas the pack or packing is the container in which multiple packages are distributed. However, packing can also create dramatic results. Not only can it be used to protect the product and reduce the price of shipping, it can often be used as an appealing point-of-purchase display.

Effects of Transportation

The effects of packaging on transportation can be quite damaging, especially if there is no preplanning involved. Unlike other forms of design, packaging can be quite fragile, and therefore the shape, dimensional size, and crush impact of the product and the designed package (paper boxes, glass bottles, plastic bottles, flexible plastics, blister packaging, folding plastic boxes, litho laminations, plastic clamshells, paper clamshells, tins, wooden boxes, cardboard packaging, and so on) need to be part of the process from the beginning. If not, the results can be quite vitiating. The relationships between designer, printer, and carrier are critical to the success of an item getting safely from A to B. The printer and carrier can help the process by researching the standard sizes of boxes and shipping containers as well as the materials that are available within the market (cardboard or wood, for example) and telling you what they would recommend.

Figure 1

Figures 1–3
Studio: Aloof Design
Art Director: Sam Aloof
Designers: Andrew Scrase,
Jon Hodkinson

Aloof designed and produced a range of branded packaging for furniture retailer twentytwentyone to celebrate reissued work by internationally distinguished designers Lucienne and Robin Day. The collection launched with a series of silkscreen printed Irish-linen tea towels selected from Lucienne's archive, and the Tricorne tray, manufactured in plywood, with birch or walnut veneer, designed by Robin in 1955. Recycled kraft packaging, handprinted with silkscreened graphics, complements the natural materials of linen and wood. The

packaging is carefully designed, assembled without the use of glue, and functions as a point-of-sale device. The graphics have been kept to a minimum with die-cut apertures allowing the products to be seen and touched. The packaging becomes part of an enjoyable consumer experience. A white ink was specially mixed to provide solid coverage, strong contrast to the corrugated kraft material and good crush/rub resistance to prevent scuffing in transit. It is silkscreened one color, die cut, and folded into shape without glue.

Figure 2

Here is a list of common factors involved when trying to determine the effects of transportation, which, when used as a point system, can help determine the design of the packaging, and packing or shipping container.

Air	Add two points
Ground	Shipped by truck or train, add two points
Water	Shipped by cargo ship, add six points (partial container), four points (half container), or two points (full container)
Handling	How many times will the container/box be handled? Add two points for each person
Stackable	How many times can the item be stacked? Add two points for each time stacked
Crush resistance	How fragile is the object when placed in the end-user packaging? Add two points (excellent), four points (good), six points (average), or eight points (poor)
Repackaging	Will the item be repackaged for shipping at any point in the delivery process? If so, add two points. If the item is going to be reshipped, add the appropriate points from the categories above

The more points accumulated, the more stout the design solution will need to be for either the package design, packing/shipping container, or both.

Taking the time to determine the effects of transportation is a crucial part of the design process, and one that should not be overlooked. In today's global market, products are often produced in one country and then shipped to their final destination. When dealing with overseas manufacturers and printers, it is prudent to get references, signed agreements on replacement of damaged goods, and printing-and-shipping insurance. These costs are normally passed on to the client. Working closely with the manufacturer or printer is critical to the success of transporting goods. They deal with it on a more regular basis, and their level of expertise is therefore often superior to that of transportation companies.

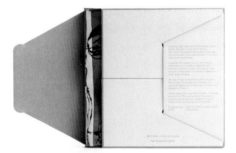

Figure 3

Figure 4

Effects of Storage and Display

While the primary purpose of packing is to protect a product throughout its transport and storage, it can also be designed with sales in mind. For example, the wooden crates that house wine bottles not only protect them from light, keep the bottles stored at the appropriate angle, and prevent breakage when palletized, they also make an excellent storefront display.

In addition, designers can consider the unique gestalt effects that can be used to their advantage when multiple packages are shown at the same time, such as alternating the sides of the package on show. Color can be used not only to heighten the product's visibility, but also to protect the contents or for repeat usage. Wine packaging often uses color to differentiate itself from competitors, but it also serves to protect the contents from being tainted by light. Likewise, packing can protect the interior product, be used to further the product's viability, and be reused for other purposes. In some cases, unique wine crates and packing for fruit have become collectors' items in themselves.

Figure 5

Figure 4
Studio: Irving
Designer: Julian Roberts

Having an exterior casing to protect the product offers great long-term storage capabilities, and, in this case, offers an aesthetic appeal unsurpassed by almost any other substrate.

Figure 5
Studio: 3PART designteam

As one can see from the package design, Royal stacks easily on the shelf and offers excellent crush resistance for storage. Having the name of the product on all four sides offers good display value.

Diagram 1
Depending on the direction of the package, the flutes of corrugated cardboard protect a product from shock or pressure.

Shock resistance
is perpendicular to
corrugations (flutes)

Flutes

Pressure resistance is parallel
to corrugations (flutes)

When contemplating the design of a package, the physical and chemical properties of the product will help determine the requirements. These include: size; weight; fragility; viscosity (solid, liquid, gas, paste, powder); the abrasive and/or corrosive nature of the product; odor, taste, and smell; and possible contaminants, such as water, oxygen, odor, light, and heat. The degree of protection needed for a package or packing is determined by these properties as well as the conditions placed upon it and the environment. Conditions may be determined by consumer demand—such as the guarantee of quality or quantity—or external governing bodies defining nutritional considerations, product composition, and information on usage. Environmental considerations include the atmospheric conditions at the packing house, during transportation, and at the final destination, and will include temperature, light, and humidity. In addition, the possibilities for contamination through the introduction of static, microorganisms, light, air, odors, tastes, off gassing, corrosion, insects, and rodents must be explored. These issues will determine whether the package and packing must be composed of soft (paper, paperboard/cardboard, fabric/textiles, plastic films) or hard (wood, glass, hard plastic, metal) materials, the degree of protective barriers needed, and whether the product will be shipped by land, sea, or air.

Figure 6

Figure 6
Studio: Irving
Designer: Julian Roberts

Preserving fruits, vegetables, and meats has empirically been proven to provide one of the longest storage methods for food products. In this case, the exterior wooden case protects the somewhat fragile glass preserve container, creating a wonderful display.

Figure 7

Harsh and Normal Environments

As discussed in the section on glass (see Chapter 6), sunlight can be quite damaging to printed material. A constant pounding of sunlight can reduce a four-color image to a faded cyan in no time. Day-Glo inks are extremely sensitive to sunlight and will fade even more rapidly. UV varnishes are available to help protect ink pigments from changing their molecular structure, thereby altering color appearance, and to reduce damage from sunlight over the same period of time. However, this is a battle that can't be won, so it needs to be managed.

Any common light source will eventually cause damage over time, be it direct sunlight, indirect sunlight, incandescent, or fluorescent. The more directly an object is exposed to a light source, the more rapidly the object will visually deteriorate. Almost everyone has seen a back-lit restaurant menu sign displaying four-color photographs of their dishes, and when the sign is first presented the entrees look appetizing, but after a time the same food looks washed out and unappealing. When dealing with most papers and plastics, sunlight also breaks down the tensile strength, thus causing not only discoloration, but also making

the substrates themselves more brittle. Talking with manufacturers about different substrates should yield invaluable insight into a given substrate's life expectancy so that clients are not disappointed.

Most often the exposure of package design to light is in a somewhat controlled environment. However, many food products do not fare well at room temperature and need to be chilled or frozen, so the packaging needs to be suitable for that environment. With food products that have an expiration date or freshness date, the design becomes somewhat easier to manage, as that date will establish how long the packaging has to last. For example, Yoplait Trix® Yogurt is designed for relatively short-term storage in a refrigerator. Of course, other factors are involved in the design of this product—including ergonomics, price point, and target audience—but the design is not created to withstand a prolonged period of time before use. Therefore, the choice of substrates for packaging can be applied more economically, thus reducing the price point without an effect on the target audience and with minimal or no effect on the ergonomics of the design.

To understand client needs better, and thus create a package design that will satisfy expectations, a list of questions defining the delimitations for the project is necessary. As follows:

1. What is the price point for each package?

2. Who is the target audience?

3. Is the product perishable?

4. What is the length time from production to "sell-by" date?

Figure 8

Figure 9

Figure 7
Studio: Irving
Designer: Julian Roberts

Sunlight can be extremely harsh on sensitive material. The dark-green glass container offers good protection against damaging sunlight. The exterior container uses single-weight fluted cardboard for excellent crush resistance and 100 percent opacity against harmful UV light.

Figure 8
Studio: Gouthier Design
a brand collective
Creative Director: Jonathan Gouthier
Designers: Gouthier Design
Creative Team

Making use of the company's corporate colors made for effective branding, and also provided an excellent technical feel. The double-wall package offers good crush resistance for multiple stacking and storage.

Figure 9
Studio: Irving
Designer/Illustrator: Julian Roberts

Porcelain containers offer a fantastic UV protection, and, when sealed properly, offer excellent storage capabilities on the shelf.

5. What is the suggested freshness timetable from production to point of purchase?

6. Is the product fragile?

7. What is the crush resistance of the product— excellent, good, average, or poor?

8. Will the product need to be refrigerated?

9. Will the product need to be frozen?

10. Will the product need to be heated, and, if so, under what conditions (microwave, stove, propane grills, etc.)?

11. Where is the product being manufactured?

12. Is the intention to place the product in the package design at the manufacturing plant?

13. Will the package design and/or product need to be repackaged?

14. How stackable is the product?

15. In what countries will the product be sold?

16. If the product is to be sold locally or regionally, what is the estimated maximum distance?

17. How will the package design be shipped (air, ground, water)? If the package design and product (as one) are using multiple forms of shipping, please indicate.

18. What is the size of the run?

19. Are there any substrates that need to be utilized for packaging purposes? If so please specify.

20. What is/are the substrate(s) used to produce the product?

21. Are there any specific/specified colors that need to be used?

22. Can full color be used if meeting a set price point?

23. How do you envision the package design being handled after point of purchase?

24. Do you require the package to be a tamperproof pack?

25. Will the packaging need to be watertight?

26. Is it a toiletry product?

27. How do you envisage the product being displayed on the shelf?

28. Will the package design need to be stackable on the shelf?

29. How many times do you think the product/ package design will be handled from point A to final destination?

30. After manufacturing and placing the product in the package design, what would be the optimal shipping quantities to retailers?

31. Where do you envision the package design being stored after point of purchase, for example, in what room of the house?

Through a list of questions such as this a thorough understanding of expectations can be determined and met. Involving clients in the process early and often invests them and makes the project more likely to succeed.

When dealing with refrigerated packaging, understanding the ergonomics as well as if and how the packaging is going to be recycled will help to determine how you approach the job.

Figure 11

Figure 10

Figure 10
Studio: Irving
Designer: Julian Roberts

Box packaging/construction, such as the Cioccolatini Misti, offers good insulation against moderate heat and excellent crush resistance.

Figure 11
Studio: Irving
Designer: Julian Roberts

Plastic substrates offer some of the best protection for dried foods. In this case, wrapping the food in a clear-plastic substrate allows the consumer to determine quickly whether the dried food has been damaged by moisture. This type of container offers no crush resistance, but it does have some rigidity against punctures.

Figure 12

Taking the example of beer bottles, generally each bottle has a paper label applied. When refrigerated and then brought back out into room temperature, condensation forms on the bottle, thus dissolving the glue and loosening the label—the same happens when bottles are placed in a cooler filled with ice and water. Using a different type of glue might seem the obvious solution, one that isn't water soluble, but most beer bottles are recycled, so when they go through a cleaning process before they are reused (in some countries only damaged bottles are melted back down and reformed) a nonwater-soluble glue would mean the recyclers would have to use hazardous waste chemicals to remove it. This would be a far more expensive process, and ecologically unsound. It is critical, therefore, for a designer to comprehend fully the life cycle of any package design.

Another example is packaging for dairy products. This type of packaging is usually flexography printed on plastic that is resealable. Economic considerations play an important role in the overall design. With that said, paper and plastic substrates will function properly in a refrigerated environment. A good design solution takes into account how often the package will be taken out of the refrigerator and used, opened, cut, torn, and resealed.

Many different substrates are used for frozen-food packaging. The most common are paper and plastic, and each of these has its own strengths and weaknesses. Under freezing conditions paper is more flexible than plastic, but does not seal the product as effectively; plastic can be formed to fit the product and thus creates a better seal. However, under frozen conditions plastic can become brittle, and it is more likely to tear apart if stressed.

Figure 12
Studio: XO Create!
Photographer: Michael J. Robins

This type of container, using multiple substrates of paper and plastic, is fantastic for harsh environments such as refrigeration. The exterior paper container is designed for ease of storage and the ability to stack the item on a shelf.

Therefore, ergonomics and environmental conditions play a key role in choosing the most appropriate material. It is also quite common to see both substrates being used at the same time to create a package design.

When setting up a frozen-food packaging mechanical for press, it is imperative not to extend the ink area over the area reserved for glue. Most glue used is water soluble, and most ink is oil based. Everyone has heard the expression "Oil and water do not mix," and under frozen conditions this becomes a simple truth—the glued areas will pop, releasing their hold. This is a common mistake made by designers. If using a flood varnish, set up the mechanical to avoid the glued areas, thus allowing it to penetrate into the paper and keeping the side panels locked even under the harshest conditions.

People say "What you see is what you get," and in the field of package design there is no truer statement. It is the designer's responsibility to do the research and get it right the first time. Design flaws may appear to cheapen the product and may erode consumer confidence. This is made apparent in one of the harshest environments for package design, the bathroom—if oil and water do not mix, then neither do water and paper. This is why most bathroom and toiletry products are made from plastics. However, many are not constructed well, simply because the designer did not fully understand the ergonomics. As we've seen, ergonomics plays an important role in package design, one that simply cannot be overlooked if quality is paramount. This does not mean that expensive materials need to be used to create quality. What is

Figure 13

Figure 13
Art Director: Pia Grumeth
Designer: Simone Gauss

Plastic and foil containers offer great durability in harsh refrigerated environments. A semitransparent plastic was used so that the consumer can readily see how much fruit and yogurt was used for each container. A foil lid was used to seal it, and is ergonomically easy for consumers, including children, to use.

needed is a full understanding of how and for what duration the product is going to be used. For example, Pantene Pro-V Hair Conditioner is an excellent hair product, with thick conditioner that dispenses easily if stored with the cap on the bottom. The cap on the bottom allows the consumer to ergonomically squeeze out the conditioner and eliminates the need to shake the bottle in frustration. However, since the hinge of the cap takes the most force when stored or even dropped, the plastic hinge tends to break, especially on bulk sizes. In this case ergonomics is weighed against the design and perceived product value within a given price point. The same issues arise with squeezable condiments. Ultimately, it is the designer's responsibility to do the research and get it right the first time.

All substrates used for package design give the conditions under which the manufacturer has tested the product, which provides an understanding of how it behaves under certain conditions. They should also supply swatch books, which will list recommended uses as well as what the substrate is made of, along with its colors, finishes, weights, and thicknesses available. The samples are usually large enough to create empirical tests—and if they are not, most manufacturers or dealers will provide full-sized sample sheets upon request.

When creating package design that will be exposed to extreme heat or a repetitive action, understanding how the material will behave is essential. For example, what types of plastics

Figure 14

Figures 14–17
Studio: Graham Hanson Design
Designers: Graham Hanson,
Dorothy Lin

Health-and-beauty products can encounter some of the harshest environments—they can be subjected to long periods of steam and heavy moisture. This is why most of these products—such as Therapie—are stored in plastic containers. Note how the tubes have wide caps so that they can be displayed and stored upside down.

Figure 15

used for packaging will hold up under microwave conditions? What is the melting point of different packaging plastics, and under what conditions? What is the burn point for different types of paper? How many times can a substrate be bent back and forth before it breaks? If using a package container that dispenses liquid, what is the average amount dispensed, and how much will the container hold? These types of questions need to be asked and answered before any aesthetic values are considered. So, if a container holds 25 fl oz (739ml) and the average amount dispensed is 1/8 fl oz (3.7ml), the amount of times the cap will open and shut is 400 times, and the hinge on the lid has to be able to withstand a stress greater than 400 openings.

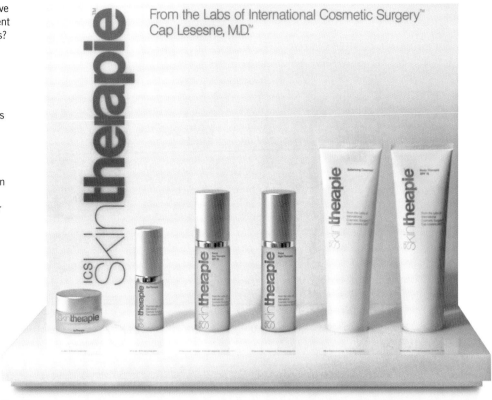

Figure 16

Figure 17

Figure 18

Impact on the Shelf

In today's technological environment, many marketing agencies use computer software that tracks the eye movement of test subjects to determine the impact of a package design when it is placed on a virtual shelf. The subjects wear special glasses that are capable of determining where the eye fixes when scanning the scene of this environment—an aisle of canned goods in a grocery store, for example. This strategy is a very high-tech way of helping to calculate the visual impact of a package design upon consumers. However, other, more traditional methods can also be of use—and the whole process starts with research.

Before any designer sits down to contemplate a package, they should have a thorough understanding of the context in which the product will be used, how the product will be displayed in a retail context, how competitors' products and packages will be displayed alongside it, the kind of packaging they use and why (most often the "why" can be determined by the type of packaging they are using—see Chapter 6 and "Effects of Transportation" and "Harsh and Normal Environments" in this chapter). This understanding should also include competitors' color schemes, typography, imagery, shapes—both in graphic elements and actual package shapes—and compositional balances. This activity will yield an understanding of the marketplace and help set delimitations and objectives for the package design so that it can have a greater impact on the shelf.

Copper Mountain Beer is one example of a product where the packaging was decided upon after employing the strategy above. The design team looked at the delivery systems and display of their competitors' products so that a unique labeling and branding system could be applied to maximize the impact of the new product. By doing so, any unoriginal initial ideas were eliminated straight away, allowing for the more unique. Beer products have some set packaging standards for their glass bottles and labeling systems that help to minimize the cost. So, a careful study was conducted to analyze trends in labeling and packaging within the American microbrewery market, and this revealed that certain graphic shapes, colors, symbols, and containers were being overused, thus minimizing visual impact. Out of 91 craft-beer labels, they found that 75 were square, 15 had die cuts, and five were directly printed on the bottle. In addition, the graphic shapes found on the labels were telling, with 37 having a dominant shape of oval, 22 used a square, 18 a circle, four a diamond, four a slant, four a triangle, and two were rectangles. Furthermore, over 95 percent of the craft beers had a container that contained six bottles.

By avoiding the pitfalls they found with this study, a more unique packaging, labeling, and branding system was devised, and in this case the conceptual ideation was engendered from the empirical study. By researching the subject, a list of environments and the indexical information found within was devised. Comparing the indexical list with the list found in the empirical study immediately eliminated the over-

Figures 18 and 19
Studio: Exhibit A: Design Group
Art Director: Cory Ripley
Designers: Cory Ripley,
Robert Spofforth

Based around the theme "Walk Your Dog," Kudos Collars' distinct and attractive packaging adds value to the product—designer dog collars and leashes—and makes them stand out from their competitors in a retail environment. The packaging can be positioned to feature the company logo or, alternately, the "theme statement," allowing retailers to create their own in-store combination display. A custom, bone-shaped hangtag allows the customer to determine easily what's inside the collector tin. A sample of the product material is also attached to the tag.

Figure 19

used and obvious. A list of symbolic and iconic information could also be devised. However, iconic information most often tends to be obvious. Through the use of indexical and/or symbolic information, metaphor relationships can be devised to foster ideation. These metaphor relationships are often brought about through simile, irony, and parody—simile is most often used within a visual construct. However, irony and parody can be very effective.

In the case of Copper Mountain Beer, the pretzel-shaped label and metallic copper ink are indexical references of two environments— a bar and Copper Mountain itself—that have been transformed into an overriding symbol that now represents the microbrewery, and is a visually cogent agreement of appearance, freshness, and quality.

Figure 20

Figure 21

Figure 22

Figures 20–22
Art Director: John T. Drew
Designer: Steve Gonsowski

This unique package design uses indexical references to visually separate itself from the multitude of beers and brewing companies that are displayed on the shelf. This includes using metallic inks and diecuts to help create separation.

Figure 23

Life Cycle

The life cycle of a product is determined by a number of issues, including its shelf life and, for food, its expiration date. The shelf life is the length of time that a perishable product is considered viable (nutritional and palatable) whereas the expiration date is the point at which an edible product is no longer considered safe for consumption. Although these two aspects of product life cycle are distinctly different, they are inherently connected and conceivably far more complex for the package designer. A package designer must also consider the use of the product after purchase and the functionality of the package once the product is bought and used. Therefore, the life cycle of a package includes that of the product as well as the length of use after purchase. For example, the life cycle of milk packaging will take into consideration the retail refrigeration, point of purchase, home storage, and ease of consumption after purchase. Likewise, products that have an indeterminable shelf life—a toy, for instance—must have packages that not only accommodate the distribution and marketing of the toy, but may also serve as a functional receptacle or imaginative container for the toy long past its initial purchase.

To accurately account for the life cycle of the product and the package, the designer should be aware of the product's characteristics (see "Effects of Storage and Display" in this chapter) as well as the product's perishability,

Figure 23
Creative Director: Karel Golta
Designer: Anne Carls

Plastic containers are some of the most durable materials for package design, and when sealed properly, placed in storage temperatures, and not exposed to direct sunlight, they will aid in the longevity of a product. Note: The embossing around the neck is a nice ergonomic touch. It allows for a better grip when the bottle is pulled from refrigeration on a hot summer day.

bulk density, and the potential effects of a product in a concentrated form. These issues will require numerous consultations with, to name a few, product designers, packaging manufacturers, distribution experts, and nutritionists. Design solutions should be framed around questions such as the following:

1. When does degradation of the product begin, and how long does the product last?

2. How does the product react in bulk packaging or when in concentrated form (gas, odor, water vapor transfer, or package–product interaction)?

3. What are the climatic and physical constraints of the distribution environment (light and heat)?

4. What are the possible contaminants (water, oxygen, odor, light, heat, or grease)?

5. Are there any unusual physical, chemical, or mechanical stresses that the product will be subject to?

6. How will the product be maintained (refrigerated or heated, for example)?

7. Are tamper-resistant packaging or childproof closures mandatory?

Factors controlling shelf life may also affect product expiration and viability. For example, the packaging of electronic devices in certain containers has been known to cause enough static to build up to render the product useless. Thus antistatic packaging is required for

Figure 24

Figure 25

Figure 24
Studio: Wallace Church, Inc.
Creative Director: Stan Church
Designer: Clare Reece-Raybould

Packaged goods become lost when even the smallest supermarket stocks thousands of similar products. In this environment, consumers gravitate toward products with identifiable origins. To enhance the "Swiss" equities and create a more premium package, a deeper, richer color palette and an updated Alpine background illustration was applied. The logo was updated with stylish flavor bands, gold piping, and flavor cues, including chunks of chocolate.

Figure 25
Creative Director: Bettina Gabriel

The foil wrapper offers flexibility: it conforms to a shape easily, and can readily be printed with flexography. Depending upon the shape of the product, this type of substrate can easily be used for display purposes, however, it does not offer much in the way of insulation.

Figure 26

sensitive devices such as computers and their components. In other instances, the distribution of materials in concentrated form or in bulk may create emission issues for an unwitting designer. For example, kitty litter and bananas can emit low levels of radiation that may be a problem in customs screening. More obvious is the relative positioning of natural products. This can often be seen in grocery stores where cut flowers are placed next to fresh produce, such as apples, which give off gas and significantly shorten the life of the nearby flowers. Given all of these factors, extending shelf life through packaging requires a degree of understanding of the aseptic conditions and container types used within the packing industry.

Aseptic packaging is loosely defined as a method of extending shelf life through the elimination or control of unwanted organisms. Two methods for producing aseptic packaging are hermetic sealing and commercial sterilization. A hermetically sealed package is sealed airtight in an effort to exclude organisms from entering and to prevent gas or vapor from entering or exiting. Canned food is often considered hermetically sealed. A commercially sterile package does not eliminate all microorganisms, but eliminates the microorganisms' ability to reproduce under nonrefrigerated conditions. Examples of aseptic packaging include the presterilized/sterilized packages used for milk, soup, and fruit juice, as well as the nonsterile packaging for yogurt. Other methods of extending shelf life are irradiation, heat, and chemical treatment, including dehydration, freezing, canning, and oxygen deprivation. A packaging designer must consider these options and conditions at length to determine the appropriate design solution. For example, vacuum packaging is a highly successful and simple method of modifying internal gas for the extension of shelf life, but it will crush and deform soft products such as bread.

In addition to the product viability, a designer has to define the visual appeal and use of three container types within the package. The primary container is the package that directly contains the product—the bag that contains lettuce or potato chips is primary. A secondary container houses the primary packaging barrier within another source, typically a box. Breakfast cereal

Figure 26
Art Director: Christopher Rimel
Designer: Crystal S. Chin

Beautifully executed, these types of substrates are classified as luxury materials that offer durability, crush resistance, and longevity.

Figure 27
Art Director: Fabian Barral
Designers: Jordan Mauriello,
Fabian Barral

This is a wonderfully executed design that has the appearance of a hand-tinted photograph and is placed in a traditional brown-paper bag for delivery. A crack-and-peel label is applied to the exterior of the bag to seal it. This type of packaging is inexpensive and offers good scuff resistance for items other than food. Depending on how this substrate is used, the life cycle is relatively short.

Figure 27

utilizes an interior primary bag and a secondary box to increase its shelf life and protect it from being crushed. A tertiary container is usually defined as the distribution packaging or pallet and wrappers that hold the primary and secondary containers for transport. Many packaging types can be used to create the containers, commonly paper, glass, plastic, metal tins, textiles, and wood. These materials can be made into retortable pouches, water-soluble pouches, antistatic materials, paper-board, boxes, tins, cans, bottles, cups, sachets, pouches, cellophane, plastic foils, and films, to name a few. Of these, paper is often considered for its light weight and strength. Glass is used for its transparency and resistance to gas, moisture, and noxious odors; it is, however, very fragile. Plastics often present the best of both paper and glass. Some plastics are odor and gas proof and atmosphere resistant, and they can be hermetically sealed. All materials are usually tested optically and mechanically as well as for their ability to provide a barrier. Packaging is a vibrant industry in which new designs and materials are continually made available to the designer. No one material can be defined as the best solution for any given environment or product—there are simply too many factors that must be tested.

Figure 28

Figure 29

Figures 28 and 29
Studio: WE RECOMMEND
Art Directors/Designers: Martin Fredricson, Nikolaj Knop

This box construction with a slide wraparound lid and a foam insert offers fantastic crush resistance. This type of packaging is expensive, but offers longevity and, if properly handled, can last for years.

Color Management
for Print

Unlike motion graphics and web design,
package design and print-based graphics deal
with three-dimensional color space, making
accurate color rendition far more complex and
often difficult to achieve. With that said, over
the last few years, manufacturers of different
color-calibration devices have improved the
accuracy of their equipment and made them
economical options for monitors and printers.
As technology advances, designers are required
to digest more and more information, yet at
the same time, the equipment utilized within the
field is becoming more user-friendly. Such
a consolidation of information is engendering a
new type of designer, one who is more rounded
in all aspects of design.

This environment creates new challenges
for any practitioner. Graphic design is no longer
a static technological industry, but one that is
in constant flux. Today's new and ever-changing
technology is continually absorbing information
and skills from related fields into the landscape
of a designer's responsibilities. The ability to
constantly learn and grow as a designer has
never been more important.

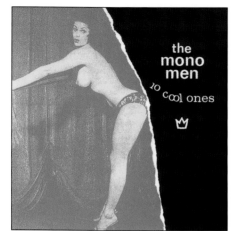
Figure 1

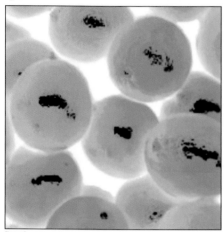
Figure 2

Color Calibration

Since the 1980s a technological explosion has transformed the way in which designers manage, process, and produce color, and this has resulted in both benefits and drawbacks in the way color is communicated visually. Since the introduction of the computer as a tool and a medium, designers have found it frustrating to color calibrate and color sync their monitors to printing devices. Many color swatch books, monitor devices, and application programs are overly complex and do not yield effective results. Because of the physical nature of color, these devices are not accurate enough in the presentation of color. Color is light; it changes from environment to environment and from device to device, thus making color calibration and color syncing devices very complex.

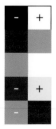

The first step in color syncing a monitor to a color printer is to create a color matrix comprised of 5-percent increments, from 0 percent to 100 percent (see "Building Spot-Color Matrices for Overprinting" in Chapter 4). Such a matrix is appropriate for ink-jet, plotter, color laser, Fiery, Iris, and Color Key proofs. It can be used for any six-color ink-jet printer. For high-end color proofs, a color matrix comprised of 2.5-percent increments is warranted. This type of matrix is appropriate for eight-color and 12-color ink-jet printers, Cromalins, Matchprints, and press proofs.

There are many different color matrices on the market, some having finer steps than others. All of these are used to simulate color appearance, and for good reason: this is by far the most accurate way of determining the subtle differences found within the spectrum of hues created using set primaries. However, some of these color matrices are worth owning and others are not.

Designers are responsible for understanding how subtractive, additive, and three-dimensional color theories are used within the field and in practical applications. Contemporary design requires that designers work both on and off the computer. In doing so, we are moving back and forth from subtractive, additive, and three-dimensional color spaces. In most cases this requires a set process to create a controlled outcome. The mechanics of each color theory are different, but they are interrelated to create a cohesive whole. Each color theory is based on different stages of how the human eye sees color or light. Hue is likely to shift appearance from one color model to another—so, for example, when a hue moves from an additive

Figure 1
Art Director/Designer: Art Chantry

A traditional fake duotone. Note how the lightest and warmest of the two hues is used as the background color, and the darker of the two hues is used to create the continuous-tone image. The yellow hue has a Y tristimulus value of 85.382, and the green has a value of 24.817, a CVD of 60.565. It is not recommended that you create fake duotones and duotones with less than a 20-40 percent CVD.

Figure 2
Studio: design@qirk.com
Designer: Daryl Geary

The chroma value of hues in this CD package would likely be outside the color gamma for a four-color ink-jet printer. In this case, creating a color matrix of the hues selected for commercial printing, and printing the job out from an ink-jet printer, would allow for visual verification and color adjustments.

Diagram 1
Primary sets within their respective color theory. When a pure hue is applied to another paradigm, some hues become semipure or achromatic.

Traditional color

Four-color process

Additive color

Subtractive color

3-D color

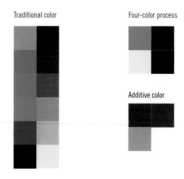

environment to a subtractive one, the color is likely to shift. This can create frustration for a designer.

There are several ways to color calibrate a package design, depending on how the design is constructed. Some package designs use spot colors from a standardized color-communication system such as PANTONE—and more often than not these designs use fewer than four plates when printing, keeping within budgetary constraints. (The more printing plates, or colors, used in the more expensive the job is to print—each plate is capable of printing only one hue.)

If color accuracy is critical and budgetary constraints are pressing, choosing spot colors that fall inside the CMYK color spectrum is prudent. This decision allows the color palette to be reproduced on almost any four-color-process ink-jet printer, whether low-end or high-end. Choosing paper that has the highest brightness rating (98 percent or higher) or printing on the actual paper stock specified for the job is critical for accurate color appearance. In this way, color calibration between the hue chosen, computer monitor used, comprehensive printer, and commercial printer for press can easily be achieved with minimal cost. To verify whether a spot color falls in or out of the CMYK color spectrum, use the Color Picker and Custom Colors under Set Foreground Color in the toolbox in Photoshop. In the Color Picker dialog box, on the right-hand side, click on Custom. This will bring up the Custom Colors dialog box. Choose the PANTONE color you want, and the chosen hue will appear in the swatch window. If the hue chosen falls outside of the CMYK color spectrum, a three-dimensional box will appear to the right of the swatch. Click on the box and

Figure 3

Figure 4

Figure 5

Figure 3
Studio: Irving
Designer: Julian Roberts

The Carluccio's Caffè Napoli Espresso packaging uses a foil bag with a crack-and-peel label applied, which uses three hues and the white of the paper to create four distinctive hues. In other words, the label uses three plates.

Figure 4
Studio: Irving
Designer/Illustrator: Julian Roberts

In this case, four-color process printing was used on the exterior tin. Different hues of foil-colored paper were used with a crack-and-peel gold seal to cut cost. Printing a foil stamp onto the multiple-colored foil paper would have been far more expensive.

Figure 5
Studio: Irving
Designer: Julian Roberts
Illustrator: Jonathon Stewart

A slip-cover wraparound with three vivid hues was used to lower production costs. The white of the substrate created the fourth additional hue.

Figure 6

the closest CMYK color will appear below this swatch, to the left.

For example, if you choose PANTONE 7488 U, you will find that the CMYK color spectrum is incapable of matching this, so trying to create this color on a comprehensive four-color-process printer is pointless; a higher-end—and more expensive—printer or printout will be required. The designer can see what the CMYK hue looks like when compared with the chosen PANTONE color by clicking with the mouse on the swatch below. The CMYK facsimile (C62 percent, M0 percent, Y85 percent, and K0 percent) will appear above the PANTONE hue—in this case, a dramatic shift in color appearance. By adjusting to a higher percentage of cyan and yellow, the chroma will intensify, but the hue will still not be an accurate match.

Despite this, an enormous array of colors can be reproduced through the CMYK color spectrum. The fact that this book and all the package designs that appear within it are built from this spectrum is testament to its versatility.

Figure 6
Studio: Irving
Designer: Julian Roberts

Similar to Figure 3, three distinctive hues were used with the white of the substrate to create the fourth additional color. In this case, if multiple hue variations are created to identify a different product, having the hues specified fall inside the four-color process gamma is cost effective. In doing this all labeled variations can be printed at the same time—a technique known as ganging up. By making the labels crack-and-peel, the same foil bag can be used for multiple products, thus cutting costs further.

Diagram 2
Traditional 12-step color wheel.

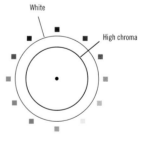

White

High chroma

CMYK Document Calibration

In Photoshop or Illustrator different processes for color calibration are required. However, the starting point is the same: the PANTONE four-color process guides. Color calibration requires that the hue on the screen be calibrated to something off screen. In this case, PANTONE four-color process guides give visual verification of hue appearance. Both Photoshop and Illustrator contain a multitude of color-management profiles from which to choose. To color calibrate using the standardized color-management profiles, follow these steps:

1. Purchase the PANTONE four-color process guides. If a different color-matching system will be used for visual verification, the relevant swatch book(s) will need to be obtained. If the swatch books are not affordable, see step 6 below.

2. In either Photoshop or Illustrator, create a 12-step color wheel using the following CMYK color builds. Each one of these CMYK colors matches the builds of a PANTONE process hue. For example, the colors listed below are based upon PANTONE PROCESS GUIDE uncoated, published 2000. For an exact match, please refer to the current PANTONE Publications.

Color	CMYK	PANTONE
Red:	C000 M100 Y100 K000	PANTONE DS 73-1-U
Red-orange:	C000 M070 Y100 K000	PANTONE DS 49-1-U
Orange:	C000 M050 Y100 K000	PANTONE DS 32-1-U
Yellow-orange:	C000 M035 Y100 K000	PANTONE DS 18-1-U
Yellow:	C000 M000 Y100 K000	PANTONE DS 1-1-U
Yellow-green:	C050 M000 Y100 K000	PANTONE DS 294-1-U
Green:	C100 M000 Y100 K000	PANTONE DS 274-1-U
Blue-green:	C100 M000 Y050 K000	PANTONE DS 254-1-U
Blue:	C100 M020 Y000 K000	PANTONE DS 225-1-U
Blue-violet:	C100 M050 Y000 K000	PANTONE DS 207-1-U
Violet:	C100 M100 Y000 K000	PANTONE DS 184-1-U
Red-violet:	C050 M100 Y000 K000	PANTONE DS 164-1-U

3. Select Color Settings in either program. In Photoshop CS, Color Settings can be found under the Photoshop heading, and in CS2 it can be found under Edit in the main menu. In Illustrator, select either Color Settings or Assign Profile, which can both be found under Edit in the main menu.

Figure 7

Figure 7
Studio: Irving
Designer: Julian Roberts
Illustrator: Christopher Brown

When creating a line of labels such as Carluccio's, it is cost effective to keep the hues specified within the four-color process range. All labels can be printed at one time by ganging them up—multiple impressions on one sheet of paper—on press and ultimately saving the client money.

Figure 8

4. In the Color Settings or Assign Profile dialog boxes, choose either Working Spaces CMYK in Photoshop or Working CMYK in Illustrator. Both of these settings are scroll-down menus. Choose one of the following color-management profile settings.

> ColorSync CMYK-Generic CMYK profile
> Euroscale Coated v2
> Euroscale Uncoated v2
> Japan Color 2001 Coated
> Japan Color 2001 Uncoated
> Japan Web Coated (Ad)
> U.S. Sheetfed Coated v2
> U.S. Sheetfed Uncoated v2
> U.S. Web Uncoated v2
> 150-Line (PANTONE)
> Canon CLC500/EFI Printer
> Generic CMYK Profile
> Japan Standard v2
> KODAK SWOP Proofer CMYK-Coated stock
> KODAK SWOP Proofer CMYK-Newsprint
> KODAK SWOP Proofer CMYK-Uncoated Stock
> Photoshop 4 Default CMYK
> Photoshop 5 Default CMYK
> SWOP Press
> Tekronik Phaser 111 Pxi

Figures 8 and 9
Studio: XO Create!

The labels were produced on digital presses, which are notorious for their lack of color consistency. To overcome this, XO Create! worked closely with the print provider to develop a series of colors that could be produced consistently and with a minimum of variation. The rich patterns and shapes further disguised any remaining variances. As part of the process, the printer indicated which color-profile setting best suited their digital needs to help create a qualitative job. Talking with the printer first to understand if they want an early or late bind will help assure a quality job. (See "Color Work Flow" in this chapter.)

Figure 9

5. Scroll down and select each profile setting in the swatch book. In a separate Word file, indicate the hues that are accurately represented within each profile setting. Some settings do better than others in each family of colors; no one-color profile setting can accurately match every hue or even family of hues. Conduct a series of tests by printing out each profile setting to verify if color appearance is altered. Make sure that you write down the overprinting RGB and L*a*b* numbers from 10 to 100 percent in 10-percent steps.

6. Without a color swatch book, create two 12-step color wheel documents. The first is the same as above. However, the second document needs to be set up differently:

    i.   In Photoshop and through the foreground color in the Toolbox palette, select each individual PANTONE hue specified above. Write down both the RGB numbers and L*a*b* coordinates. For Illustrator use RGB, and for Photoshop use L*a*b.

    ii. Create either or both the Photoshop or Illustrator document and save it (or them). Both will create an accurate depiction of the hues specified with the exception of their chroma value—the colors will look right except for their brightness. Either document can be used to match colors.

    iii. Open both 12-step color wheel documents—either the L*a*b* or RGB document—and the 12-step document, using the specified PANTONE hues above.

    iv. Repeat step 5 above.

Figure 10

Figure 11

Figures 10 and 11
Art Director/Designer:
Darren Hoffman

The L*a*b* values are a device-independent ordinance used within the design industry to translate hues specified from one system to another, for example, a PANTONE hue converted into RGB or CMYK color.

Figure 12

Figure 12
Studio: Reisigl Associates
Creative Director: James K. Reisigl
Art Director/Designer: Marianne Young

In this case, even the liquid found
inside the different-flavored bottles
of the Shakka Display can be
translated to print specifications
using L*a*b* values.

Spot-Color Document Calibration

When creating packaging in Photoshop or Illustrator using spot colors
that fall outside of the CMYK color gamma, the color-wheel verification
document should be set up for the standard ink-matching system used.
For example, if spot colors from PANTONE are specified, then the
PANTONE Formula Guide Coated/Uncoated swatch book primaries/base
colors should be used to create the color wheel. If another ink-matching
system is used, the base inks/primaries that produce the multitude of
hues found within the system create the color-wheel verification document.
The base inks/primaries for the PANTONE Coated/Uncoated system
are listed below.

For Coated Basic Colors

Primaries	RGB equivalent	L*a*b* equivalent
PANTONE Yellow C	R252 G225 B0	L89 A4 B112
PANTONE Yellow 012 C	R255 G214 B0	L87 A2 B114
PANTONE Orange 021 C	R255 G92 B0	L63 A63 B95
PANTONE Warm Red C	R252 G61 B50	L57 A71 B53
PANTONE Red 032 C	R244 G42 B65	L54 A74 B41
PANTONE Rubine Red C	R211 G0 B95	L44 A78 B8
PANTONE Rhodamine Red C	R229 G15 B159	L52 A79 B19
PANTONE Purple C	R183 G39 B191	L46 A68 B48
PANTONE Violet C	R79 G3 B169	L24 A54 B74
PANTONE Blue 072 C	R0 G25 B168	L19 A40 B79
PANTONE Reflex Blue C	R0 G32 B159	L19 A32 B74
PANTONE Process Blue C	R0 G130 B209	L47 A33 B57
PANTONE Green C	R0 G175 B138	L60 A78 B2
PANTONE Black C	R50 G44 B36	L18 A2 B6

For Uncoated Basic Colors

PANTONE Primaries	RGB equivalent	L*a*b* equivalent
PANTONE Yellow U	R255 G229 B0	L91 A2 B96
PANTONE Yellow 012 U	R255 G220 B0	L89 A3 B94
PANTONE Orange 021 U	R255 G113 B41	L67 A57 B66
PANTONE Warm Red U	R255 G98 B93	L63 A61 B36
PANTONE Red 032 U	R248 G81 B99	L60 A65 B28
PANTONE Rubine Red U	R217 G61 B122	L52 A64 B3
PANTONE Rhodamine Red U	R230 G75 B163	L57 A66 B14
PANTONE Purple U	R189 G84 B195	L53 A54 B39
PANTONE Violet U	R113 G80 B178	L42 A31 B48
PANTONE Blue 072 U	R54 G65 B162	L31 A21 B55
PANTONE Reflex Blue U	R59 G77 B160	L35 A14 B48
PANTONE Process Blue U	R0 G125 B200	L48 A17 B51
PANTONE Green U	R0 G163 B134	L57 A61 B1
PANTONE Black U	R87 G83 B79	L36 A1 B3

**Note that these values change based on the edition of the PANTONE
Publication being used. These values may no longer be current.
Please refer to current PANTONE Color tools for current values.**

Figure 13

Figure 13
Studio: Exhibit A: Design Group
Art Director: Cory Ripley
Designers: Cory Ripley,
Robert Spofforth

Jack and Lily packaging increases the product's in-store presence when displayed—hung or placed side by side. The chocolate-brown and blue color bars boldly frame the product and create a distinct Jack and Lily area in any retail environment. Additionally, the combination of the graphic elements and color palette matches beautifully with both "baby girl" and "baby boy" shoes, and make for a standout, yet subtle unisex design. Note how the printed hues match the various substrate colors; by having the L*a*b* ordinance for each hue, mixing pigment and dyes for different substrates becomes a manageable hue experience.

Figure 14

By using this system a color profile can be selected for both client proof and electronic mechanical. In some cases, the color-profile setting may be different for the client proof than the electronic mechanical. For example, a printer may want a particular color-profile setting, but when printing it out on your color-proofing systems the colors shift, creating an undesirable comprehensive. In many cases, shifting the color profile settings to something that is more advantageous to the color-proofing system is warranted. If so, it is advisable to create a duplicate copy for client purposes. In short, switching back and forth between color-profile settings is not recommended.

It is also recommended that you color calibrate your monitor on a monthly basis, using the software provided with your computer. This will ensure better results when verifying colors on screen. However, to get a higher level of calibration between monitor, printer, scanner, and digital camera, additional hardware and software will need to be purchased.

GretagMacbeth/X-rite is one of the industry leaders in this field, with an array of hardware and software products. (See the "Color Work Flow" section in this chapter for more details.)

Figures 14 and 15
Studio: The Hively Agency
Art Director/Designer: Sarah Munt

The Chocolate Sauce labeling system utilizes an unusual uncoated paper and hue combination to achieve individuality on the shelf.

Figure 15

Color Work Flow

Color work flow is the management of color between one device and another in the daily context of a working environment. A simple example of this is how colors are built and perceived by the human eye within the document created, how a monitor displays these colors on the screen, and the representation of hue when the document is finally printed. However, for print-based graphics, management of the color-work-flow environment is far more complex, and it is therefore much harder to control the perception of hue.

Today, advances in technology allow for more precise perceptual management of color within this highly complex work environment—while it is still not perfect it improves all the time. There are three elements to the technology: calibration, characterization, and conversion. Calibration is straightforward, and it is the first step in creating a truly color-managed environment. All devices that deal with the perceptual display of color need to be calibrated, including digital cameras, scanners, printers, monitors, and sometimes overhead digital projectors for client presentation.

Characterization is the determination of the color space needed when creating color profiles that help to simulate the gamut need for perceptual appearance—both individually and uniformly—throughout the working environment. Conversion is the uniform color optimization from one device to another for the purpose of reproduction, and this includes RIPS, the Raster Image Processor, which is a device that transforms digital images into

Figure 17

Figure 16

Figure 16
Art Director: Mary Ann McLaughlin
Designer: Zeina Said Hamady

This wonderfully intriguing design would not be hard to color manage—all hues are relatively muted and tinted, and would therefore be less likely to color shift.

Figure 17
Studio: 1972dg
Art Director/Designer:
Carlos Marques

An incredibly bold, but subtle piece is achieved through a warm color palette with gold-foil stamping. The intensity of hue makes this design hard to color manage within a working environment if the environment has not been properly set up.

Figure 18

(printer) that has a smaller color spectrum, or gamut, than the hues specified within the document. The printing device must always have a larger color gamut than the hard proof for accurate color appearance or the colors will never match those on screen. To determine if the printing device being considered has a larger or smaller color spectrum, you can use software programs such as Chromix ColorThink Pro 3. These help to manage the color-work-flow environment, and can even lower production costs by defining the appropriate hard-proofing system. Many different hard-proofing systems are available today, and the costs vary greatly. High-end color proofs cost a great deal, and may not be necessary for a given job, so to use them can waste money. Being able to determine which type of proofing system is needed for what job is incredibly helpful.

Unless told otherwise by the commercial printer that will be doing the job, always specify an early bind for CMYK images. An early bind or late bind is the time a working color space is assigned or embedded into the digital file. For the US market, US Web Coated SWOP v2 is recommended for press. In many cases a late bind is preferred by some printers (depending upon the color system being used), and finding this out is key to creating a high-quality print job, so communication is essential. Assignment of a working color space (color profile) in Photoshop is located under the Advanced setting in the New Document dialog box.

a bitmapped format for output to press. Leaders in the color-management industry such as GretagMacbeth/X-rite, Adobe, Epson, and Apple Macintosh all supply software and hardware that help create, calibrate, and manage color profiles and hardware equipment throughout a graphic-design studio, thereby making conversion easier.

The biggest frustration designers face is the discrepancy between the colors they see on a soft proof (the screen) and a hard proof (ink-jet, Iris, Matchprint, Cromalin, for example). The most common reason for this discrepancy is when a hard proof is created on a device

Figure 18
Studio: Gouthier Design
a brand collective
Creative Director: Jonathan Gouthier
Designers: Gouthier Design
Creative Team

Extremely elegant and sophisticated, this design would be all but impossible to manage within a working environment if the environment had not been set up properly. Although most of the hues are muted, because of the multiple substrates and printing processes, the color-workflow environment becomes even more critical to the success of this design.

Diagram 3
Snapshot of a screen after calibrating the computer monitor using Eye-One Display 2 system (hardware and software).

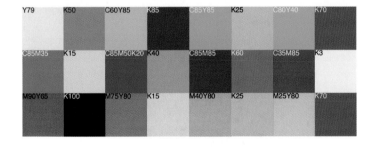

Manually Calibrating LCD Monitors using a Mac

In the System Preferences dialog box, click on Displays and choose Millions of Colors. Slide the Brightness level to the full amount, and click on Automatically Adjust Brightness as Ambient Light Changes. Then click on Color. Once you are in the Color System Preference dialog box, click on Calibrate. In this dialog box click on the Expert mode and then hit Continue and follow the step-by-step instructions.

The problem in the past has been how to verify if the manual calibration you have just created is accurate. In the Applications folder under Utilities, launch the software program called DigitalColor Meter. This program will measure the projected light or colors the monitor is creating in many different color systems: RGB As Percentage, RGB As Actual Value 8-bit, RGB As Actual Value 16-bit, RGB As Hex Value 8-bit, RGB As Hex Value 16-bit, CIE 1931, CIE 1976, CIE L*a*b*, and tristimulus.

Once the monitor has been calibrated manually in Photoshop, create a CMYK document (see Diagram 3) and specify US Web Coated SWOP v2 for the color profile. Set the DigitalColor Meter for CIE L*a*b* and scroll over each hue within the document, making sure to write down the L*a*b* values. Once all the L*a*b* values are recorded, double click with the Eye Drop tool in Photoshop on each individual hue and go to the Foreground

Figure 19

Original file
Epson calibration, gamma 1.8, photorealistic with natural color setting
LCD (control) uncalibrated printer using Colorsync setting
Laptop Eye-One Display 2 printout 1
Laptop Eye-One Display 2 printout 2
Laptop Eye-One Display 2 printout 3
Laptop Eye-One Pro printout 1
Laptop Eye-One Pro printout 2
LCD Eye-One Pro printout 3

Figure 19
Studio: 1972dg
Art Director/Designer: Carlos Marques

A beautiful design, this package illustrates how both coated and uncoated colors can be used to create a dynamic color palette.

Diagram 4
This diagram is a comparison of the hue variance found between the built colors in the original files and printouts using Eye-One Display 2, Eye-One Pro, uncalibrated printer using the ColorSync setting (control), and an Epson calibrated printer using a gamma setting of 1.8, Photorealistic with a Natural Color setting. The hues found in the original document all fall within the color gamma that can be reproduced with a Epson 2200, and the job was printed on Staples Photo Supreme Matte paper with a brightness rating of 111 percent. Standard Epson inks were used for printouts, and the computer monitors were calibrated for lines four though nine with Eye-One Display 2, and a color profile was created by Eye-One Pro for lines six through nine. Lines three through nine used the ColorSync setting in the Print Dialog box.

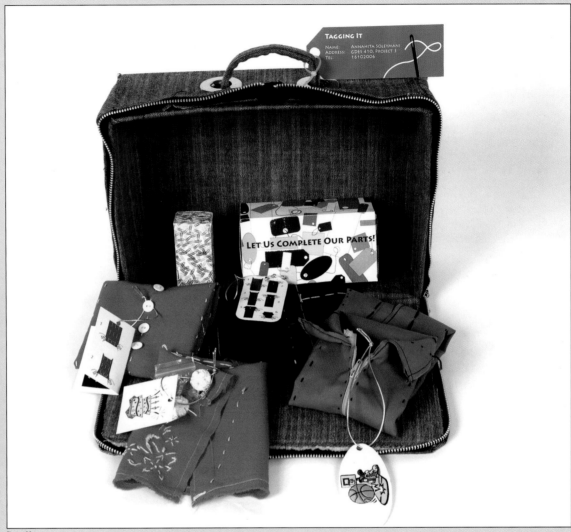

Figure 20

Figure 20
Art Director:
Pornprapha Phatanateacha
Designer: Annahita Soleymani

When employing multiple substrates,
pigments, and dyes, using the
PANTONE® Color Cue® can help to
assure color accuracy between one
printing process and another, or from
printing process to dyeing process.

Color dialog box. Within this dialog box the L*a*b* colors are presented for each hue and can be verified against the L*a*b* numbers already written down. To verify visually the accuracy of the manual calibration, type in the L*a*b* values taken from the DigitalColor Meter. There should be little or no variation in color appearance. In most cases a deviation of more than 2 or 3 percentage points either way will create a distinct perceptual difference.

L*a*b* colors represent the second stage of color perception. RGB colors represent the first stage. The Commission Internationale de L'Eclairage (CIE) developed the L*a*b* system—lightness (L), red/green value (A), and yellow/blue value (B)—that is device independent, meaning this system runs true. The system is not altered by any software or hardware application, and can act as a translator for color systems that are device dependent, such as CMYK.

Once an accurate calibration has been accomplished, try using the ColorSync setting for ink-jet printers. This setting is in the Print dialog box, and seems to create the most accurate hard-copy proof for low-end printers. To set Epson printers up for flat artwork, you can try using Epson Calibration Gamma 1.8, Photorealistic with Natural Color setting (see Diagram 4).

As a side note, use the Y of the tristimulus value setting in the DigitalColor Meter to ensure proper Color Value Differential (CVD) for the Americans with Disabilities Act, and to ensure proper type and color legibility. As a rule of thumb, 20 percent CDV is recommended between foreground and background colors when using type and color combinations for 20/20 vision, and a 40 percent CDV for the visually impaired, as defined by the Americans with Disabilities Act. The act further states that the foreground color needs to have a 70 percent or higher Y tristimulus value and the background color needs to have a 30 percent or lower value. Although this section of the act pertains to signage, this system yields invaluable insight into how and why package design needs to be legible for all walks of life.

Calibrating LCD and CTR Monitors using Eye-One Display 2

GretagMacbeth's Eye-One Display 2 is a great and inexpensive device for color calibrating a multitude of monitors quickly and accurately (see Diagram 5). It will work with LCD, CRT, and laptop monitors, and will create a working color profile for the color printers in a work-flow environment. These profiles work with the ColorSync setting in print-dialog boxes and are seamless. To use them with Adobe products, go to the Convert to Profile dialog box under Edit and click on the Destination Space profile setting. Scroll down to the color profile the Eye-One Display 2 created, and select the profile that works best for the printers connected to the working environment. The Eye-One Display 2 software and hardware are simple to use, and the interface walks you through the clear step-by-step instructions.

Diagram 5
This diagram is a comparison of the color variance found between the monitors after using Eye-One Display 2 calibration. The CRT control monitor was measured before calibration and was selected randomly as a comparison. All colors were measured using L*a*b* coordinates and translated into CMYK colors for relative appearance.

CRT monitor 1
CRT monitor 2
CRT monitor 3
Laptop monitor 1
Laptop monitor 2
LCD monitor 1
CRT control monitor 1

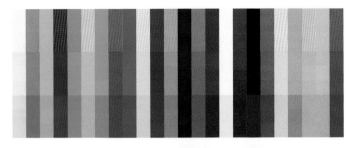

Laptop file 1
Laptop file 2
LCD file 3
Laptop monitor 1
Laptop monitor 2
LCD monitor 3
Laptop printout 1
Laptop printout 2
LCD printout 3

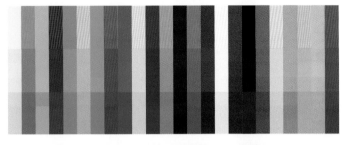

Laptop file 1
Laptop file 2
LCD file 3
Laptop monitor 1
Laptop monitor 2
LCD monitor 3
Laptop printout 1
Laptop printout 2
LCD printout 3

Laptop file 1
Laptop file 2
LCD file 3
Laptop Eye-One Display 2 printout 1
Laptop Eye-One Display 2 printout 2
LCD Eye-One Display 2 printout 3
Laptop Eye-One Pro printout 1
Laptop Eye-One Pro printout 2
LCD Eye-One Pro printout 3

Profiling Multiple Devices using Eye-One Pro

GretagMacbeth's Eye-One Pro is a moderately expensive device that will create color profiles for printers, digital cameras, scanners, and digital overhead projectors, and is excellent for graphic-design studios, helping to create a better-managed color-flow environment (see Diagrams 6, 7, and 8). The Eye-One Pro (hardware) with the Eye-One Share (software) will also measure the amount of light (in Kelvins) in a given working environment, and color samples (in L*a*b* coordinates) for targeting artwork to be archived digitally, so it is great for art galleries, private art collectors, libraries, and museums. The Eye-One Pro can also be used to determine how far off a color printout is, in the work-flow environment, from the colors originally specified. To do this, set up a document similar to Diagram 3. Make sure you print this document out on different types of paper to determine the correct paper for color accuracy.

Eye-One Pro makes creating color profiles for printers, scanners, and overhead projectors quite easy, and the tutorials are built into the software; however, creating color profiles for digital cameras can be difficult. For quality results, it is recommended designers use professional-grade equipment when setting up color profiles for still lifes and copy-stand work.

Diagram 6 (above top)
This diagram is a comparison of the hue variance found between the built colors in the original files, monitor displays, and printouts from each computer on the same printer. The hues found in the original documents all fall within the color gamma that can be reproduced with an Epson 2200, and the job was printed on Staples Photo Supreme Matte paper with a brightness rating of 111 percent. Standard Epson inks were used for printouts, and the computer monitors were calibrated using Eye-One Display 2. The calibration information was set up as standard within the ColorSync setting in the Print Dialog box.

Diagram 7 (above middle)
The specifications in this diagram are as for Diagram 6, with Eye-One Pro creating a color-printer profile used for all printouts from each computer. The ColorSync setting was used for printing.

Diagram 8 (above bottom)
The specifications in this diagram are as for Diagram 6. The computer monitors were calibrated using Eye-One Display 2, and a color profile was created by Eye-One Pro for three of the printouts. In both cases the ColorSync setting was used as standard for printing.

Diagram 9 (a–d)
A wide variety of choke and spread settings. Note that as type is choked, the hairlines of letterforms become more compressed and therefore may lose some legibility, as in b. In contrast, type that is spread may become thicker than was intended.

a   1-pixel choke

b   2-pixel choke

c   2-pixel spread

d   4-pixel spread

Trapping

Trapping is when one plate/color is choked or spread so that a small amount of ink is over-lapping an adjacent hue. This is achieved through film or digital methods and implemented on the plate or directly on the digital printing press. Choking (down) or spreading (out) a color creates a slight overlap of adjacent hues so that a print job looks perfect.

Dark trapping involves reversing the order of cyan and magenta, a process that improves image quality, because the trap cannot be detected by the eye. These effects typically take place in a visible color tint of the hue that was printed last. Depending on the colors used, this effect can range from slight to drastic. For example, printing black on top of yellow will create a neutral black, but printing yellow on top of black will create a warm black with a slight tint of yellow. Another example is printing 100 percent cyan over 100 percent magenta, which creates purple with a bluish tint, while reversing the order of printing creates purple with a reddish tint.

Most packaging created today often has more than one hue. The trap needed to accommodate a package can be drastically different depending upon the printing technique, materials used, and substrate printed on. These factors are critical in determining the flexibility inherent in the color palette chosen to brand the package, company, and/or product. For example, most

silkscreen printers need between ¹⁄₁₆ and ¼in (0.06 and 6.4mm) to hold the trap—in other words, for the job to appear in register without any unwanted paper color showing between printed hues. Typically a trap is much smaller for offset printing, and therefore not visible to the naked eye. With this said, a package-design color palette should be devised so that the hue scheme can accommodate different printing techniques.

Many color combinations will not be effective when silkscreening or with any other type of printing that requires a trap setting of greater than 0.144pt (c. 0.05mm). All printing inks are translucent, and some are more translucent than others; the more pure the color is, the more translucent it will be. In most cases, a color that is pure or semipure will create, when overprinted, an additional third hue that is noticeable. (See "Overprinting" in Chapter 4.) Additives can be mixed into ink to make it less transparent; however, these additives tend to alter the hue. When a large trap value is assigned, this third color may overpower the design, creating legibility and readability problems or making the product simply look bad. Most designs are meant to be used for an extended period of time, and therefore require forethought to accommodate any printing technique or medium on which the design may be used. Such planning will allow the client tremendous flexibility in the print delivery of a design over time.

Figure 21

Figure 22

Diagram 10 (a–d)
Optimal trapping conditions would be to balance the choke and spread of an image or mark so that each will be minimally affected. Generally, the background is choked down while the foreground, in this case type, is spread out. Type that is filled with 100% of a color that is built into the background will not need to be choked or spread. For example, yellow type on a red background (d) will not need to be altered because the red has yellow in it.

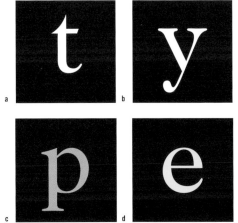

Figure 21
Studio: Irving
Designer: Julian Roberts
Typographer: Rob Clarke

In this case, the label used trapping by choking down the typography and spreading the silver plate. Metallic ink was used to achieve the silver. The individual chocolate truffle wraps do not use trapping: trapping is not used on a one-color job.

Figure 22
Art Director/Designer: Art Chantry

Each printing process has its own characteristics that define the accuracy of printing/holding something in register. In this case, a crude printing process was used, and therefore a larger trap is necessary to hold the job in register. If you look at the black hue around "The Makers," you can see a reddish-black tint around it—the trap. In this case, the printing process adds to the aesthetic appeal. In many ways different printing processes are like different illustration styles. Having a mastery of the subject, like Art Chantry, can help aid in the aesthetic appeal.

Figure 23

Figure 24

In 1994 we conducted a color study with PANTONE-identified silkscreen inks (see pages 152 and 153). Although this study was originally designed to test color legibility, due to the printing method chosen some type and color combinations were illegible because the trapping area overpowered the legibility of the original two-color combination. Nonetheless, this color study indicates the basic color principles that govern the visibility of a trap. To ensure accuracy within our findings, we created an additional color study (in 2005) with the hues found on the 12-step color wheel. (This also included 50-percent tints of the 12 hues and 20-percent tints of cyan, magenta, yellow, black, yellow-magenta, yellow-cyan, and cyan-magenta.) The general principles that govern the visibility of trapping are listed below. These guidelines are particularly important when using printing methods that require a trap setting from $\frac{1}{16}$ to $\frac{1}{4}$in (0.06 to 6.4mm) or greater.

- The cruder the method of printing, the more likely the trap will be visible.

- The higher the CVD, the less visible the trap.

- The higher the substrate brightness rating, the more likely the trap will be visible.

- The lower the substrate brightness rating, the less likely the trap will be visible.

- Printing on coated paper will make the trap more obvious than printing on uncoated.

- Using a color combination that is analogous will yield an almost invisible trap.

- Using a color combination with the colors two steps away from each other (on a 12-step color wheel) will yield an invisible to

visible trap; however, in almost every case the trap is not overpowering (see Diagram 18, sample 17).

- Depending upon the hue scheme, a color combination in which the colors are three steps away from each other will create a visible to overpowering trap. The exceptions to this rule follow. These color combinations tend to yield an almost invisible trap:

  - The violet family in combination with the blue-green family

  - The green family in combination with the yellow-orange family

  - The yellow family in combination with the red-orange family

  - The yellow-orange family in combination with the red family

- Any color combination that is created with a cool color and a warm color of the same visual intensity will create a trap that is overpowering.

- So long as black is printed with the proper ink density, the trap, with any other hue, is virtually invisible.

The best way to determine whether a potential color combination will yield a visible to over-powering trap is by checking in Photoshop or Illustrator. Select the spot colors you wish to use. (Photoshop and Illustrator allow use of any standard ink-matching system, as well as the choice of one spot color from one system and a second spot color from another.) Put each spot

---

Figure 23
Art Director/Designer: Art Chantry

Distressed typography is used to help harmonize the large trap necessary for this printing process. The trap is visible within the green components of this design, but seems perfectly normal given the context.

Figure 24
Art Director/Designer: Art Chantry

Once again, Art Chantry is a master of understanding different printing methods to achieve the look and feel of a design. In this CD cover, blocks of red are used under the black hue to create large areas that trap, and at the same time work conceptually within the design.

Diagram 11
As seen in this diagram, a visible trap is created when using different printing processes. Note, the offset trap is unnoticeable due to the amount of choke and spread needed to hold the type in register.

Diagram 12 (a and b)
A change in printing order on a two-color job comprised of magenta and cyan. In a, the magenta is printed over the cyan; and in b, the cyan is laid over the magenta. In most cases, the image will subtly shift to the hue of the last printed color.

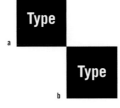

a

b

Diagram 13
A visual demonstration of hues that are two steps away from each other on a 12-step color wheel. Note how these hues yield a trap that is not overpowering.

0.625 trap

0.125 trap

0.25 trap

Offset trap

hue on its own layer, then select the Multiply feature. (In Photoshop, Multiply is under the Layers dialog box, and in Illustrator it is under the Transparency dialog box.) This will show how apparent the trap will be when printed.

Creating a document that uses overprinting colors is a prudent choice if the trap is visually apparent. Understanding how the hues will overprint can yield innovative color designs and mechanicals that will print more effectively, considering the visual anomaly has been built into the design or mechanical. For example, instead of using trapping, one can simply knock out through the overprinted color to reveal the color that is laid down first on press.

The electronic mechanical will often have to be constructed differently when changing the designated ink order for printing. For example, when printing small yellow type on a black background, the mechanical will be set up in the traditional manner. However, to create yellow type on a warm-black background with a yellow tint, either the black ink will need to incorporate a large percentage of yellow (between 50 percent and 100 percent) or the black plate will need a type reversal, and the yellow plate will need a solid overprint covering the black plate. The first option involves a change to the normal printing procedure and will create a more visible color tint. The scenarios above can be designated for a change in printing order. Both mechanicals are set up properly to accommodate this experience because the trap is eliminated or virtually undetected.

The printing order of inks is often defined because the print job tends to trap better with the darkest color printed last. However, in two-color jobs it is sometimes a toss-up as to which ink should be the hue that traps because the print job will not be adversely affected either way. In these cases, changing the printing order may give rise to a printing effect where the colors create a more pleasant hue experience.

Figure 25

Diagram 14
These hues are an exception to the rule that states colors three steps away from each other will yield a visually overpowering trap.

Diagram 15
Color combinations with cool and warm hues of the same visual intensity will create a trap that is overpowering.

Diagram 16
Choking and spreading is unnecessary when building a composite in this manner.

Diagram 17
When black is printed with the proper ink density the trap will be near invisible.

Figure 25
Art Director/Designer:
Dusan Jelesijevic

This job was run on offset lithography, which means the size of the trap would be minimal. In this case, the trap is near invisible with the blue package. The yellow hue at 100 percent overprinted with a blue hue also at 100 percent creates green, a near analogous color palette. Using a small portion of red within the overall color scheme minimizes visible traps. The same can be said for the orange-and-purple package design. Red, the common denominator within both hues, helps to minimize critical registration.

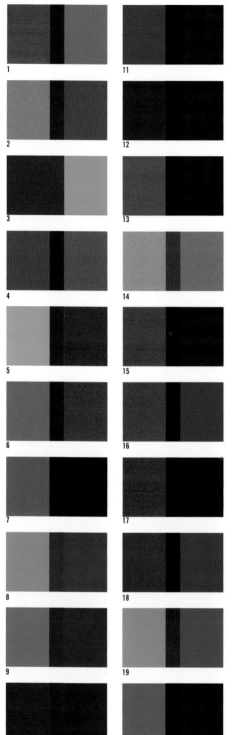

Extremely Bad Color Combination for Trapping

	PANTONE Hue 1	Y-T	CMYK	PANTONE Hue 2	Y-T	CMYK	CVD	Base Inks
1	PANTONE Red 032 C	21.79	0/91/87/0	PANTONE 348 C (K3%)	16.02	100/0/79/27	DT 5.77	1/3
2	PANTONE 416 C (K9.4%)	28.02	0/0/15/51	PANTONE 5473 C (K13.6%)	13.91	90/42/55/22	DT 14.11	3/3
3	PANTONE 288 C (K5.9%)	7.11	100/65/0/30.5	PANTONE 3272 C	29.95	100/0/47/0	LT 22.84	3/2
4	PANTONE 357 C (K20%)	12.52	79/0/87/56	PANTONE 431 C (K15.6%)	18.12	65/51/43/15	LT 5.6	3/3
5	PANTONE Process Blue C	17.40	100/0/0/0	PANTONE 485 C	18.22	8/98/100/1	LT .82	1/2
6	PANTONE 3005 C	22.11	100/30.5/0/6	PANTONE Red 032 C	21.79	0/96/74/0	LT .68	2/1
Average		8.30						

Poor Color Combination for Trapping

	PANTONE Hue 1	Y-T	CMYK	PANTONE Hue 2	Y-T	CMYK	CVD	Base Inks
7	PANTONE 335 C (K5.9%)	17.69	100/26/71/12	PA NTONE 295 C (K11.2%)	7.76	100/83/33/32	DT 9.93	2/3
8	PANTONE 334 C (K1.5%)	23.14	100/9/70/1	PANTONE 293 C	13.47	100/75/4/1	DT 9.67	2/2
9	PANTONE 327 C	20.34	100/20/62/6	PANTONE 286 C (K5.9%)	10.44	100/83/6/1	DT 9.9	2/3
10	PANTONE 186 C	17.54	11/100/85/2	PANTONE Blue 072 C (K1.5%)	2.92	100/92/2/2	DT 14.62	3/1
11	PANTONE 287 C (K3.0%)	8.27	100/83/16/5	PANTONE Black C (K100%)	3.77	63/63/70/66	DT 4.5	3/1
12	PANTONE 221 C (K5.9%)	11.73	32/100/50/20	PANTONE Black C (K100%)	3.77	63/63/70/66	DT 7.96	2/1
13	PANTONE 513 C	14.47	48/99/1/0	PANTONE Black C (K100%)	3.77	63/63/70/66	DT 10.70	2/1
14	PANTONE Orange 021 C	30.67	0/78/100/0	PANTONE 2727 C	30.67	76/53/0/0	0	1/2
15	PANTONE 485 C	18.22	8/98/100/1	PANTONE 2617 C (K5.9%)	7.53	84/100/20/15	DT10.69	2/3
16	PANTONE 485 C	18.22	8/98/100/1	PANTONE 343 C (K20%)	9.92	94/41/79/39	DT 8.3	2/3
17	PANTONE 192 C	19.63	2/100/66/0	PANTONE 2756 C (K11.2%)	2.31	100/98/24/17	DT 17.32	2/3
18	PANTONE 253 C	17.41	45/92/0/0	PANTONE 287 C (K3%)	8.27	100/83/16/5	DT 9.14	2/3
19	PANTONE 334 C (K1.5%)	23.14	100/9/70/1	PANTONE 293 C	13.47	100/75/4/1	DT 9.67	2/3
20	PANTONE 300 C	16.20	100/56/2/0	PANTONE Black C (K100%)	3.77	63/63/70/66	DT 12.43	2/1
Average		9.63						

Y-T = Y tristimulus value
CVD = Color value differential

PANTONE Colors displayed here are process simulations and do not match the solid PANTONE-identified standards. Consult current PANTONE Color Publications for accurate color.

Figure 26
Art Director/Designer:
Gabriela Lopez De Dennis

In this case, the type reversal is created with no critical registration within the trap, and it is therefore easy to hold on press. Both the yellow and muddy orange have a larger percentage of yellow running through each hue, eliminating the need to either choke or spread the typography.

Diagram 18
This is a visual facsimile (simplified) of the color study conducted in 1994. Note, the information has been organized by quality of trap.

Good Color Combination for Trapping

	PANTONE Hue 1	Y-T	CMYK	PANTONE Hue 2	Y-T	CMYK	CVD	Base Inks
21	PANTONE 4525 U (K1.7%)	50.00	22/27/51/0	PANTONE Blue 072 U	2.92	100/92/2/2	LT 47.08	4/4
22	PANTONE 294 C (K5.8%)	9.45	100/82/25/16	PANTONE Black C (K100%)	3.77	63/63/70/66	DT 5.68	3/1
23	PANTONE 142 C	53.70	5/27/84/0	PANTONE 2756 C (K11.2%)	2.01	100/98/24/17	DT 51.69	3/3
Average	**17.87**							

Excellent Color Combination for Trapping

	PANTONE Hue 1	Y-T	CMYK	PANTONE Hue 2	Y-T	CMYK	CVD	Base Inks
24	PANTONE 266 C	11.42	73/85/0/0	PANTONE Black C (K100%)	3.77	63/63/70/66	DT 7.65	2/1
25	PANTONE 430 C (K87.5%)	30.16	51/38/33/2	PANTONE 280 C (K5.9%)	7.10	100/88/21/17	DT 23.06	3/2
26	PANTONE 107 C	73.50	4/5/92/0	PANTONE 356 C (K5.9%)	17.10	100/28/100/19	DT 56.4	3/3
27	PANTONE 216 C (K20%)	11.30	38/96/54/33	PANTONE Black C (K100%)	3.77	63/63/70/66	DT 7.53	3/1
28	PANTONE 320 C	26.31	100/13/35/1	PANTONE 2738 C	2.65	100/96/3/3	DT 23.66	2/2
29	PANTONE Yellow 012 C	70.95	3/12/100/0	PANTONE Reflex Blue C	17.40	100/90/8/5	DT 53.55	1/1
30	PANTONE Red 032 C	21.79	0/96/74/0	PANTONE Black C (K100%)	3.77	63/63/70/66	DT 18.02	1/1
31	PANTONE 199 C	19.03	8/100/73/1	PANTONE 287 C (K3%)	8.27	100/83/16/5	DT 10.76	2/3
32	PANTONE 165 C	31.74	0/77/100/0	PANTONE Black C (K100%)	3.77	63/63/70/66	DT 27.97	2/1
33	PANTONE 347 C	20.73	100/10/100/2	PANTONE Black C (K100%)	3.77	63/63/70/66	DT 16.96	2/1
34	PANTONE 153 C (K5.9%)	21.62	20/67/100/7	PANTONE Black C (K100%)	3.77	63/63/70/66	DT 17.85	3/1
35	PANTONE Yellow 012 C	70.95	3/12/100/0	PANTONE 199 C	19.03	8/100/73/1	DT 51.92	1/2
36	PANTONE 226 C	18.88	13/100/17/0	PANTONE Black C (K100%)	3.77	63/63/70/66	DT 15.11	2/1
37	PANTONE 420 C (K1.1%)	62.75	19/15/16/0	PANTONE 477 C (K5.9%)	8.95	40/77/78/52	DT 53.8	3/4
38	PANTONE 485 C	18.22	8/98/100/1	PANTONE Black C (K100%)	3.77	63/63/70/66	DT 14.45	2/1
39	PANTONE 321 C (K1.6%)	20.84	100/27/41/4	PANTONE Black C (K100%)	3.77	63/63/70/66	DT 17.07	3/1
40	PANTONE 206 C	19.16	10/100/60/1	PANTONE Black C (K100%)	3.77	63/63/70/66	DT 15.39	2/1
41	PANTONE 109 C	65.73	2/16/100/0	PANTONE 2593 C	9.86	62/97/0/0	DT 55.87	2/2
42	PANTONE 185 C	21.02	2/100/82/0	PANTONE 286 C	10.44	100/83/6/1	DT 10.58	2/2
43	PANTONE Warm Red C	26.78	0/90/85/0	PANTONE Reflex Blue C	17.40	100/90/8/5	DT 9.38	1/1
Average	**25.35**							

Y-T = Y tristimulus value
CVD = Color value differential

PANTONE Colors displayed here are process simulations and do not match the solid PANTONE-identified standards. Consult current PANTONE Color Publications for accurate color.

Figure 26

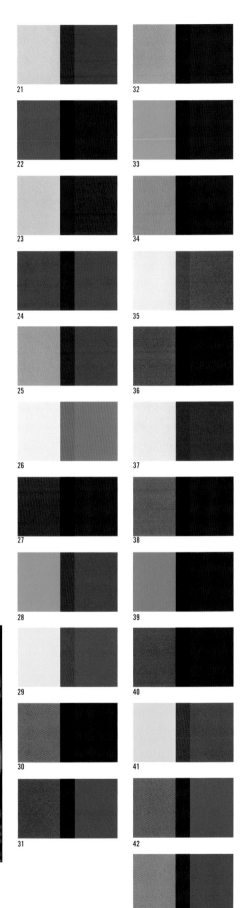

Figure 27

Color Correcting

In today's marketplace, package designs can take on an array of continuous tones and gradients. With gradients, the control from light to dark, including split-fountains, is easily achieved. The blend of the gradient is of concern when preparing a job for press. To safeguard against any unwanted banding, make sure the blend steps are maxed out at 256 steps. Banding is especially evident when using the 3-D feature in Illustrator. Assuring that the blend steps are done this way will help to alleviate any problems.

To color correct continuous-tone packages for press—whether four-color, grayscale, monotones, duotones, fake duotones, or tritones—the tonal values from light to dark must be set up correctly. For press there are seven major concerns when dealing with color correcting:

· The quality of the original image.

· The quality of the scanned image (if applicable).

· Ensuring proper contrast from light to dark within the photograph. Without this the image will look flat. Typically, a lack of contrast is caused by the overall image being too light, too dark, or too even (a lack of lights and darks). When continuous-tone images appear flat, the color primaries throughout the overall image tend to be relatively proportionate.

· Avoiding the light areas dropping out.

· Preventing the dark areas filling in (dot gain), which, as with the light areas dropping out, will cause a loss in detail and an improper tonal range from light to dark.

· Compensating for the printing process, including the substrate being utilized.

· With duotones, fake duotones, and tritones there is usually a seventh factor, that of maintaining tonal range when overprinting takes place. This can be achieved through the curve settings in the duotone dialog box.

The quality of the original image is the primary factor that determines whether it will print well—what you start with is what you get. An image that is flat, out of focus, or constructed incorrectly will never yield a reproduction of high quality. The image in question must be in focus, be properly color balanced, and have the proper tonal range from light to dark—this includes grayscale images that have gradients or continuous tones.

Having the right tool to color correct photographs is paramount, and there is no better program for this than Photoshop. Once the image is scanned and saved in the right color mode (RGB, CMYK, or grayscale), determine the proper contrast. There are several ways to achieve this. The first step is to try using the Auto-contrast and Auto-level features under Image in the main menu. This is accurate half of the time. For press, however, dropout and dot gain must be taken into account.

Figure 27
Studio: 1972dg
Art Director/Designer: Carlos Marques

The use of multiple continuous-tone images, both color and black and white, required them to be color corrected properly in order to create a quality branding strategy. In the case of the Tia Maria bag, the photo corrections are superbly done, creating a qualitative message.

Diagram 19
The higher the quality of printing, the more likely banding will be noticeable. To safeguard against it, set the banding features to their highest settings.

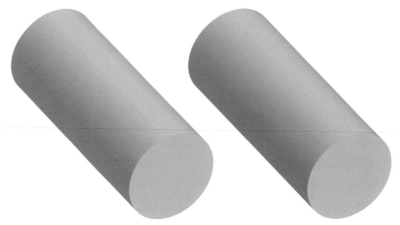

If these automated features do not properly color correct the image for press, open the Information dialog box under Windows in the main menu. The Information dialog box reads the color builds found within the image at any given point, including grayscale. For press, the highlights and lowlights or shadow areas within the image should be properly determined, and their builds should be retrieved. The general rule for highlighted areas is no less than 2 percent to 3 percent of color information for each channel, totaling no less than 8 percent. (Color information is the amount of image data found on each channel—use the Information dialog box under Window in the main menu to retrieve this information.) Correcting the image to fall within this percentage range will alleviate most of the dropout on press. On press, between 2 percent and 3 percent typically translates to 0 percent color information. In other words, if the image is not properly adjusted for press, a 5 percent highlight area will appear on press anywhere from 0 percent to 2 percent, resulting in the dropout of a considerable tonal area.

For press, the general rule for color information in dark areas is a value of no more than 98 percent. By properly adjusting the contrast to achieve this percentage, dot gain will be counteracted on most coated and less absorbent papers. If using a highly absorbent paper, a maximum of between 94 percent and 97 percent is recommended—on such papers, these areas will completely fill, creating a solid, 100 percent color field. If these rules for press

cannot be met through the automated features, the Brightness and Contrast feature under Image in the main menu of Photoshop will need to be adjusted. Using this along with the Information dialog box will ensure that the image has the proper contrast and color for press.

Figure 28

Figure 28
Studio: Wallace Church
Creative Director: Stan Church
Designer: Lawrence Haggerty

This is an iconic message that primarily relies on the four-color images, which are superbly color corrected to maximize the qualitative level of the intended message.

Diagram 20
This diagram demonstrates an image that has been properly color corrected, and one that has not. Using the steps outlined above will safeguard against improper color balance.

Figure 29

Figure 30

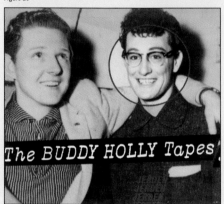

Figure 31

Figure 32

Duotones, Fake Duotones, and Tritones

For duotones, fake duotones, and tritones, a few more steps must be taken in order to properly color balance and color correct continuous tone within the images. Prior to the mid-1980s, duotones were created with two separate pieces of film, one for each color. Each piece was taken from the original image and exposed to light differently to create the base art. In Photoshop, this is no longer the case. A duotone is created from one piece of film or one channel and split into two pieces of film for press. Therefore, color correcting a duotone, fake duotone, or tritone in Photoshop creates visual verification problems—when using two spot colors, including black and one other, what appears on the computer screen is not what will appear on press.

Figures 29–32
Art Director/Designer: Art Chantry

These duotone CD covers are created using black and an additional hue. When color correcting for duotones, first correct in grayscale mode before converting.

Diagram 21
A demonstration of how a duotone is created.

 +  =

Verifying Spot Colors

You can use several methods to create a document, all of which allow for visual verification when color correcting a duotone, fake duotone, tritone, or setup for press. The first is to refer to a color guide. PANTONE offers a duotone guide for both coated and uncoated colors, the PANTONE Studio Edition Duotone Guide. Each duotone color combination offers four distinct curved setups for black and another spot color, and the guide offers a comprehensive compilation of 11,328 setups, with an explanation of how to work with duotone curves in Photoshop.

This information is excellent when working with duotones created with black and another color, but many duotones are created with two spot colors, such as PANTONE 102 and PANTONE 2415, both of which fall within the CMYK color gamma. The method listed below works only with spot colors that fall within the CMYK color gamma. (A method for dealing with spot colors that cannot be matched by the four-color process is described later in this chapter.) There are two ways to verify whether a spot color falls within the CMYK gamma. The easiest is to check in one of the color guides that display which spot colors meet this requirement, such as PANTONE® COLOR BRIDGE®.

A less expensive way to visually verify whether a spot color falls within the CMYK gamma is to use the QuarkXPress Colors features under Edit. (Photoshop CS or higher will also allow you to do this.) Using the Colors features in QuarkXPress, you can simulate any solid-to-process guide for any color-matching system, including PANTONE, Toyo, Trumatch, and Focoltone.

1. Open the Default Colors dialog box by clicking on Colors under Edit in the main menu.

2. Within this dialog box click on New, choose the spot color to be verified, and click OK to return to the Default Colors dialog box.

3. Choose Edit within this to return to the Edit Colors dialog box.

4. Choose the CMYK mode under Model. The spot color along with the four-color-process equivalent will appear in the New and Original color swatch section within this dialog box, allowing for visual verification. If the two colors match, the spot color can be created within the CMYK gamma. If the two colors do not match, then the method listed in Creating Duotones Outside CMYK Color Gamma should be used.

Figure 33

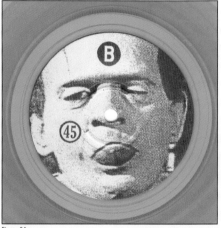

Figure 34

Diagram 22
A demonstration of how a fake duotone is created. A fake duotone is when one of the two channels is utilized at 100% of color to create a flat color field. The darker of the two colors used (in this example, cyan) creates the continuous-tone image. A fake duotone is an excellent way to make an image more graphically inclined.

 +  =

Figure 33
Art Director/Designer: Art Chantry
Photographer: Jini Dellaccio

When creating duotones that fall outside of the CMYK color spectrum, special care needs to be taken in order to verify accurate color rendition. In this case, the duotone has been pushed to create a high-contrast image, thus minimizing the need for verifying color.

Figure 34
Art Director/Designer: Art Chantry

In this case, the Frank En Stein image found on the 45 label uses a crude screen percentage, and at the same time the image is pushed, making verifying color accuracy less important.

Diagram 23
A demonstration of how a tritone is created.

 +  + 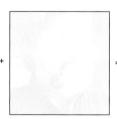 =

Figure 35

Figure 36

Creating Duotones within the CMYK Color Gamma

When creating a duotone for a package with two spot colors other than black, follow the method below to create an accurate color appearance for final output. The PANTONE Studio Edition duotone curves can also be used with any image in Photoshop by loading the curve setting.

1. Create a duotone using your spot colors—for example, PANTONE 102 and PANTONE 2415—in Photoshop.

2. Open up the original grayscale image and create a monotone using PANTONE 102.

3. Create a PANTONE 2415 monotone using the same grayscale image as for Step 2.

4. Copy each monotone into a new CMYK document in Photoshop. There should be two layers, each having a monotone image and a background layer (white).

5. Click on layer 2 to make it active, and then apply Multiply under Normal in the Layers dialog box to see how the two spot colors are overprinting in Photoshop in process color. At this point, a difference in color between the Photoshop duotone and the hybrid facsimile just created should be discernible. Check any PANTONE coated or uncoated spot colors from the PANTONE COLOR BRIDGE® guide to see if they match (the newer swatch books indicate whether a PANTONE color can be matched through CMYK means), or use QuarkXPress or Photoshop to determine color gamma. The duotone facsimile

Figures 35–38
Art Director/Designer: Art Chantry
Photographer: Charles Peterson

In the case of the Tad CD, color verification is critical. Note how the image (above right) dodges the area around Tad's face, creating visual separation between the other two band members.

facsimile created in the CMYK mode is more color accurate than the Photoshop duotone and can be used as a guide to color correct the Photoshop duotone image for press. (The CMYK duotone facsimile is created from two grayscale images, unlike its Photoshop counterpart, thus creating a color facsimile closer to what will appear on press.)

6. If the spot colors match the CMYK color gamma, color correct each layer in the Curves dialog box (only), under Image in the main menu of Photoshop, and save both curve settings. Keep the image in CMYK mode, and do not add any channels.

7. Click back on the Photoshop duotone and reopen the duotone setting under Image in the main menu.

8. Click on each duotone Curve setting individually. The duotone curve matrix will appear.

9. Load the Curve settings saved for each color. The duotone will be properly color corrected.

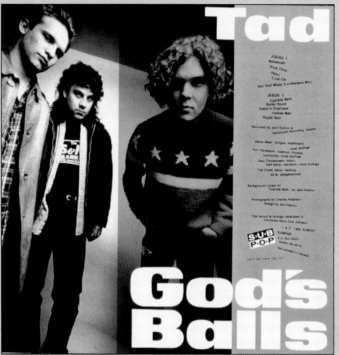

Figure 37

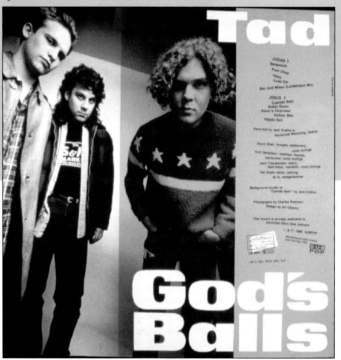

Figure 38

Figure 39

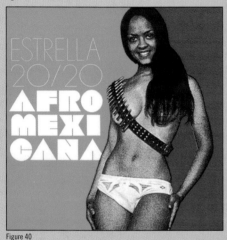

Figure 40

Creating Duotones outside the CMYK Color Gamma

When creating a duotone for a package outside the CMYK color gamma, the computer monitor will need to be set up differently so that it holds, or emits, only the colors that are specified for creating the duotone. A large percentage of spot colors are outside the CMYK color gamma. The primaries that make up these colors have a higher chroma rating than those that can be created through process colors, therefore, the computer monitor's color space needs to be changed to reflect more accurately the chroma value of each individual hue. Two of the CMYK color primaries within Photoshop must be altered each time a duotone is created, as outlined below.

1. Open a grayscale image or convert a CMYK image to grayscale.

2. Convert the grayscale image to the duotone setting under Image in the main menu of Photoshop.

3. Select the Duotone mode in the Duotone Options dialog box.

4. Select the two spot colors to create the duotone. Do not adjust the curve settings.

5. After selecting the two spot hues, click back on each color and then click on Picker and write down the individual L*a*b* values for each spot color.

6. Click on the overprinting setting at the bottom of the Duotone Options dialog box.

7. Click on the color swatch found in the Overprinting dialog box and then click on the Picker and write down the L*a*b* values of the overprinted hue.

8. Open the duotone.

9. Under File in the main menu, scroll down to Color Settings and select the CMYK setup.

10. Under the CMYK Setup dialog box, select Custom within the Ink Colors slot. (For each Photoshop version, the process of acquiring the Ink Colors dialog box is somewhat different. However, it is usually found under Preferences or Color Setup under File in the main menu of Photoshop.)

11. Click on the L*a*b* coordinates, bottom left of the dialog box. The L*a*b* setting must be activated for this process to work.

12. In the Ink Colors dialog box, enter the L*a*b* values for the first duotone color in the three cyan slots.

13. Enter the second duotone color in the three magenta slots.

14. Enter the overprinting duotone color in the three cyan/magenta slots.

15. Click on OK in the Ink Colors dialog box.

16. Save the ink-color settings by clicking on Save in the CMYK Setup dialog box and then click OK.

17. Open the original grayscale image, copy it to the clipboard, and then close the grayscale image.

Figure 39
Art Director/Designer: Art Chantry

The Coyote Men CD cover is an excellent example of a monotone image using a crude screen pattern. In this case, the hue black falls within the CMYK color gamma. However, the other two hues are spot colors that cannot be reproduced using CMYK process hues.

Figure 40
Art Director/Designer: Art Chantry

The Estrella 20/20 CD cover is a masked-out monotone image. The green, yellow, and red hues are spot colors—the red hue cannot be reproduced through CMYK process colors. A crude screen pattern is intentionally applied to the figure to help create visual separation from the smooth, flat color background.

Diagram 24 (a and b)
As is clearly demonstrated, this method will yield a better understanding of how the image will print on press.

 +  =

a

Standard duotone

18. Open a new CMYK document in Photoshop. Copying the original image on the clipboard will prompt Photoshop to automatically create a document the size of the original grayscale image.

19. Paste the original grayscale image into the cyan and magenta channels.

20. Select and delete any information found on the yellow and black channels within the document. Do not delete the channels.

21. Click on the composite CMYK channel to view the facsimile duotone. If the spot colors chosen are outside of the CMYK color gamma, the Photoshop duotone, already open on the computer screen, and the facsimile duotone color composite should look dramatically different. The facsimile duotone is an accurate color representation for press.

22. Within the facsimile duotone, click on the cyan channel and open the Curves dialog box.

23. Adjust the curve setting and save it to the appropriate folder.

24. Once the cyan channel curve setting has been saved click OK.

25. Repeat steps 22 to 24, above, for the magenta channel.

26. Within the Photoshop duotone, load the curve settings for each spot color and save the document. The duotone is now mechanically ready for press.

PANTONE has done an outstanding job in compiling 11,328 duotone curve settings for use with its colors. These settings can also be used by loading the desired settings in steps 23 and 26. Furthermore, they can be used with other ink-matching systems, such as Trumatch, Toyo, and Focoltone. To use these curves effectively, select colors that are similar in value and chroma. The hue does not need to match. By altering the two hues that create the duotone, the secondary and tertiary colors and their corresponding tints will be different.

Figure 41

 +  =

b

Duotone within CMYK color gamma

Figure 41
Art Director/Designer: Art Chantry

In this case, a fake tritone is used—the image was originally created as a tritone and then converted into CMYK process colors.

Figure 42

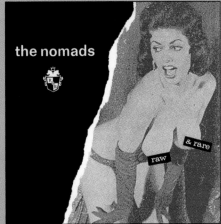

Figure 43

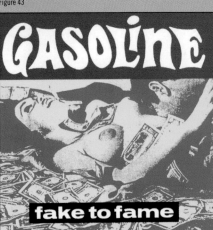

Figure 45

Figure 44

Creating Fake Duotones

For fake duotones only one curve setting needs to be saved, not the solid color. Under Duotones in Photoshop, set the curve setting for the spot-color solid. In the duotones matrix set both the 0 setting and the 100 setting to 100. This will ensure that the second color of the duotone prints 100 percent of color. When creating fake duotones, the darker of the two colors should always be the continuous-tone image. The process for color verification and mechanical preparation is as described above.

Figures 42–45
Art Director/Designer: Art Chantry

In each of the CD covers presented, fake duotones are utilized to create vivid images. In each case, a warm, high-chroma hue is used for the background color. With the exception of *Last Straw*, the background hues have a Y tristimulus value of 73.4 or higher, and the foreground hue/continuous-tone hues have a Y tristimulus value no greater than 22. In the case of *Last Straw*, the red hue is warm, and it has a CVD from the background hue of 20.26. *Raw & Rare* has a CVD of 87.22, *Don't Like You* has a CVD of 67.3, and *Fake to Fame* has a CVD of 51.8, making all four images clearly legible.

Diagram 25
A demonstration of how a fake duotone is created. Note, the lighter of the two hues has been used as the background color.

 +  =

Type and Color

When setting up a document for press, it is the little formal details that most often cause printers to have fits. They are most often also the elements overlooked by designers, and they tend to create readability, legibility, and registration problems. Some simple rules, when applied properly, can facilitate the process of setting up the mechanical for press.

Reversals

A reversal is when type or a graphic element is dropped out from a solid color or color tints and shades to the color of the substrate. However, choosing the right color and substrate combination is critical to alleviate any legibility problems. For example, a type reversal with a color tint or a solid yellow-orange on white paper will more than likely not be legible because either the color tint or the solid yellow-orange does not have a 20 percent differential from white paper. In this scenario, the type would be presented rather small. If the type was presented large enough for the proper viewing distance on the package design, and having less than 20 percent CVD, the visual angle would need to be grossly exaggerated (5 degrees is the norm for 20/20 vision). Then again, the type may be so large that it does not fit on the package. The software, Acuity 1.0, can determine the proper viewing distance for any type and color combination.

Every paper stock has a brightness rating or color-value number that can be obtained from a paper representative or a paper swatch. The color in which the type reverses can also be an issue because of the number of plates/channels the type reversals have to go through. There is not usually a problem if the background hue is pure, semipure, or a spot color, but there can be a problem mechanically when dealing with four- and six-color processes. If the color is made from all process primaries, it will be very difficult to hold the job in register on press, especially with small type, small graphics, or fine detail. The solid color background in which a reversal takes place should not be made from more than two of the process primaries. This may seem limited, but with the addition of color tinting there are thousands of colors from which to choose. If color shading (the addition of black) is desired, one of two strategies can be employed to create a proper electronic mechanical. If two colors already make up the solid background, then color shading should be applied uniformly to both the background and the reversal. In this case, the type or graphic is no longer a reversal, but rather a knock out, and registration is still held to only two plates. Because black is uniformly applied, registration is not a problem. The second strategy is to eliminate one of the two colors and replace the second color with black. In this scenario shading and tinting can still be used.

Figure 46

Figure 47

Diagram 26
As shown here the color value differential (CVD) is critical in determining if the object can be seen or not at a distance. With that said, some hue combinations that have a 2% CVD or less are perfectly legible. The 20% CVD rule is good for normal eyesight. However, a 40% differential will alleviate any doubt and is more inclusive.

Figures 46 and 47
Studio: Ruadesign
Art Director/Designer: Diogo Paulo

When using type reversals, understanding how the mechanical is put together will lead to better print quality. In this case, yellow and green possess no critical registration because 100 percent of yellow is used to create green. Furthermore, a black outline is utilized throughout the illustration and typography, eliminating critical registration.

Diagram 27 (a–c)
This diagram illustrates the difficulty of holding numerous plates in register when on press. In other words, the more plates that are used to create the specified knockout or reversal, the more chances the job will not be in register.

a

b

c

Figure 48

Figure 49

Simultaneous Contrast

Simultaneous contrast is a strobing effect resulting from the use of unequal portions of colors, and it is most pronounced with an imbalance of large and small areas of color. A pronounced simultaneous contrast of color opposites can be quite unpleasant on the eye.

To some degree, simultaneous contrast occurs with all colors, but it is most noticeable when pure complementary colors are juxtaposed. This phenomenon is caused by retinal-cone fatigue. The photoreceptor cells found within the cones near the fovea of the eye become overworked because each cell can process only one color at a time, and the resultant switching back and forth overstimulates the photoreceptor cell, thereby creating the visual phenomenon of simultaneous contrast.

We can use this effect to our advantage, however. As stated above, pronounced simultaneous contrast is predictable when using pure complementary colors. As the complementary colors become less pure, the effect lessens, which means we can control the degree of the strobe, and learning to harness this effect can lead to innovative color work. For example, we can create a package that makes use of this back-and-forth motion— a perfect solution for any company associated with movement-oriented activities such as sports—giving rise to all kinds of possibilities.

Figure 48
Studio: REFLECTUR.COM
Art Director/Designer: Gwendolyn Hicks

When applied correctly, simultaneous contrast can be used as a visual magnet to obtain greater attention. In this case, the near complementary color palette of a high-chroma teal-green and red creates pronounced simultaneous contrast. The typography is managed beautifully by making sure that the teal-green and red do not butt register.

Figure 49
Art Director: Marcos Chavez
Designers: Marcos Chavez,
Mark Naden

With small type, simultaneous contrast should be avoided. In this case, tinting the teal-green by impregnating the plastic bottle with white pigment (an ingenious idea) eliminates simultaneous contrast.

Diagram 28
A visual depiction of the color primaries for 3-D color theory. A photoreceptor cell responsible for detecting color within the human eye can only process one color at a time. The photoreceptor cells found within the rods can process black, white, and shades of gray at the same time. This is why simultaneous contrast does not occur to any great degree in black and white form.

3-D color

Simultaneous contrast must be considered every time graphics and type with detail are created within a color field. To read when pronounced simultaneous contrast occurs can be difficult or impossible. Getting the design off the computer and testing it in different light sources is the best way of predicting outcome. Remember, the computer screen lies for print—it often gives a inaccurate representation of color appearance. Pull accurate color proofs and verify the color combination in different light sources—in daylight, under fluorescent lighting, under incandescent lighting, and on a computer screen.

Because of the design process and the production phases associated with print-based graphics, it is far more complicated to visualize the final outcome without viewing the finished work. The quality of any comprehensive printer will affect the result. If the area in question is made up of four-color-process builds, it is easy to predict outcome. If the design is made up of spot colors that fall outside of the CMYK spectrum, a more accurate color proof should be pulled—such as an Iris (which matches most spot colors for the lowest price), Fuji Final Proof, Agfa Print, Cromalin, Matchprint, Waterproof, or Kodak Approval.

Today, graphic-design programs have a color component built in. This feature allows designers to retrieve the color builds of any hue used within the document. Pronounced simultaneous contrast occurs when pure complementary colors are juxtaposed. By reading builds of the hues in question, we can predict the amount of simultaneous contrast that will occur and then make the appropriate adjustments.

Several strategies can be employed to adjust the amount of simultaneous contrast occurring within a piece:

· Add a portion of one color to another by setting up a color matrix with 10 percent increments. This matrix will help to determine the point at which simultaneous contrast does not affect the readability or legibility of the color combination in question.

· Tint the color or type-and-color combination with a third color; this also requires the building of a color matrix.

· Shade the color combination with black to reduce the amount of simultaneous contrast.

· Combine all of the above.

· Switch the color combination to a harmonious color palette, one that has an equal portion of one color running through both color fields—for example, yellow type on a green background, which is harmonious because the amount of yellow is stable in both the foreground and the background.

In print-based graphics, the first, second, and fifth techniques above will still create a two-color combination, with no additional ink necessary to complete the job. In other words, if the paper is white, the job is still considered two color and not three color. When tinting or shading one or both of the colors, select a color swatch that has additional white, black, or another color. In addition, a color percentage of one of the two hues found within the combination would still be considered a two-color job.

Figure 50

Diagram 29

These techniques can be utilized to either decrease or increase simultaneous contrast.

Tinted red type/green background
100%;90%;80%;60%;40%;20%;10%;0%

Tinted green type/red background
100%;90%;80%;60%;40%;20%;10%;0%

Tinted green background/red type
100%;90%;80%;70%;60%;50%;40%

Tinted red background/green type
100%;90%;80%;70%;60%;50%;40%

Shaded red type/green background
5%;10%;15%;20%;25%;30%;35%;40%

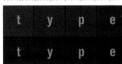

Green type/shaded red background
5%;10%;15%;20%;25%;30%;35%;40%

Green type/red background with percentages of cyan
10%;20%;30%;40%;50%;60%;70%;80%

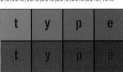

Red type/shaded green background
5%;10%;15%;20%;25%;30%;35%;40%

Red type/green background with percentages of magenta
10%;20%;30%;40%;50%;60%;70%;80%

Figure 50
Studio: milkxhake
Art Director/Designer: milkxhake

This is a project commissioned by a paper company, Antalis (Hong Kong) Ltd., to design a New Year calendar for 2006. Instead of creating a general calendar paper sample, the studio came up with the unusual idea of publishing "The Very First Magazine 2006," mixing the concepts of "calendar," "magazine," and "visual diary" in an unconventional approach. Twelve contributors from Asia-Pacific Region (Hong Kong, China, Singapore, Malaysia, and Thailand) were invited to make their unique issue based on a given month. Their personal thoughts and creative views on paper medium were deeply explored. Note how the high-chroma hues are stored side by side intentionally, creating simultaneous contrast. By doing so, a strobing effect within the eye is created, and in this case will gain more attention by the viewer.

Color Legibility

The theory behind color legibility and the practical application of color begins and ends with understanding color in three-dimensional form. Within three-dimensional color theory are the triadic relationships between the source, the object, and the observer. In order to predict color legibility accurately, these three components must be considered both individually and together, and each involves numerous factors. Understanding how to account for natural or man-made environments will enable you to ensure color appearance and legibility. Without a full understanding of color appearance and/or light, the final outcome becomes unpredictable.

With additive color theory, the source changes with each scenario depending on the intensity of light. Since the early 1700s scientists have been conducting experiments into light and what is visible to humans. Through these endeavors, basic principles governing the nature of lightwaves (color) have been revealed: the intensity of light has a direct impact on the chroma and value of color, and the wavelength of light has a direct bearing on color appearance (hue). These factors help shape the way humans see color, and this, in turn, affects color legibility.

In the past, designers were taught how to work with an object using subtractive color theory—and for good reason. This theory teaches us how to mix paint pigment, dyes, and colorants to create an array of colors. On the computer, using traditional software applications, simple subtractive color mixing is simulated to demonstrate how objects will appear when paint, dyes, or colorants are applied. However, there is more to subtractive color theory than just mixing paint. Pigments, dyes, and colorants possess no color; the process of mixing paint involves altering those wavelengths that are absorbed/subtracted, and scattered, and which are reflected back to the viewer by manipulating the paint pigments. Changing the object's physicality, whether or not it is apparent to the naked eye, alters the object's appearance through its effect on the absorption, reflection, and scattering of wavelengths.

Figure 1

Figure 2

Figure 3

Readability

Defining readability—as distinct from legibility—is not a simple task. The printed word is composed of symbols. For the observer to understand their meaning, visual perception, identification, and recognition are necessary. A word need not be legible to be identifiable— there need be only enough visible information for it to be recognized as a word picture.

Readability enables us to understand quickly, both visually and mentally, the complex codes and structures that make up written and visual language. Written language has physical properties that help speed up the process of cognition, including the position of letterforms on a page or screen, the structure of individual letterforms, regardless of font characteristic, and the total word structure, which creates its silhouette and internal patterns—that is, the word picture.

Figure 1
Studio: The People's Design
Art Director: Chris Komashko

The thick and thin strokes of this face reiterate the lushness of poured chocolate, while the curvilinear set width can be easily associated with the round chocolates.

Figure 2
Studio: Curiosity
Designer: Gwenazi Nicilas

The white space of the Equilir product line pulls the eye to the understated typography and aids in the recognition of individual letterforms, while capital letters also slow reading letter by letter.

Figure 3
Studio: Fourillusion
Art Director: Flavio Hobo
Photographer: Thiago Fantinatti

For this Brazilian line of sandals, two-color imagery imparted the seasons of the tropical country. The type is consistently neutral and identifiable in all lowercase, reflecting femininity and the Greek goddess of love.

type

a

type type

b

type type

c

Diagram 1 (a–f)
Position, color, size, spacing, and line length of type all play a role in its readability and legibility.

Type is **typographical** in nature.

d

Position

The position of typographic forms on the printed page can either help the process of reading or hinder it. The eye moves along the printed line in a procession of small, rapid jerks called fixation points. It is only at these points that the eye is in focus. Movement continues or regresses, depending upon the complexity of the information and on its position. Approximately 94 percent of the time spent reading is dedicated to these pauses.

If there is a time limitation for viewing, it makes sense that, as designers, we understand how best to use position to reduce the time needed to recognize the intended message. The following points describe and illustrate factors that promote or impair readability:

- Type aligned vertically is all but impossible for Westerners to read. This arrangement should be avoided for signage, and for a Western audience with a time limitation (see Diagram 1a).

- Type that is positioned at a 90°-angle is less readable in an upward than a downward direction (see Diagram 1b).

- Type that is positioned at lesser angles (45° for example) is more readable in an upward than a downward direction (see Diagram 1c).

- The optimum reading distance for type set in traditional book format (between 8 and 12pt type) is on average 12 to 14in (30 to 35cm) away. At this distance, the fovea is capable of focusing clearly on a space that is about four letterforms in length. With peripheral vision, we can see 12 to 15 letterforms at each fixation point (see Diagram 1d).

- The optimum line length for type of 8 to 12pt is between 18 and 24 picas, which is around ten to 12 words per line. This word count should be maintained for any viewing distance, with the appropriate adjustment made to the size of the type (see Diagram 1e).

- For the best results, leading should be 3pt, although if the line is longer than 24 picas, more leading seems to promote the readability of information. Difficulty in reading long lines of type is attributed to the eye having difficulty in relocating the next line. Difficulty with short lines (18 picas or less) is attributed to the eye's inability to pick up horizontal line cues—in this case more leading is appropriate.

- The format of body copy has no effect on good readers, but poor readers find justified type more difficult to read.

- In signage or viewing at a distance, generous white space (tracking) around individual letterforms or numbers aids in their recognition (see Diagram 1f).

- Generous white space in a typographic treatment has always served to "activate" the page and increase the attention of the viewer. Filling the page with information creates a psychological aversion to the point where some individuals will not bother to read it at all.

f

In this example, the letterforms are tracked out equal to the stroke width, providing ample white space for viewing at a distance. If the letterforms are less than a stroke width apart, they will converge when viewed at a distance.

Knowing the number of words per line is helpful for package design.

e

Structure of Individual Letterforms

As the weight of information available on the subject shows, the structure of individual letterforms has a significant impact on readability. This section concentrates on structural factors that enhance or contribute to the readability of the printed page. Letterforms fall into four major groups, based on their structure: vertical strokes, curved lines, both vertical strokes and curved lines, and oblique strokes. Some letterforms have a more dominant role than others in the readability of a word:

- Words composed of ascenders and descenders perform the most important role in the creation of a word picture (see Diagram 2).

- Letterforms with no ascenders or descenders provide few visual cues (see Diagram 2).

- In both capital and lowercase letterforms, the right half of the form provides greater cues for cognition than the left half (see Diagram 3).

- The upper halves of lowercase letterforms are more readable than the lower halves (see Diagram 4).

- With capital letterforms, the lower half of the form provides more cues for cognition than the upper half (see Diagram 4).

- Capital letterforms have a distinct order of ranking for cognition. In 1930 the Council of British Ophthalmologists advised that

Figure 4

Figure 4
Art Director: John T. Drew
Designer: Letty Avila

Specific traits of the typeface were linked to the psychological effects, perception, and interpretation of the color.

Diagram 2
The ascender and descender in "picture" provide visual cues to ease the reading of the word, whereas "no cues" lacks a defined word picture. The spelling of the word or the design of the typeface can determine the amount of ascenders and descenders.

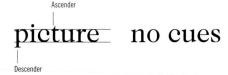

Ascender

picture　no cues

Descender

Diagram 3
The right half of a letterform is easier to recognize than the left half.

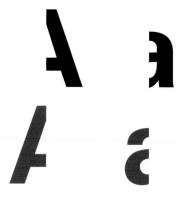

some letterforms are difficult to read, whereas other letterforms are easy. Numbers and capital letterforms have an inherent order of cognition and can be categorized into four groups:

· Easily recognized:
  A C J L D V O U 7 1 4

· Intermediate:
  T P Z I G E F K N W R 6 2 3

· Difficult:
  H M Y X S Q B 5 8 9

· Letterforms that can be confused with one another:
  C D G O Q H K M N W

· Copy set in all capital letterforms interferes with the speed of reading. In fact, using all capitals decelerates the process of reading more than any other factor, by slowing the activity to a letter-by-letter process (see Diagram 5c).

· Many researchers have found that italic letterforms reduce the speed of reading by up to 15 percent when compared with roman (see Diagram 5d).

· Old-style numerals are more easily recognized than those of modern typefaces. This is because they are constructed with ascenders and descenders, thus giving the word picture-identifiable cues for recognition (see Diagram 6).

Figure 5

Figure 5
Studio: Phoenix Creative
Designer: Carlo Irigoyen

The packaging and mailer for Pacific Life promotional items reflects the connectivity of circuitry that is reinforced in the navigable type.

a

The format of body copy has no effect on good readers, but many readers find justified type more difficult to read.

b

The format of body copy has no effect on good readers, but many readers find justified type more difficult to read.

c

COPY SET IN ALL CAPITAL LETTERS DECELERATES THE PROCESS OF READING MORE THAN ANY OTHER FACTOR.

d

Italic letterforms reduce the speed of reading by up to 15 percent.

Diagram 5 (a–d)
Notice the effect the word picture and alignment have on readability in the above boxes. Diagram 5a shows optimal conditions. The justified type in 5b degrades readability through disproportionate kerning and equal line lengths. The irregular kerning destroys the word picture and equal line length provides the reader few visual cues as to the start of the next line. Set in all caps, 5c eliminates the word picture and significantly hinders readability. Diagram 5d, in italics, also slows readability by distorting the letterform and manipulating the clarity of the word picture.

Diagram 6
The Helvetica numerals below lack ascenders and descenders, making the number more difficult to read than when set in the old-style face to the right.

56 *56*

abcdefghijklmnopqrstuvwxyz
abcdefghijklmnopqrstuvwxyz

ABCDEFGHIJKLMNOPQRSTUVWXYZ
ABCDEFGHIJKLMNOPQRSTUVWXYZ

Diagram 4
The upper halves of lowercase letterforms provide more cues for cognition, but the reverse is true for capital letterforms.

Figure 6

Word Pictures

A word picture is a combination of typographic forms with an external and internal pattern that is recognized by the reader at a glance. The reader need not see all parts of the letterforms within a word for the word to be recognized. The eye can recognize a word as fast as a single letterform, and, by memorizing these word pictures, mature readers can familiarize themselves with the total characteristic shape of individual words. The following points will influence the readability of a design:

· Longer words are more apt to be recognized at a glance than shorter ones because they provide more cues for the reader.

· The prefix and first half of a word provides more cues—or a better word picture—for recognition than does the second half (see Diagram 7). Words to the right of the fixation point furnish meaningful cues for perception and further fixations (see Diagram 23 on page 182).

Figure 6
Designer: Bradley W. Baker

When bundled on a shelf, the string calls attention to this T-shirt packaging and slows down the viewer's eye. However, because of the size of the numbers, the string and reversal of colors do not diminish readability.

Diagram 7
In this example, the word is easily recognized by its identifiable prefix. The suffix increases the amount of visual cues and provides grammatical context, but is indistinguishable from many other words.

Diagram 8
As exemplified above, words set in all lowercase are easily read due to their identifiable word picture. A word set in upper- and lowercase will retain its word picture to some degree, but a word set in all uppercase will completely disintegrate the word picture.

- Words that are set in headline type, with capital and lowercase letterforms, retain their word pictures and are therefore easy to read (see Diagram 8).

- Under normal reading conditions, reversing black letterforms on a white background to white letterforms on a black background will decelerate the process of reading by up to 14.7 percent. This is caused by a loss of normal word picture (see Diagram 9b).

- With any one of the factors above, adding color that is preconceived as abnormal will decrease the speed at which the letterform, word, line of text, paragraph, column, or document is read by up to 14.7 percent. However, this may be a desirable effect (see Diagram 9c).

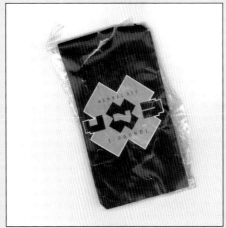

Figure 7

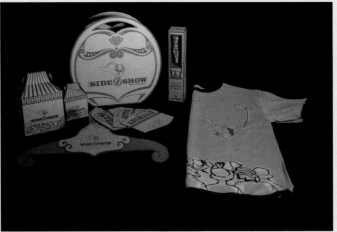

Figure 8

Black letterforms on a white background produce the usual speed of reading, and set the standard by which other deviations are measured.

White letterforms on a black background will decelerate the process of reading by up to 14.7 percent.

Adding color that is preconceived as abnormal will decrease the speed at which the letterform, word, line of text, paragraph, column, or document is read.

a   b   c

Figure 7
Studio: schönereWelt! swelt.com
Art Director: Sven C. Steinmeyer

The condensed countershapes and loose tracking of this logotype reflect the techno rave culture of the 1990s and add instant recognition to this cost-conscious package without sacrificing readability.

Figure 8
Art Director: Babette Mayor
Designer: Danny Giang

As a series of versatile packaging for a wide range of products, the typographic choice and consistent application unify the brand.

Diagram 9 (a–c)
The type set in the boxes above illustrates the effect that type and background can have on readability.

readability

legibility

legibility

legibility

Diagram 10
Readability defines that a word, such as that above, can be read even though every part of the letterform is not revealed. Legibility defines that every element of a word must be distinguishable in the prescribed usage. In this case, each variation of "legibility" is completely legible for the viewing distance of a book.

Figure 9

Legibility

Now that we have defined some of the factors that help or hinder reading, we can turn to those that contribute to legibility—the visual clarity of printed words, letters, numerals, and simple symbols as defined by the scientific standardization of visual acuity. There is a considerable difference between readability and legibility. Readability is concerned with the speed of reading, whereas legibility is more concerned with visual clarity. We have already stated that in order for something to be readable only enough information need be visible for it to be recognized as a word picture. In order for something to be legible, errors of communication must be avoided. Some letterforms and numerals are more apt to be misread than others. Your first concern as a designer should be with legibility and clarity of communication. This is of particular importance in the creation of signage systems or viewing typography for packaging at a distance—you do not have to look far to find signage that does not serve the purpose for which it was intended.

There is a formula for determining the distance at which a letterform is legible: for every 1in (2.54cm) of letterform height equates to 42ft (12.8m) of viewing distance. This formula is accurate for typefaces that are monoweight, with a breadth of line similar to that of the typeface Helvetica 75. Most typefaces, however, have a wide ratio of thick to thin strokes, making this formula too broad to predict the visual outcome with complete accuracy for standard 20/20 vision.

Figures 9–11
 Studio: AG Adriano Goldschmied
Photographer: Nina Ng

AG-ed by AG is a seasonally changing line of jeans with specialty washes. Each season, four years are selected from the vintage archive for marketing and sales.

This package for celebrity clientele and magazine editors promotes authenticity and harks back to the cigar boxes and wanted posters of yesteryear. The hangtags utilize distressed typography to provide readable word pictures and inform the viewer of the vintage. Even the back patch on the waistband and the subtle stitching on the pocket reinforce the AG name while diversifying the product line.

Figure 12
Studio: Positiu Design Consultants
Art Director/Designer: Oriol Llahona

The enlarged "g" increases the overall readability of the minimal contrasting colors, whereas the smaller type benefits from the contrasting orange color.

Figure 12

Scientific Standardization of Visual Acuity

Dr. Hermann Snellen, MD, a Professor of Ophthalmology at the University of Utrecht, developed the scientific standardization of visual acuity in 1862, and this standard remains the basis for all eye testing in the medical field today.

In Snellen's development of letterforms for his Standardized Eye Chart, it was necessary to contain the shape within a square matrix five times the thickness of the width of the letterform itself. The formula allows for a visual angle of 5 degrees—the proper angle for standard 20/20 vision—on the surface of the retina wall when the letterforms are placed at the correct distance. If the angle decreases or increases by moving the object or chart in space, the object is no longer presented at the proper distance for standard 20/20 vision, and the image on the retina wall either becomes too small to be seen or it becomes larger and therefore easier to see. The visual acuity test, Snellen's Standardized Eye Chart "was based upon this [above statement] theoretical resolving power of the eye as deduced from the density of the receptor cell matrix. To separate two visual stimuli, at least one unstimulated receptor cell must lie between two stimulated cells and on this basis the resolving power of the eye should be about one minute of arc." (Rose, F. Clifford (ed.). *The Eye in General Medicine*, London: Chapman and Hall, 1983.)

The density of the photoreceptor-cell matrix in the human eye governs the visual-acuity test. Two visually stimulated cells within the matrix must be separated by one unstimulated

Figure 10

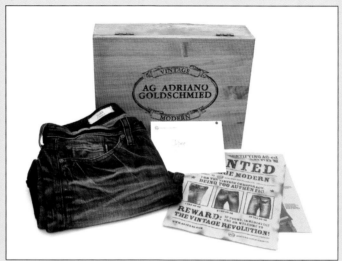

Figure 11

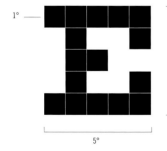

1°

5°

5°

Diagram 11
Dr. Snellen's letterforms are composed of a square matrix in which the width and height of the letterform is five times the thickness of the stroke and counterform. The stroke of the letterform is 1° and the entire letterform is 5° of visual angle on the retinal wall at a predefined distance. In this way, Dr. Snellen's letterforms are used to establish standardized eyesight.

Figure 13

Figure 14

The time needed to recognize an individual letterform is less than a fraction of a second if it is clear and sharp. If we have 20/20 vision, recognition of the first letterform within the line of type occurs almost instantaneously. The process of recognition occurs letter by letter, in rapid succession, until we reach the point at which legibility is hard to define and readability begins to take over. (Diagrams 11 and 13, on pages 173 and 175, depict Snellen's monoweight typeface as viewed from different distances.)

Snellen created his letterforms based on mathematics so that the entire form operates at the same visual angle. The font is a perfect monoweight typeface, with its counter and positive shapes equal in size. This allows for the rate of convergence at a distance to be equal as well. For example, if we view Snellen's typeface at distances further than that used for testing 20/20 vision, at each distance, the counter and positive shapes move closer to one another until the form converges on itself. The typeface is designed so that when viewed at any distance, the size of the counterforms is the same as the width of the lines composing the letterforms.

In condensed typefaces, convergence usually occurs with the countershapes of the letterforms whereas, with other types of fonts, it occurs at the thinnest part of the line composing the letterform, which converges to the color of the background. Most type designers vary both the thickness of the lines composing the letterforms and the sizes of the countershapes. Thus, convergence occurs in different areas at different rates with most typefaces, and so typefaces have more than one visual angle when

cell to create an electrical impulse that represents an object. The receptor-cell matrix, or simple matrix, is one of three matrices found within the eye (the others being the complex and hypercomplex matrices). The simple matrix works by a system similar to a string of binary numbers: on-off-on, or stimulated-unstimulated-stimulated. At a minimum, a wavelength needs to cross over three cells of the simple matrix in the specific order of stimulated-unstimulated-stimulated in order to register as an object seen by the mind's eye.

Figure 13
Studio: AG Adriano Goldschmied
Photographer: Nina Ng

The typography of AG Adriano Goldschmied is diversified on the back pocket of each pair of jeans, but consistent on AG's signature label called a thermopatch. Made of poplin, the thermopatch is dyed and screenprinted with the name of each AG style. After die cutting, the thermopatch is adhered to the inner waistband through a heat-transfer process that assures the patch will not come off when laundered and always informs the consumer of the fit they are wearing.

Figure 14
Studio: AG Adriano Goldschmied
Photographer: Nina Ng

All trim within the AG Adriano Goldschmied collection resonates with the overall packaging line. Even type that is distressed, all capitals, or embossed on metal grommets/buttons is readable as AG, because of the overriding typographic consistency, tracking, and unified color.

Diagram 12
AG's typographic composition assures legibility in varying materials, such as this mechanical for copper buttons.

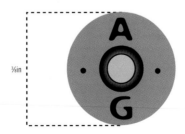

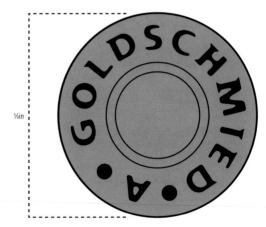

presented at a distance. For most typefaces, the possibilities for convergence are numerous. Like human fingerprints, each font is unique, having certain characteristics that make up its structure. Some letterforms are inherently more visible than others if they are of equal size. The following factors affect legibility:

· Kerning letters tighter than the breadth of the line composing the typeface will result in a decrease in the distance at which the letterforms can be deciphered. In this case, the word or words become one long ligature, decreasing legibility and readability (see Diagram 14 on page 176).

· The legibility of a letterform is determined by its thinnest line. In the case of a condensed letterform, legibility is determined by the character's counterform if the counterform is thinner than the breadth of the stroke composing the letter (see Diagram 15 on page 176).

· The maximum legibility of type in relationship to distance will occur when letterforms are of a consistent width. A medium-to-bold extended letterform should be used so that the line thickness will be one-fifth the size of the letter squared, allowing for ample counterspace. This is mathematically correct if all typefaces are of the same letter height (see Diagram 17 on page 178).

Figure 15

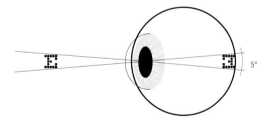

5°

Diagram 13
If the letterform is increased or the viewing distance decreased, more than 5° of the retina wall will be covered and the legibility will increase. Likewise, if the letterform is decreased or the distance of the letterform is increased, less than 5° of the retina wall will be covered and the legibility will decrease. If the observer does not have 20/20 vision, the visual angle will increase or decrease as though the scale and distance of the letterform has been increased or decreased.

Figure 15
Studio: Elf Design, Inc.
Designer: Erin Ferree

With color signifying the variety of scents available, the ascenders and descenders of this rounded sans serif type visual cue a water droplet and help to increase recognition of individual letterforms.

Figure 16

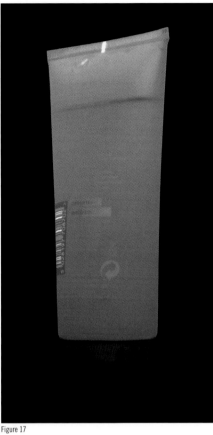

Figure 17

Contrast

Myths about color contrast have persisted in the arts and in subtractive color theory for some time. These myths concern the perceived color differential between, for example, a color presented to the viewer from 100 percent of color to 0 percent of color in 10-degree increments, or two different colors, side-by-side, presented for viewing. In either case, color contrast does not exist, only the color value rating—or, to be more accurate, the Y tristimulus values and their corresponding differential numbers. Color contrast is determined by form/silhouette, motion, depth, and color. In order to obtain color legibility, these factors must be clearly defined. Diagram 16 illustrates how an individual would see the world if color perception were the only factor that he or she had to determine color contrast. Without form/silhouette, motion, and/or depth, objects are unrecognizable and there tends to be a multitude of colors varying in hue, value, chroma, and shade, with no clear distinction of form. Simply put, any discussion of color contrast must include all the factors that determine it.

Figure 16
Studio: Positiu Design Consultants
Art Director/Designer: Oriol Llahona

In this package the cap height of some letters is equal to the X-height of others within the same word. Because of the unified thicks and thins throughout the word, visual clarity is retained.

Figure 17
Studio: DESIGNLAB
Designer: Cyrille Charbonnier

When sitting on the shelf, color calls the viewer's attention to this tone-on-tone package as the type is barely readable. However, when held, the color contrast of the matte bottle to the type creates a unique sheen thereby increasing legibility appropriate to the viewing distance.

optimal

tight kerning

Stroke width

Diagram 14
For optimal legibility, the kerning of a word should not be less than the stroke width of the letterform. Tight kerning will decrease the legibility of a word viewed at a distance.

Diagram 15
Not all letterforms are equally legible. The legibility of a letterform is hindered by different factors for each face. For example, the counterform in this condensed typeface will appear to converge to black at a distance, while the thins of this Old Style typeface will converge to white at a distance. In addition, different letterforms at the same point size have significantly different proportions. For instance, in this case, both "gs" are set in 163 points.

Form/Silhouette

Humans have the physical and mental ability to use and determine the difference between readability and legibility. Readability is both universally and culturally defined—most of this interpretive function takes place in the mind. As a viewer matures, recognition quickens, even though the object is not seen in its totality. This is because of the bank of imagery a mature viewer has built up. Legibility, on the other hand, deals with visual clarity, with how well the visual pathway detects, in this case, the form/silhouette of the object. This function of human perception is attributed to the simple matrix field located at the end of the visual pathway. It is responsible for detecting properly oriented moving slits, edges, and dark bars. The simple matrix field receives binocular input.

When dealing with type-and-color combinations, clarity of form/silhouette is just as important as any of the other three factors determining color contrast. Three published rules of thumb apply to viewing type-and-color combinations at a distance—although two of these are grossly inaccurate.

The first—that every 1in (2.54cm) of letter-form height equates to 42ft (12.8m) of viewing distance—is inaccurate for several reasons, particularly the assumption that form/silhouette is the only consideration that determines type-and-color legibility at a distance. It does not take into account the factors that determine the source, the object, and the viewer, nor does it take into account motion, depth, and color. Without having a full understanding of these

factors and how they fit a particular scenario, accurate type-and-color prediction for viewing at a distance is impossible.

United States federal law, through the *Americans with Disabilities Act of 1990* and subsequent amendments, mandates the second rule: "Letters and numbers on signs shall have a width-to-height ratio between 3:5 and 1:1 and a stroke width-to-height ratio between 1:5 and 1:10." However, just because the rule is law does not mean it is effective, as it is based on several unsound assumptions regarding color contrast and form/silhouette. The most damaging of these is the width-to-height ratio and the stroke width-to-height ratio. When we apply these ratios to a site, some configurations will work better than others, and illegible type-and-color configurations will emerge. In the case of the width-to-height ratio, the document fails to specify from what part of the typographic anatomy the measurement should be taken (arm, stem, terminal, stroke, shoulder, tail, ascender, leg, eye, spine, hairline, crossbar, fillet, apex, bowl, ear, link, descender, loop, serif, counter, spur, etc.). The importance of specifying a designated location or methodology within the font anatomy is twofold: first, the location assures that the visual angle of 20/70 vision (visually impaired) is guaranteed, thereby producing the proper density within the photo-receptor-cell matrix; second, density is produced through both size and mass. In order to achieve 20/70 vision, the visual angle must be displayed at the proper size on the retina wall, thereby creating enough density for the object to be seen at the specified eyesight.

Figure 18

Diagram 16
Under normal conditions the black type can be easily determined due to the distinguishable color contrast including form/silhouette. However, if color perception or the Y tristimulus value were the only method of determining color contrast, the type would appear to be a hazy field of color.

Figure 18
Designer: Theo Williams

The Lexon business-card holder subtly reveals typography through the transparent plastic skin of the package, forcing the viewer to push the aluminum, thumbprint-sized catch to read more.

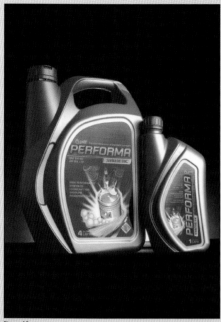

Figure 19

Figure 20

Figure 21

A width-to-height ratio of between 3:5 and 1:1 is too broad in some respects and too narrow in others. The premise of the width-to-height ratio and the stroke width-to-height ratio is flawed. Snellen's Standardized Eye Chart is the basis for all visual form sense testing worldwide. In this, the width of the lines comprising the letterform "E" is five-times squared (1:1). This produces the correct visual angle when presented at the proper distance for any standardized eyesight including the visually impaired or legally blind (20/200). Use of the 3:5 ratio or anything in between 3:5 and 1:1 will produce an inferior angle, thus reducing the size and density of the image when displayed on the retina wall and interpreted by the photoreceptor-cell matrix. In other words, when letterforms from different fonts that meet the current standard are presented at 3in (7.62cm) letter height, they will all have different visual distances at which someone possessing 20/20 or 20/70 vision can see them—some will vary little with distance, others drastically.

The stroke width-to-height ratio of between 1:5 and 1:1 allows for condensed letterforms to be used for the purpose of signs and signage systems. Because of the way in which the Americans with Disabilities Act is written, some condensed fonts that meet the requirements will converge before the specified distance. In other words, the anatomy of these fonts and their countershapes will collide before the proper distance is achieved, thereby making legibility and readability impossible. If condensed letterforms are to be used, the measurement should not be taken from the stroke width, but from the smallest counterform within the font, the part of the typographic anatomy that is weakest for viewing

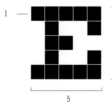

Helvetica Bold

Diagram 17
This example shows the optimal legibility in Dr. Snellen's "E" and its prescribed relationship to the Americans with Disabilities Act. Dr. Snellen's "E" falls within this law, while the Helvetica Bold "L" narrowly misses the constraints of the mandate. In addition, as we have seen previously, the counterform has significant impact on the legibility of a letterform. The Americans with Disabilities Act does not take into account the width of the counterform, as exemplified in the "M."

at a distance. In the majority of condensed letterforms the counterforms are narrower than the stroke. The 1:5 ratio is in keeping with Snellen's visual form sense testing (which includes the Standardized Eye Chart), but the 1:1 ratio creates an inferior angle for the object to be displayed on the retina wall. This may not seem like much to do with package design, but it has everything to do with viewing typography at a distance and creating impact on the shelf.

The third published guideline for visual acuity can be found in Snellen's research. For this guideline, specific typographic anatomy within each font specified was measured under 7-degree magnification in order to ensure that the visual angle for all standardized eyesight, including 20/200 vision, would be met. In doing so, the proper density within the photoreceptor-cell matrix is assured. Other mathematical equations were used in order to make the proper translation of Snellen's visual form sense testing to incorporate the form/silhouette component of the complex receptor field matrix and the other factors that define color contrast (motion, depth, and color).

Figure 22

Figure 23

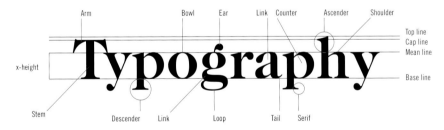

Figure 24

Figure 22
Studio: Domot Antistudio

The variety of typefaces and sizes conform to a wide array of viewing distances, attracting the viewer and forcing one to handle the package in order to read the information.

Figure 24
Studio: milkxhake
Art Director/Designer: milkxhake

The 135-film (35mm) canister provides an interesting packaging-redesign problem for an alternative pop-culture magazine from Hong Kong. As a slogan, "Shoot better" is reinforced in the cross hairs of each typographic form.

Figure 23
Studio: Exhibit A: Design Group
Art Director: Cory Ripley
Designers: Cory Ripley, Robert Spofforth

Capsoles™ corporate colors were selected as the best combination to visually portray the term "sportmedical" and are easy to replicate with different methods of print production. The unique typeface and substitution of the legs in the "A" reiterate this message.

Diagram 18
The Americans with Disabilities Act mandates the proportionality of the letterforms, but fails to specify from what part of the letterform the measurements should be taken. As can be seen from this diagram, the anatomy of a letterform is complex and varied.

Figure 25

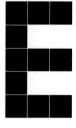
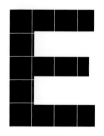
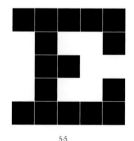

Figure 26

Distance and Motion

All three of the photoreceptor fields—simple, complex, and hypercomplex—respond to moving stimuli. When dealing with type-and-color combinations in static form, as with package design, simple and hypercomplex photoreceptor fields do not play an important role in color legibility; however, when a person is walking, they play a crucial role. Motion is one of the most effective forms of visual communication. The human eye naturally gravitates toward anything that is moving, particularly objects moving in a distinct orientation and pattern. Objects that move in a seemingly random order do not hold the viewer's attention because of the way in which the receptor fields physically operate. These photoreceptor-cell matrices are a product of evolution, and the development of a receptor field that detects random movement was not required in our ancestors' daily lives.

The process of deciphering messages takes time, and, when time limits are placed on viewing an object, details evaporate. The visual acuteness of the viewer, the placement of the object, and the pattern it forms in motion or static representation all have a direct bearing on color legibility. (This statement only hints at the complexity encountered when motion enters the equation.)

Figure 25
Designer: Aldo Bastos Filho

A unified packaging concept from delivery to storage and display will often give the viewer additional reaction time prior to the actual consumption of the product, such as in this cart.

Figure 26
Studio: Reisigl Associates
Creative Director: James K. Reisigl
Art Director/Designer: Marianne Young

Reisigl Associates developed the ingenious concept of putting color on the inside of a back label on a frosted bottle. This simultaneously diffuses and magnifies the text "Cruzan flavored rums" through the depth of the faceted glass and the curve of the bottle. This makes the color appear to glow, and beckons the consumer from multiple viewing distances.

3:5

3.75:5.2
Helvetica Bold

5:5
Snellen

Diagram 19
In order for the Helvetica Bold "E" to meet the strict definition of the *Americans with Disabilities Act*, it would have to appear more uniform—like the "E" to the left.

Diagram 20
As driving speed increases, foreground details begin to fade and the clear silhouettes of letterforms diminish. Because of this, elaborate detail in highway signage is meaningless.

Figure 27

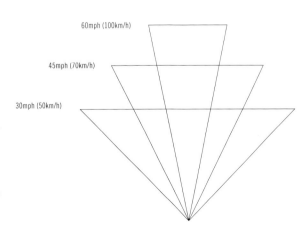

60mph (100km/h)

45mph (70km/h)

30mph (50km/h)

Diagram 21
The above "Ms" are set in 28pt and show the variety of stroke width-to-height ratios that occur in diverse typefaces.

Diagram 22
Left: As the speed of the viewer increases, the peripheral vision decreases and the need for additional distance and thereby time to view the object increases. For example, a person moving at 60mph (100km/h) will need signage to be legible at a greater distance than a person moving at 30mph (50km/h). In addition, the peripheral vision of a person moving at 60mph (100km/h) will be approximately half that of a person moving at 30mph (50km/h).

Figure 27
Studio: estudiocrop
Art Director/Designer: Dado Queiroz
Photographer: Fabiano Schroden

This shopping bag and gift box is an excellent way of advertising the brand because each will be seen at varying degrees of distance for diverse reaction times. For example, the shopping bag will reach multiple viewers—drivers, passengers, and pedestrians—as the shopper walks down an ordinary street.

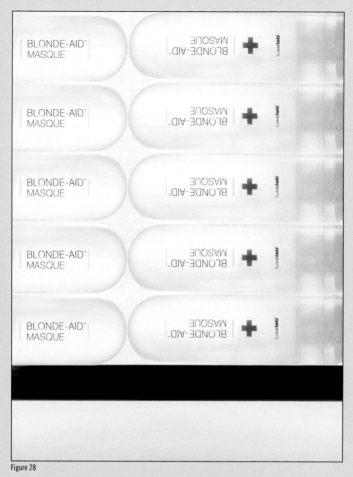

Figure 28

Depth

The perception of depth is created by input from both eyes—their corresponding rods and cones (including ganglion cells); the optic pathway (including the right and left lateral geniculate bodies); the simple, complex, and hypercomplex fields located in the primary visual cortex and many other parts of the brain. Without binocular input from both hemispheres of the visual pathway, depth perception would be very limited—for example, we could still see a package design in the distance, but we could not tell how far away it was. This phenomenon increases as the visual-acuity rating of the viewer deteriorates. Depth perception gives us the ability to judge time and space as we move through our environment. Without it, depth and varying distances become difficult to navigate and judge.

Figure 28
Studio: Dustin Edward Arnold
Art Director/Designer:
Dustin E. Arnold

Keeping in line both with the salon's aesthetic and strict modernist tastes, the packaging and ensemble shelf display for Luxelab Blonde-Aid Masque is quickly identifiable and readable as a salon-grade luxury product.

Diagram 23
With our peripheral vision, we can see about 12–15 letterforms at each fixation point while standing still. Our peripheral vision decreases as speed increases. In addition, as the eye scans forward, words to the right of the fixation point furnish meaningful cues for perceptoin and further fixations, and words to the left fade from view. This, in combination with the fact that, on average, a motorist can perceive only 7–10 items, must be considered when designing for motion.

Diagram 24
The mind's eye detects oriented moving slits, edges, and dark bars. Visual perception and legibility deals with visual clarity, and how well the visual pathway detects this form/silhouette.

[text right] of the fixation point furnish meaningful clues for perception and further fixations.

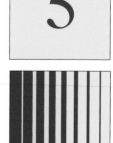

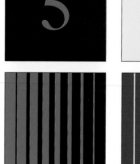

Figure 29

Figure 30

Figure 31

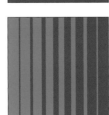

Diagram 25
The natural environment slits can consist of the whole gamma of color. Pure red type on a split complementary or near split complementary will strobe, due not only to simultaneous contrast, but also to the eye's inability to keep pace with slits and edges.

Figure 29
Studio: The Grafiosi
Art Director/Designer: Pushkar Thakur

Regardless of distance, the impact of a package begins the moment it is seen. These steel hangtags and size dividers impart quality and sophistication as the consumer approaches and the typography slowly comes into the correct viewing distance.

Figure 30
Studio: The Grafiosi
Art Director/Designer: Pushkar Thakur

The blind emboss on these tags invites the viewer to absorb in a tactile way the information, slowing down the process and drawing the consumer closer for a viewing distance appropriate to a condensed typeface.

Figure 31
Studio: Bohoy Design
Designer: Johanna Bohoy

As a promotional item given to Triumvirate Environmental clients on Earth Day, even chocolate packaged in earth-friendly, recycled materials can convey luxury while maintaining commitment to the statement "The Earth is our nest."

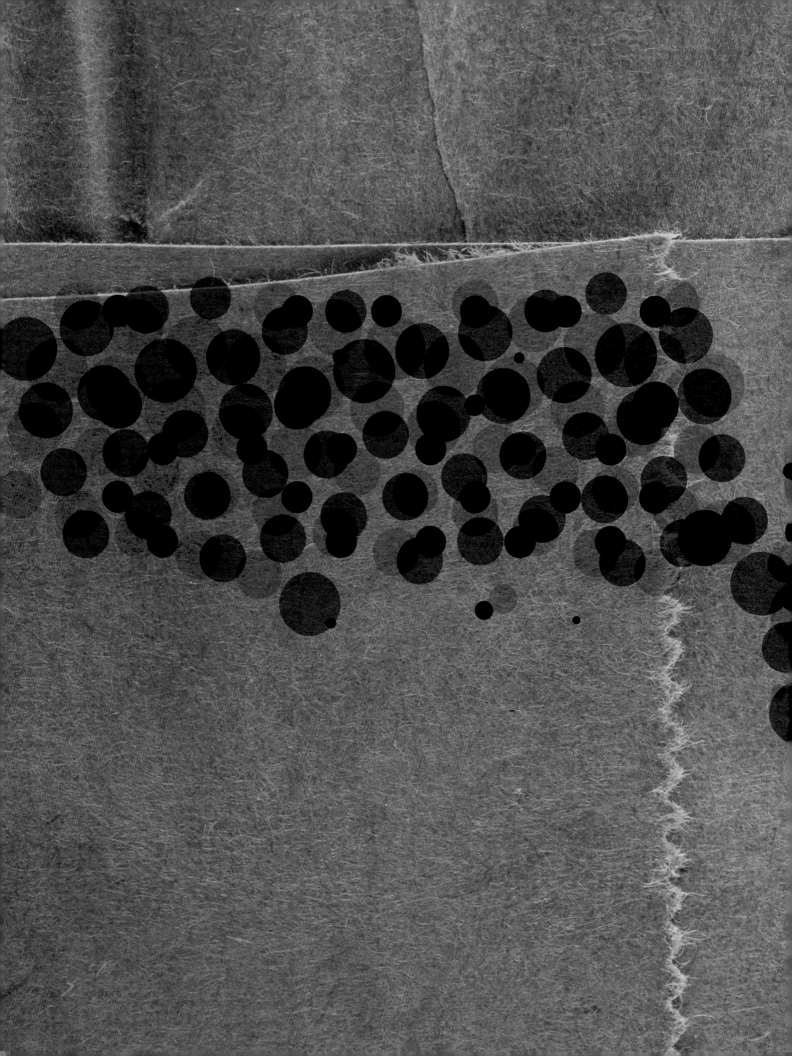

Color Association

Physical, psychological, and/or learned behavioral attributes can be assigned to all colors. Depending upon the culture in which an individual is raised, certain colors will convey certain meanings. Throughout history humans have assigned meaning to color, both consciously and unconsciously, in order to understand and define the environment around them. Modern medical science has been actively pursuing the understanding of physical, psychological, and/or learned behavioral effects associated with color for more than a century, and anthropologists and historians have also been studying the effects of color on human endeavors.

Within the design field, the physical and psychological effects of color have not been widely taught. More often than not, designers are taught to tell people how they should feel about art, including color, regardless of any scientific basis. To ignore this wealth of color information is to overlook the most powerful communicative tool designers have.

(Bearing in mind the often culture-specific nature of these responses, we have limited our discussion here to Western cultures.)

Figure 1

Figure 2

Micro Color Responses

Color affects humans physically because of its psychological associations. These effects can be classified according to two general categories: warm and cool. Three basic responses to color are associated with human behavior—motor, glandular, and conscious—and each of these responses holds clues to human reactions. Muscular contraction or relaxation as a response to color is referred to as a motor response. With a glandular response, particular glands in the body are activated, which prompts a chemical secretion that brings about a specific change in the body. With a conscious response, the activation is in the brain, and the viewer is immediately aware of the response. Warm colors (red, red-orange, orange, orange-yellow, and white) possess a longer wavelength than cool colors, and in general elicit a response of warmth and hardness; cool colors (blue, blue-green, and green), on the other hand, tend to elicit a response of cold and scattered, or diffuse, space. Both warm and cool evoke a conscious response. (There is evidence to support the idea that these responses to warm and cool colors may be a learned cultural response.)

Motor and Glandular Responses

An individual placed in a high-chroma red room will experience, for a short period, accelerated heart rate and increases in blood pressure, pulse rate, respiration rate, and muscle-reaction rate. This is a motor response. Low-chroma greens and blues cause the opposite effect, slowing down muscle-reaction time, calming nerves, and generally

Figure 1
Studio: SOLUTIONS Branding & Design Companies
Creative Director: Martin Weber
Designer: Kathrin Blank

Warm yellow and red emote baking and enrich this relaunch of Aurora flours.

Figure 2
Studio: FiF DESIGN House Team

Complemented by bright colors, the devilish attitude of the Zab icon and cheeky smile of the Pizza icon promote this unconventional instant food in the Thai market.

relaxing the body. However, this response can be counteracted if the chroma level of secondary and primary greens and blues is intensified. Both of these color categories, warm and cool, also trigger galvanic skin responses. The skin's response, its resistance to color, indicates the immediate emotional reaction of an individual to color. The higher the chroma rating in both categories, the greater the motor response induced.

Psychological Responses

The psychological effects of any color can be altered by changing its chroma, tinting, purity, saturation, shading, and texture rating. For example, the intensity, or chroma, of a color is significant in triggering arousal or excitement irrespective of hue. The perception and interpretation of color is very complex and can be altered by properties not normally associated with color—silhouette/form, depth, and motion of an object, for example. The psychological interpretation of color is not a precise language, but in general, along with all other factors associated with visual communication, color can be used to shape visual messages.

There is some evidence to support the theory that for children in Grades 1 through 6 (four to ten years of age) blues and reds are highly desirable colors. In general, red is preferred over blue in Grades 1 through 3, but blue is preferred over red in Grades 3 through 6. Color preference is also gender related. Boys prefer (in order of preference) blue, red, green, violet, orange, and yellow; girls prefer blue, green, orange, violet, red, yellow, and white. High-chroma primary and secondary colors are

Figure 3

Figure 3
Studio: RED8 Comm
Art Director/Designer: M. Piotrowski

The hue and intensity of this packaging emphasize the nature of the KFC sandwich.

preferred by all schoolchildren over muddy and neutral-gray colors. Saturated reds and blues are preferred over shades and tints of reds and blues. When children enter their teens, warm colors are still preferred over cool, but as they grow, their color preference develops with them. Children less than a year old have no color preference, supporting the statement that the responses to colors are cultural, and that we often have a physical response opposite to what is culturally learned—meaning one response takes place in the conscious mind and the other, for example, can be motor or glandular responses that do not register consciously, but operate on a more primeval level. Adult men prefer blue, violet, and green, whereas adult

women prefer red, orange, and yellow. For both men and women, Color Value Differential (CVD) is paramount in the preference of color combination—the more contrast, the more pleasing the combination. However, compositional balance also plays an important role in influencing a pleasing CVD. The greater the CVD, the greater the kinetic energy within the composition.

Color, in all its forms, can also influence the perception of taste. Color taste preferences and color associations are influential in the success or failure of a product, an important consideration in food packaging. In general, yellow and yellow-green have a low appetite rating, whereas orange, red, white, and pink foods are perceived as being sweeter. In a study conducted with wines, white and pink labels were perceived to be sweeter than wines colored yellow, brownish, or purple, regardless of actual taste. Foods not conforming to preconceived ideas tend to be rejected. For example, any natural food dyed an unnatural color will be rejected by most consumers. High-chroma white or bleached white foods and food packaging are seldom chosen. They tend to be perceived as unhealthy. Foods and food packaging in the blue-green family need to be handled with care, as blue-green is typically associated with mold and mildew. Nature does not create many edible foods that are colored a high-chroma blue, light blue (sky-blue or cyan), or high-chroma blue-green, and therefore most consumers find blue food unnatural because it elicits a strong negative response correlating to an appetite suppressant. There may be

Figure 4

Figure 4
Studio: XO Create!

A strong color palette and bold graphics grab the attention of young consumers for Long John Silvers' first ever kids' meal line of packaging. Imaginative use of illustrations with bold black outlines and bright primary hues differentiate the packaging from other chains' overly saturated and often chaotic designs.

Figure 5
Studio: XO Create!

This muted, warm family of colors translates well on various substrates and media for The Grind's coffee- and cold-beverage packaging, point-of-sale, environmental, and signage design. By choosing a more muted color scheme, reproduction across a range of coated and uncoated substrates and printing methods—including silkscreening, digital, and offset printing—was ensured.

Figure 5

a self-preservation correlation associated with blue and blackish-purple foods—many poisonous fruits and berries have these hues.

Red and orange fruit juices are perceived to be sweeter than juices of other colors. If food coloring is added to juices to intensify the chroma, the juices are perceived as sweeter, regardless of actual taste. With baked goods (breads, cereals, and nuts), a medium golden-brown is expected by consumers, and many of these products have golden-brown labels and packages as well.

Not everyone responds to color in the same way. There is evidence to suggest that, depending upon a person's innate personality, a color may produce an effect opposite to the typical stimulus response. A person who is more naturally introverted may not feel comfortable in a high-chroma environment, and this may induce a reaction opposite to what normally happens. The same can be said for someone who is excitable. Placing such an individual in a room decorated with low-chroma hues will serve only to make them uncomfortable. For interior and environmental graphic designers, understanding the personality traits of the individual is critical for success. That is, both the culture and the individual within the culture must be taken into consideration. Having the client answer a series of questions designed to profile his or her personality traits will help you decide on an appropriate solution.

It is said that color influences the perception of noise, temperature, weight, time, and volume. Color can change not only the mood of a person within a given environment, but also their perception of space. For example, cool and dark colors, regardless of hue, can make a room seem smaller; warm and light colors produce the opposite effect. Color may also influence the perception of time. A 1975 study conducted by Dr. Goldstein indicated that individuals placed under red light tended to overestimate how much time had elapsed, whereas those placed under green or blue light underestimated it. The effect of light/color on humans is a very complex and powerful one. Designers may tailor color to evoke a more meaningful response. However, when this is not possible (for example, with design for the masses), understanding the cultural norms of the intended audience is paramount in creating an effective design solution. Regardless of whether a color has psychological associations for the audience, or whether the response is simply learned, a wealth of responsive color information can govern informational color palettes.

Figure 6

Figure 6
Studio: Fuelhaus
Art Director: Ty Webb
Designer: Etel Garaguay

The richness of the cookie is communicated through the warm reds, while silver-gray adds a touch of elegance and sophistication.

Figure 7

Macro Color Associations

Color must be placed in context in order to understand the implications associated with its meaning. This hue association, along with the other factors that influence a color's associative interpretation—form/silhouette, motion, and depth—create a complete mental picture, one that can be amplified, reduced, associated with, or learned. In very general terms, each of the above factors can be broken apart and used separately to convey messages and prompt emotions, associative responses, and/or learned behavior. This section, through charts, will explain the positive associative responses to color, the negative associative responses to color, the appetite rating of different colors, and their associative taste.

Figure 7
Studio: Light Publicity Co., Ltd.
Creative Director: Kimiko Ida

Chocolife is marketed at seniors, using a wide, easy-open package, large, centered type, and recyclable paper. In this series, color imparts a sense of taste—rich milk chocolate.

	High-chroma red family	Dark-red family (burgundy, brick-red)
Positive associative responses	Surging, brilliant, intense, energizing, sexy, dramatic, stimulating, fervid, active, cheer, joy, fun, aggressive, hope, powerful, hotness, excitability, solid, aggression, provocative, strength, virility, masculinity, dynamism, imposing, dignity, benevolence, charm, warm, overflowing, ardent, power, not dissipating, irresistible, extrovert, saints, patriots, compassion, counteraction, comedy, vigor, severe, traditional, fire, opaque, dry, hot, heat, blood, Christmas, Fourth of July, St. Valentine's Day, Mother's Day, flag, passionate, excitement, happiness, love, school, dignity, charm, graciousness	Rich, elegant, refined, taste, expensive, mature, earthy, strong, warm, country, serious, important, passive, grown, ripe, developed, experience, sincere, earnest, selective, exquisite, wealthy, worldly, significant
Negative associative responses	Brutal, war, restless, tension, sinners, communists, anarchists, hate, melancholia, anger, falling profits, red herring, fire, intense, opaque, dry, heat, blood, danger, Christmas, Fourth of July, St. Valentine's Day, Mother's Day, flag, rage, fierceness, rapacity, pain, hunger, revolt, aggression	Serious, problematic, passive, doubtful, ambiguous, uncertain, submissive, inactive, grave
Appetite rating for package design	Excellent	Poor
Associative taste	Very sweet	No associative taste

Figure 8

Figure 9

	Earth-tone red family
Positive associative responses	Warmhearted, rural, rustic, earthy, warm, wholesome, country, welcome, good, healthy, fit, sound
Negative associative responses	Earthy, country, rural, rustic
Appetite rating for package design	Poor
Associative taste	No associative taste

Figure 8
Studio: Light Publicity Co., Ltd.
Creative Director: Kimiko Ida

The color of chocolate is superseded by the need to communicate flavoring through color and image, in this case strawberry. Although the color of the chocolate changes, the texture of the package remains consistent.

Figure 9
Studio: Light Publicity Co., Ltd.
Creative Director: Kimiko Ida

Brown sugar is infused into this chocolate.

Mid-range pink-red family	High-chroma pink family	Pastel-pink family
Restrained, toned down, soft, subdued, quiet, sentimental, sober, tame, domestic	Stimulates, aggressive, genial, exciting, happy, high, fun, excitement, attention-getting, promising, color of love, energetic, youthful, spirited, fun, trendy, wild, bright, hot, high-energy, sensual, cheer, joy	Soft, sweet, tender, cute, comfortable, snug, rarefied, delicate, female babies, delicate, cozy, subtle, animated, energetic, joyful, beautiful, expressive, emotional, shy, romantic, feminine, gentle, affectionate, intimate, active, guileful
Subdued, quiet, domestic, toned down, tame, soft	Girlish, lusty, infant, young, callow, immature	Weak, fragile, wavering, unsure, stereotyped color response for female baby, delicate, feeble, frail
Good	Excellent	Excellent
Sweet	Very sweet	Sweet

Figure 10

Figure 11

High-chroma orange family

Positive associative responses

Producing, healing, tasty, growing, fire, warm, cleanliness, cheerfulness, masculine, fearlessness, curiosity, antithesis, thought, whimsical, childlike, happy, vital, sunset, harvest, autumn, hot, juicy, tangy, energizing, gregarious, friendly, loud, radiant, communication, wholehearted, receptive, intimate, comedy, pride, ambitious, joy, happy, dramatic, cheerful, lively, exciting, bright, luminous, metallic, Halloween, Thanksgiving, jovial, energetic, hilarity, exuberance, satiety, cheer, joy, fun, stimulates, aggressive, happiness, school, youth, strength, impetuosity

Negative associative responses

Danger, hot, loud, fire, forceful, pain, restlessness, antithesis, gloom

Appetite rating for package design

Excellent

Associative taste

Very sweet

Figure 10
Studio: Light Publicity Co., Ltd.
Creative Director: Kimiko Ida

The rich taste of citrus is suggested not only by the orange color, but also through the icon.

Figure 11
Studio: Light Publicity Co., Ltd.
Creative Director: Kimiko Ida

The wide array of colors allows the consumer to ponder the selection. For example, the background hue for milk chocolate (Figure 7) differs from this white chocolate only in tint. While the icon remains consistent, the product color is displayed in a contrasting white.

Mid-range orange family	Dark-orange family	High-chroma yellow-orange family
Gentle, entice, good spirits, glad, nurturing, soft, fuzzy, delicious, fruity, sweet, inviting, mellow, ripened, livable, cheerful	Exhilarating, inspiring, stirring, stimulating, moving, provoking, most exciting, passive	Enterprise, drive, target, goal, luxuriance, cheer, joy, fun, excitement, stimulates, aggressive, powerful, energy, splendid, warmth, delight, glow, pleasant, agreeable, cheerful, energetic, healthy
Unclear, obscure, undetermined	Passive, submissive, idle, quiet, inactive, resigned, yielding	Pride, pushy, target
Good to excellent	Poor	Excellent
Sweet	No associative taste	Very sweet

Pastel-yellow family	
Positive associative responses	Pleasant, sunshine, glad, compassionate, tender, kindhearted, cheerful, happy, soft, sunny, warm, sweet, extrovert, good smell
Negative associative responses	Bland, mild, subdued, foolish, simple, silly, softhearted, cowered
Appetite rating for package design	Poor to good
Associative taste	Sweet

Golden-yellow/beige family	Dark-yellow family	High-chroma yellow family
Dignified, pleasant, autumn, flowers, harvest, rich, sun, exalted idea, splendid, warm, wheat, comforting, sunbaked, buttery, classic, sandy, earthy, natural, soft, new idea	Flavorsome, long, active, appetizing, thirst	Anticipation, agreeable, pleasant, noble, welcome, vigorous, youthful energy, speed, movement, enlighten, sunshine, cheerful, friendly, hot, luminous, energy, magnanimity, intuition, intellect, loudest, most luminous, brightest, young, vivacious, extrovert, comedy, celestial, favorable, biological, safety, warmth, joy, spontaneity, active, projective, aspiring, investigatory, original, expectant, varied, exhilaration, spring, summer, incandescent, radiant, sunny, inspiring, vital, high-spirited, life, health, cheer, fun, excitement, stimulates, aggressive, honesty, happiness, strength, brilliant, admixture, picture, great density of light, substantial, real, satisfying, intrigue
Bland, smooth, mild, flat	Shame, disgust, unease, palatable, sicken, tension	Loudest, lacks weight and substance, scoundrel, coward, caution, yellow journalism, sickness, dense, deceit, treachery, yellow dog, yellow streak, incandescent, envy, jealousy
Excellent (for baked goods); good to excellent (for products other than baked goods)	Good	Good
No associative taste	Semisweet	Very sweet

Figure 12

	High-chroma yellow-green family
Positive associative responses	Lemony, tart, fruity, acidic, sharp, bold, trendy, strength, sunlight, biology
Negative associative responses	Sickly, slimy, most tranquilizing, tacky, acidic, gaudy, tart, disagreeable, shame, disgust, unease, bankrupt
Appetite rating for package design	Excellent (for produce other than meats); poor (for meats)
Associative taste	Very sweet, lemony

Figure 12
Studio: Light Publicity Co., Ltd.
Creative Director: Kimiko Ida

In Western countries, green tea
could be confused for mint
chocolate. In this case, the
typography becomes essential.

High-chroma green-yellow family	Pastel-green family	High-chroma green family
New growth, lemony, tart, fruity, acidic	Empathy, innate, completely, calm, quiet, smoothing, natural, sympathy, compassion	Life, use, motion, ebbing of life, springtime, infancy, wilderness, hope, peace, plenty, mature growth, fresh, grass, Irish, lively, spring, foliage, outdoorsy, sympathy, adaptability, quiet, undemanding, soft, not angular, pacific, not nervous, tranquil, thinking, concentration, meditation, cool, abundance, healthy, hope, fertile, sea, fields, greenbacks, clean, moist, nature, water, clear, St. Patrick's Day, refreshing, peaceful, nascent, calm, security, peace, mountains, lakes
Acidic, bitter, sour	Calm, quiet, sympathy, silence, stillness, inactive, idle	Sympathy, no direction, no expression, middle-of-the-road, soft, not muscular, jealousy, inexperienced worker, envy, greenhorn, disease, terror, ghastliness, guilt, radioactive
Excellent (for produce other than meats); poor (for meats)	Excellent (for produce other than meats, and baked goods); poor to average (for meats and baked goods)	Excellent (for produce other than meats); very poor (for meats)
No associative taste	No associative taste	No associative taste

	Dark-green family
Positive associative responses	Nature, mountains, lakes, natural, mature growth, versatility, traditional, money, trustworthy, refreshing, cool, naturalness, restful, stately, forest, healthiness, quiet, woodsy, ingenuity
Negative associative responses	Restful, quiet
Appetite rating for package design	Good (for produce other than meats); poor (for meats)
Associative taste	No associative taste

Mid-green family	Blue-green family	High-chroma purple family
Warlike, forces, military, camouflaged, safari, classic	Pristine, pure, serious, cleanliness, incorruptible, pensive, tranquillity, lively, mellow, cheerful, clarity, certainty, firm, consistent, great strength, inner coolness, lakes, flattering	Celibacy, rage, deep, nostalgia, memories, power, spirituality, infinity, dignified, sublimation, meditative, mystical, coolness, night, conservative, thought, royalty, nobility, subducing, athletic, important, soft, atmospheric, mist, Easter
Military, camouflaged, drab, warlike, forces, combative, militant	Irritable, disagreeable, peevish	Conservative, melancholia, priggishness, darkness, shadow, mourning, pompous, loneliness, desperation, sadness
Excellent (for produce other than meats); poor (for meats)	Excellent (for produce other than meats); very poor (for meats)	Excellent (for products other than food); poor (for food)
No associative taste	No associative taste	No associative taste

Figure 13

	High-chroma reddish-purple family
Positive associative responses	Sweet taste, subtle, restlessness, prolongs life, feminine elegance, tender longing, romanticism, exciting, sensual, flamboyant, creative, unique, sophisticated
Negative associative responses	Subtle, flamboyant, unquiet, rest
Appetite rating for package design	Excellent (for products other than meats); good to excellent (for food)
Associative taste	No associative taste

Figure 13
Studio: Light Publicity Co., Ltd.
Creative Director: Kimiko Ida

This chocolate has a 75%
coco content.

Mid-range red-purple family	High-chroma bluish-purple family	Pastel-blue family
Charming, elegant, select, refined, subtle, nostalgic, delicate, sweet-scented, floral, sweet taste	Meditative, restlessness, expensive, regal, classic, powerful, tender, longing, elegant, mystical, spiritual, futuristic, fantasy	Pleasure, peace, calm, quiet, hygienic, peaceful, refreshing, clean, cool, water, heavenly, constant, faithful, true, good, dependable, happy, tranquil, glory, devoted to noble ideas
Picky, breakable, frail, fragile	Tragedy, restlessness, misadventure, mishap, misfortune	Calm, quiet, peaceful, empty, restful, indifferent, blurry
Good	Excellent (for products other than food); poor (for food)	Excellent (for products other than food); poor (for naturally colored foods); good (for artificially colored foods)
Sweet	No associative taste	No associative taste

Figure 14

	High-chroma blue family
Positive associative responses	Dignity, spaciousness, sobriety, serenity, calm, height, lively, pleasing, rich, levels, vertical, honesty, strength, work, upward, deep, feminine, relaxed, mature, classy, expensive, unique, electric, energetic, vibrant, flags, stirring, happy, dramatic, recalls childhood, inner life, seized by love, not violent, quiet, cold, wet, reposed, blue bloods, once in a blue moon, bolt from the blue, flute, stringed instrument, mercury, clear, cool, transparent, introspective, summer, water, sky, ice, service, subduing, contemplative, sober, security, peace, thought-provoking
Negative associative responses	Mournful, feeling blue, the blues, insane, mental depression, blue Monday, transparent, recessive, distant, melancholy, gloom, fearfulness, furtiveness, sadness, work, solemn, shadows, empty
Appetite rating for package design	Poor to good
Associative taste	No associative taste

Figure 14
Studio: Light Publicity Co., Ltd.
Creative Director: Kimiko Ida

The overall intensity of this hue
helps communicate the high
(60%) coco content.

Dark-blue family	High-chroma bluish-green family	Earth-tone family
Serene, quiet, authoritative, credible, devotion, security, service, nautical, solemnity, gravity, traditional, basic, confident, classic, conservative, strong, dependable, great religious feeling, uniforms, professional	New, further, young, forward, ocean, tropical, jewelry, pristine, cool, fresh, liquid, refreshing, healing, wholesome, pure, recent	Rustics, delicious, deep, rich, warm, folksy, rooted, life, work, wholesome, sheltering, masculine, woodsy, warm, durable, secure, earth, dirt, strength
Authoritative, gloom, conservative, traditional, uniforms, serene, quiet, solemnity, irrationality	Inexperienced, raw, rude, unseasoned	Folksy, woodsy, rustics, dirt, work
Excellent (for products other than meats); poor (for meats)	Excellent (for products other than meats); poor (for meats)	Excellent (for baked goods, coffee, chocolate, and candy); good (for most other products; in some cases will have negative connotations)
No associative taste	No associative taste	No associative taste

Figure 15

White

Positive associative responses	Light, cool, snow, cleanliness, purity, clean, sterling, innocent, silent, inexplicable, normality, life, work, school, emptiness, infinity, refreshing, antiseptic, perfect balance, zeal, bright, glistening, awareness, pleasure, cold, spiritual, Mother's Day, flag, frank, youthful, brightness of spirit
Negative associative responses	Innocent, lightweight, inaccessible, silent, emptiness, fear, work, sadness
Appetite rating for package design	Excellent
Associative taste	No associative taste

Figure 16

Figure 15
Studio: Light Publicity Co., Ltd.
Creative Director: Kimiko Ida

The richness of the chocolate
is symbolized on the front of the
package through image, where
the side of the box has a patterned
motif that signifies the flavor.

Figure 16
Studio: Light Publicity Co., Ltd.
Creative Director: Kimiko Ida

The sweetness of strawberry is
communicated with pink, and the
lushness of the creamy center is
highlighted through the purple tones.

Black	Dark-gray family	Neutral-gray family
Winter, percussion, spatial, powerful, elegant, mysterious, heavy, basic, neutral, night, life, school, cold, classic, strong, expensive, magical, invulnerable, prestigious, sober, without peculiarity, distant, noble, elegant, blindness, piano	Wise, cultured, professional, classic, solid, expensive, sophisticated, enduring, mature	Quality, quiet, classic, inertia, ashes, passion, practical, timeless, old age, cunning, cool, sober, corporate
Dark, heavy, death, despair, void, eternal silence, no future, powerful, mysterious, nightmare, rigid, distant, negative, evil, blackmail, blackball, blacklist, gloom, hatred, malice, anger, fear, black magic, emptiness, mourning, funeral, ominous, deathly, depressing, negation of spirit, blindness	Expensive, costly, complex, complicated, disenchanted, disillusioned, debase	Quiet, ghostly, egoism, depression, nothing, neutral, indifference, autonomous, indecision, lack of energy, tragedy, selfishness, deceit
Excellent	Excellent (for products other than food); poor (for food)	Poor to good
No associative taste	No associative taste	No associative taste

Figure 17

Positive associative responses

Negative associative responses

Appetite rating for package design

Associative taste

Figure 17
Studio: Light Publicity Co., Ltd.
Creative Director: Kimiko Ida

Cho-pan's logo is printed in gold,
catching the consumer's eye through
its shine. The product is elaborate
and sweet—a chocolate cup that
is filled with praline.

Muddy-gray family	Silver family	Gold family
Quality, basic, classic, practical, timeless, natural	Futuristic, cool, expensive, money, valuable, classic	Warm, opulent, expensive, radiant, valuable, prestigious
Pragmatic, sober, utilitarian, old, bottom, primitive, elemental	Costly, expensive	Lavish, costly, expensive
Poor	Excellent	Excellent
No associative taste	No associative taste	No associative taste

Glossary

Absorbed light: Light that is absorbed by an object; the opposite of transmitted light. The lightwaves absorbed by an object are transformed into heat. The darker the color, the more waves are absorbed and thus the more heat it produces.

Achromatic: Hues made from black, gray, and white.

Additive color theory/mixing: Combining lightwaves to create colors.

Afterimage: Illusions occurring when retinal cones and neurons become fatigued or overstimulated. Photoreceptor cells are responsible for human perception of color. A photoreceptor cell can become fatigued if it fixates on a particular color, and this will cause a false electrical impulse by the photoreceptor cell, thus creating the afterimage.

Analogous colors: A color grouping in which the colors are to the near left and right of each other. An analogous color scheme is harmonious because all colors within the palette have a certain percentage of each other built into them.

Aqueous coating: One of four basic types of coatings applied to packaging including varnish, UV coating, and laminates. Aqueous coating is, as the name implies, a resin- and water-based covering.

Aseptic packaging: A method of extending shelf life through the elimination or control of unwanted organisms.

Blind emboss: An emboss that is not registered to a printed image.

Bronzing: An effect that develops when some inks are exposed to light and air that creates a false reading in the calculation of color. Bronzing causes a glare effect in 3-D color space. Most often it occurs in inks that are warm in nature, or color builds that have a mixture of warm and cool colors: the pigments in warm colors begin to rise up through the cooler ink pigments.

Calibration: Tuning an instrument or a device to obtain optimal results.

Characterization: The determination of the color space needed by creating color profiles that help to simulate the gamut need for perceptual appearance—both individually and uniformly—throughout the working environment.

Chroma: Color intensity. Sometimes referred to as the color's brightness, chroma is another word for the Y tristimulus value in 3-D color theory.

Chromatic colors: A series of colors arranged in set increments.

Color contrast: The difference between lightwaves detected by the apparatus of the eyeball. The photoreceptive fields near and around the fovea are responsible for four kinds of vision: motion, form/silhouette, depth, and color. All four of these factors determine color contrast.

Color mixing: The process by which different pigments, dyes, colorants, or lightwaves are mixed to create a new hue.

Color profile: Assignment of a working color space.

Color purity: The absence of white, black, or gray from a hue.

Color rendition: The phenomenon of two colors appearing the same in one light source, but very different in another.

Color saturation: The richness of a hue. Color saturation is controlled by the amount of gray added to a particular hue and has a bearing on the intensity, or chroma, of a color.

Color scheme: The color combinations selected for a particular design.

Color shading: Combining a color and black.

Color temperature: The degree of warmth or coolness that a color suggests.

Color tinting: Adding a small amount of one color or white pigment to another color.

Color toning: Adding one complementary color to another.

Color value: The relative lightness or darkness of the color as perceived by the mind's eye.

Color Value Differential (CVD): The difference between two hues as measured by the Y tristimulus value.

Color wheel: A matrix composed of primary, secondary, and tertiary hues or colors.

Color work flow: The management of color from device to device in the daily context of a working environment.

Commercially sterile packaging: An aseptic method of packaging that does not eliminate all microorganisms, but eliminates the microorganisms' ability to reproduce under nonrefrigerated conditions.

Complementary colors: Hues that are found on opposite sides of the color wheel.

Complex fields of vision: The mechanics of perceiving the location and orientation of an object. Complex fields help humans to interpret the shape, contour, and mass of an object.

Complex subtractive mixing: The process of removing lightwaves through absorption and scattering. Complex subtractive mixing occurs when light bounces off an object and then is either reflected back in the direction of the viewer, absorbed by the object as heat, and/or scattered in various directions.

Cones: The receptor cells responsible for our perception of bright light and color.

Conversion: The uniform color optimization from one device to the other for the purpose of reproduction.

Die cutting: One of the most common methods of engineering a score, perforation, or specialized cut for package design. Like a cookie cutter, dull and/or sharp steel rules are bent to the desired shape and then pressed into the paper.

Dry trapped: Printing over a dry ink.

Early bind: The color space is assigned early in the process, and before it is sent to press.

Electromagnetic radiation: The transfer of radiant energy as heat and light, through air, water, or vacuums. Electromagnetic radiation is produced by a light source, either artificial or natural.

Embossing: The process whereby a metal die containing a relief image presses into the paper, creating a raised image. Debossing creates a lowered image through the same process.

Engraving: A highly specialized technique used to create plates and dies for foil stamping or the intaglio and gravure printing processes.

Expiration date: The point at which an edible product is no longer considered safe for consumption.

Fixation points: Discrete points at which the eye is in focus. The eye moves along the printed line in a succession of small, rapid jerks, from one point to another. These points are called fixation points, and it is only at these that the eye is in focus.

Flood varnish: A varnish that is flooded across the whole surface of the substrate. Typically used to protect paper against scuffing and rubbing during handling or bulk processing.

Foil stamping: A process whereby a thin layer of foil is adhered to the surface through the use of a heated plate or die that is stamped onto the surface of the substrate. Also known as hot stamping, dry stamping, flat stamping, leaf stamping, foil imprinting, leafing, and blocking.

Fovea: A small spot on the retina that provides our narrow, central field of focused vision

Fugitive colors: Colorants, pigments, or dyes that change or lose color rapidly when exposed to light and air.

Glazing: The contrast created by a highly burnished blind emboss on textured paper. Glazing requires more pressure and heat, but creates outstanding contrast on dark stock.

Gloss emboss: An emboss method that uses a clear foil to create a highly varnished effect on blind-embossed stock. Works best on light-colored stock.

Gold leafing and gilding: The highly burnished metallic gold in illuminated manuscripts, paintings, etc.

Hard proof: A physical hard copy pulled from a color printer or press.

Harmonious colors: Two or more colors that have a sameness about them.

Harmony of analogous colors: Of scale—color tones that are produced through a single scale; of hue—colors that have the same relative lightness to the mind's eye (color value rating); of dominant color—hues that are related to the factors involved in color contrast.

Harmony of contrast: Of scale—two colors with the same or near same color value rating, but different hues; of hue—chromatic colors with distinctly different color value ratings mixed together in stepped increments; of color temperature—two colors with the same or near same color value rating, but different color temperatures.

Hermetically sealed packaging: Packaging that is sealed airtight in an effort to exclude organisms from entering and to prevent gas or vapor from entering or exiting.

Hue: A classified or specified color.

Hypercomplex fields of vision: Matrix fields of photoreceptor cells within the brain that respond most favorably to moving objects that behave with a set direction and definite position/pattern.

Iconic information: A sign that bears a similarity or resemblance to the thing it signifies—it is what it is.

Illuminant: Light, physically realized or not, defined by spectral power distribution.

Incongruous colors: Colors that make a discordant combination. A color used with another hue that is to the right or left of its complement (for example, yellow-orange as one color and reddish-purple, or bluish-green as another) creates an incongruous combination. Incongruous combinations have one color that runs through each hue, and one that does not.

Indexical information: A sign that arises by virtue of some sort of factual or casual connection with its object.

Integrated sphere: A hollow sphere used to collect all of the light reflected from the surface of a color sample.

Invariant pairs: Color samples or objects having an identical spectral-reflectance curve and the same color coordinates. The phenomenon of invariant pairs means that, in 3-D color mixing, one hue can occupy the same space as another. In other words, the colors in question match mathematically in all standard light sources, but they look different.

Iris: The portion of the eye that helps to focus an image, adjust the amount of light passing through the pupil to define depth of field, and give eyes their color.

L*a*b* colors: Model after the second stage of perceiving color within the human experience. The Commission Internationale de L'Eclairage (CIE) developed the (L*a*b*) system (L)ightness, red/green, value (A), and yellow/blue, value (B) that is device independent, meaning this system runs true. The system is not altered by any software or hardware application, and can act as a translator for color systems that are device dependent. CMYK is an example of a device-dependent color system.

Laminate: One of four basic types of coatings applied to packaging, including varnish, aqueous coating, and UV coating. Laminates are plastics that are glued to the surface, thus providing the highest level of water resistance.

Laser cutting: A highly accurate method of cutting highly complex cut shapes not suitable for die cutting.

Late bind: The color space is assigned late in the process, and after it is sent to press.

Light energy: Light distinguished by the human eye as colors.

Metallic inks: Inks that have metal flakes suspended in the resin of the ink.

Metameric pairs: Pairs of colors with different spectral-reflectance curves (see spectral power distribution curve) that have the same appearance in one light source but not in another.

Monochromatic colors: Hues consisting of one color, including screen percentages of tints, shades, and combinations of tints and shades (see color tinting and color shading).

Neutral color: A hue with a near equal screen percentage of one or more colors, including its complementary.

Pack or Packing: The container in which multiple packages are distributed.

Packaging: The container or material that directly houses the consumer product.

Parent colors: Two or more hues that are used to create or build an array of colors.

Primary colors: Pure hues that create the foundation of all color spectrums. Subtractive primaries: cyan, magenta, and yellow; black is added to create a full color spectrum for print. Additive primaries: red, green, and blue.

Primary container: The package that directly contains the product.

Primary visual cortex: A portion of the brain located at the end of the visual pathway, devoted to the input for and interpretation of sight.

Pupil: The pupil is the black point in the center of the eye through which light travels in order to strike the retina. It operates like the leaf shutter of a camera, opening and closing in a circular pattern.

Retina: The region at the back of the eyeball where the ganglion cells, cones, and rods are located.

Rods: Photoreceptors responsible for night vision. Rods are highly sensitive to light and operate effectively in dim light. They are responsible for distinguishing blacks, grays, and variations of white, but do not distinguish color.

Scattering: A phenomenon that occurs when light strikes an object with a rough surface, causing lightwaves to reflect in many directions.

Secondary colors: A hue formed by adding equal amounts of two primary colors to one another.

Secondary container: The container that houses the primary packaging barrier.

Shelf life: The length of time that a perishable product is considered viable (ie, nutritional and palatable).

Shell gold: A mix of gum arabic and gold-leaf particles made into a cake and traditionally stored in shells by Medieval and Renaissance artists. Shell gold was often used to create the unburnished metallic gold in illuminated manuscripts, paintings, etc.

Simple fields of vision: Photoreceptive fields that are parallel to one another and work best with moving stimuli.

Simple subtractive mixing: Removing light-waves through the absorption process.

Simultaneous contrast: A strobing effect resulting from the use of unequal portions of colors.

Soft proof: A screen color proof.

Spectral power distribution curve: The spectrum of color seen by the human eye; when combined this makes white light.

Split complementary colors: Two or more hues on or near the opposite sides of the color wheel.

Spot varnish: A varnish applied in a specified area of a design.

Standard observer: A set angle of observation that affects the response of normal color vision.

Standard source: A light source for which the characteristics—wavelength, intensity, etc.—have been specified.

Subtractive color mixing: The process of removing lightwaves or matter in physical space to create additional colors.

Symbolic information: Something that represents or suggests another by virtue of their relationship, association, conversion, or resemblance.

Tertiary colors: Colors produced by mixing equal amounts of a primary and a secondary color.

Tertiary container: The container, distribution packaging, or pallet and wrappers that hold the primary and secondary containers for transport.

Thermography: An economical option that simulates the effects of engraving without a die and in a shorter time. A heat-sensitive or ultraviolet (UV) resin is mixed into the ink. When the ink is printed and exposed to heat, the resin reacts, giving the image a raised surface similar to engraving.

Transmitted light: Light that is reflected.

Transparent: If light travels through an object uninterrupted, the object is transparent.

Tristimulus values: X, Y, and Z tristimulus values refer to the amount of light the eyes see from the three primaries—red, green, and blue—of 3-D color theory. These values are determined by the power (light source) × the reflectance × the standard observer (the equivalent of normal color vision for humans). The three most typical standard light sources are Source A (tungsten filament lamp), Source D50 and/or D65 (US and European standards for average daylight), and Source CWF (fluorescent lighting).

Undercolor addition (UCA): A method of adding color to improve image quality. In four-color process, small amounts of color added to the cyan plate (no more than 10 percent) will improve color density. Undercolor addition is achieved through the CMY plates, but the cyan plate is used most often as it is the least efficient primary of the three—yellow is the most efficient.

Undercolor removal (UCR): A method of removing color to improve image quality. In four-color process printing, the removal of cyan, magenta, and yellow from the black shadow areas will compensate for ink build up by replacing it with black ink. Also called Gray Component Replacement (GCR).

UV coating: One of four basic types of coatings applied to packaging that include varnish, aqueous coating, and laminates. UV coatings are plastics that dry when exposed to UV light.

Varnish: One of four basic types of coatings applied to packaging that include aqueous coating, UV coating, and laminates. A varnish is the ink vehicle without pigment.

Visual pathway: The pathway from the eyes to the back of the brain, the primary visual cortex, to which the electrical impulses travel to be recognized and interpreted in the mind's eye, instantly and right side up.

Warm colors: Colors that give the appearance of an object being nearer the observer than it is. Warm colors are derived from yellow, orange, and red. Any hue composed of a majority of one or more of these colors is said to be warm, including half of all specified purples.

Wavelength range: The visual range within which humans can distinguish the color spectrum.

Websafe Color Cube: An arrangement of the 216 hues, at 20 percent intervals, that can be depicted accurately with most common computer platforms. This includes black and white and their shades and tints (see color shades and color tints).

Wet trap: Printing over a wet ink.

Y tristimulus value: A mathematical representation of relative lightness to the mind's eye.

Bibliography

Abellana, M. et al. "Effect of Modified Atmosphere Packaging and Water Activity on Growth of Eurotium amstelodami, E. chevalieri and E. herbariorum on a Sponge Cake Analogue." *Journal of Applied Microbiology 88.4* (2000), p. 606.

Albers, Josef. *Interaction of Color.* New Haven and London: Yale University Press, 1963.

Alpern, Andrew. *Handbook of Specialty Elements in Architecture.* New York: McGraw, 1982.

Arnheim, Rudolf. *Art and Visual Perception.* Berkeley and Los Angeles: University of California Press, 1974.

Berryman, Gregg. *Notes on Graphic Design and Visual Communication.* Los Altos, California: William Kaufmann, 1984.

Billmeyer, Fred W., Jr. *Principles of Color Technology.* New York: Wiley-Interscience, 1981.

Binns, Betty. "Readability and Legibility in Text." *Step-by-Step 6* (1987), pp. 56–61.

Birren, Faber. *Color and Human Response.* New York: John Wiley and Sons, 1978.

—— *Color Psychology and Color Therapy.* New Jersey: Citadel Press, 1950.

—— *Color Perception in Art.* New York: Van Nostrand and Reinhold Company, 1976.

Blakistone, Barbara A. *Principles and Applications of Modified Atmosphere Packaging of Foods.* London: Blackie Academic and Professional, 1998.

Bleier, Paul. "Comprehensive Sign Plans: An Alternative to Restrictive Sign Ordinances." *Messages* (Summer 1989), pp. 7–9.

Blatner, David and Steve Roth. *Real World Scanning and Halftones.* California: Peachpit Press, 1993.

Bopst, Harland. *Color and Personality.* New York: Vantage Press, 1962.

Bowles, Susan, David S. Travis, John Seton, and Roger Peppe. "Reading from Color Displays: A Psychophysical Model." *Human Factors 32* (1990), pp. 147–156.

Bringhurst, Robert. *The Elements of Typographic Style.* Vancouver: Hartley and Marks Publishers, 1992.

Byrnes, Deborah A. "Color Associations of Children." *The Journal of Psychology: The General Field of Psychology.* Massachusetts: The Journal Press Provincetown, 1983.

Carter, Rob. *Working with Computer Type, Volume 3: Color and Type.* Switzerland: RotoVision, 1997.

Carter, Rob and Philip Meggs. *Typographic Design: Form and Communication, Second Edition.* New York: Van Nostrand Reinhold, 1993.

Carter, Rob and Philip Meggs. *Typographic Specimens: The Great Typefaces.* New York: Van Nostrand Reinhold, 1993.

Claus, Karen and James R. Claus Visual *Communication Through Signage: Design of the Message, Volume 3.* Ohio: Signs of the Times Publishing Co., 1976.

—— *Visual Communication Through Signage: Perception of The Message, Volume 1.* Ohio: Signs of the Times Publishing Co., 1972.

Craig, James. "Techniques for Display Type." *Step-by-Step 6* (1987), pp. 62–65.

DeCrevel, Jim. *Your Guide to Foil Stamping and Embossing.* S. l.: DeCrevel, Inc, 1997.

DeMao, John, John Drew, Ned Drew, and Sarah A. Meyer (eds.). *Design Education in Progress: Process and Methodology Volume 3, Visual Thinking.* Virginia: Center for Design Studies, 2003.

DeMaria, Kristine. *The Packaging Development Process: A Guide for Engineers and Project Managers.* Lancaster, Pennsylvania: Technomic Publishing Co., Inc, 2000.

Drew, John T., Ned Drew and Sarah A. Meyer, Eds. *Design Education in Progress: Process and Methodology Volume 2, Type and Image.* Virginia: Center for Design Studies, 2003.

Duke-Elder, Sir W. Stewart. *Textbook of Ophthalmology.* St. Louis: The C.V. Mosby Company, 1938.

Easterby Roland and Harm Zwaga (eds.). *Information Design.* New York: John Wiley and Sons, 1984.

Eiseman, Leatrice. *Color for Every Mood.* Virginia: Capital Books, Inc., 1998.

Eiseman, Leatrice. *Pantone Guide to Communicating with Color.* Florida: Grafix Press, Ltd., 2000.

Ewald, Willam R. and Daniel R. Mandelker. *Street Graphics and The Law.* Chicago: Planners Press, 1988.

Executive Committee AIGA/New York Chapter. *Press Wise.* New York: American Institute of Graphic Artists, 1995.

Fehrman, Cherie and Kenneth R. Fehrman. *The Secret Influence.* New Jersey: Prentice-Hall, 2000.

Finke, Ronald A. *Principles of Mental Imagery.* Cambridge, Massachusetts: The MIT Press, 1989.

Fishenden, R. B. "Type, Paper and Printing in Relation to Eye Strain." *British Journal of Ophthalmology 30* (1946), pp. 20–26.

Fleury, Bob. "Combining Type and Color." *Step-by-Step 6* (1987), pp. 66–69.

Follis, John. *Architectural Signing and Graphics.* New York: Whitney Library of Design, 1979.

Goethe, Johann Wolfgang von. "Moral Effects of Colour." *Goethe's Theory of Colour.* London: New Knowledge Books, 1970.

Hamid, Nicholas P. and Adrienne G. Newport. "Effect of Color on Physical Strength and Mood and Children." *Perceptual and Motor Skills 69* (1989), pp. 179–185.

Henrion, F. H. K. and Alan Parkin. *Design Coordination and Corporate Image.* New York: Reinhold Publishing Corporation, 1966.

Hannaford, Steven and Richard Imbro. *An Introduction to Digital Color Prepress.* Mount Prospect, Illinois: Agfa Educational Publishing, 1993.

Hine, Thomas. The Total Package: *The Evolution and Secret Meanings of Boxes, Bottles, Cans, and Tubes.* Boston: Little, Brown, 1995.

Hoeksma, Jan B. and Mark M. Terwogt. "Color and Emotions: Preferences and Combinations." *The Journal of General Psychology 122* (1995), pp. 5–13.

Karp, Eric M. "Color Associations of Male and Female Fourth-Grade School Children." *Journal of Psychology 122* (1988), pp. 383–388.

Karkkainen, Mikko. "Increasing Efficiency in the Supply Chain for Short Shelf Life Goods Using RFID Tagging." *International Journal of Retail and Distribution Management 31.10* (2003), pp. 529–536.

Kosterman, Wayne. "Turning Type Into Signs." *Step-by-Step 6* (1987), pp. 90–93.

Long, Michael E. "The Sense of Sight." *National Geographic* (November 1992), pp. 3–41.

Luke, Joy T. *The New Munsell Student Color Set: The Munsell Color System; A Language for Color.* New York: Fairchild Publications, 1946/1994.

Luscher, Dr. Max, Scott A. Ian (ed.). *The Luscher Color Test.* New York: Random House, 1969.

Mahnke, Frank H. and Rudolf H. Mahnke. *Color and Light in Man-made Environments.* New York: Van Nostrand Reinhold, 1987.

Marsili, Ray. "Testing Packaging Materials." *Food Product Design.* Northbrook, Illinois: Weeks Publishing Co, 1993.

Meyers, Herbert M. and Murray J. Lubliner. *The Marketer's Guide to Successful Package Design.* Lincolnwood, Illinois: NTC Business Books, 1998.

—— and Richard Gerstman. *The Visionary Package: Using Packaging to Build Effective Brands.* Basingstoke, Hampshire: Palgrave Macmillan, 2005.

Package Design Magazine. Malvern, PA: Lyons, 2004.

Mikellides, Byron. "Color and Physiological Arousal." *Journal of Architectural and Planning Research Vol. 7, No. 1* (1990), pp. 13–19.

Miyake, R. "Comparative Legibility of Black and Colored Numbers." *The Journal of General Psychology 3* (April 1930), pp. 340–343.

Neal, Kane (ed.). *SEGD Education Foundation.* Cambridge, Massachusetts: SEGD 1992, p. 3.

Pantone, Inc. *Pantone: Duotone Studio Addition, Colors and Black.* Ohio: Pickerbook Publishing Co., 1998.

Pantone, Inc. *Pantone: Process to Solid Guide.* Ohio: Pickerbook Publishing Co., 1998.

Pantone, Inc. *Pantone: Two Spot Color Mix Guide.* Ohio: Pickerbook Publishing Co., 1998.

Peery, Brady. *Fast Track to Duotone Success.* Ohio: Pickerbook Publishing Co., 1998.

Petrisic, Anton. *Packaging and Packaging Materials With Special Reference to the Packaging of Food.* Food Industry Studies, No. 5. New York: United Nations, 1969.

Pipes, Alan. *Production for Graphic Designers.* New Jersey: Prentice Hall, 1993.

Preston, K. "Effect of Variations in Color of Print and Background on Legibility." *The Journal of General Psychology 6* (April 1932), pp. 386–390.

Pring, Roger. *www. Color: Effective Use of Color in Web Page Design.* New York: Watson-Guptill, 2000.

Pye, David. *The Nature and Aesthetics of Design.* New York: Van Nostrand Reinhold Company, 1978.

Reger, Joan A. *Feeling States Evoked by Color Lighting.* Wisconsin: University of Wisconsin, 1967.

Rehe, Rolf F. *Typography: How to Make It Most Legible.* Indianapolis: Design Research Publications, 1972.

—— *The Visible Word.* New York: Hastings House, 1968.

Robertson, G. L. *Food Packaging: Principles and Practice (Packaging and Converting Technology 6).* New York: Marcel Dekker, 1993.

—— "Food Packaging Principles and Practice Second Edition." *Food Science and Technology 152* (2006).

Robson, Stephani K. "Turning The Tables: The Psychology of Design for High Volume Restaurants." *Cornell Hotel and Restaurant Administration Quarterly 40* (1999), pp. 56–58.

Rose, F. Clifford (ed.). *The Eye in General Medicine.* London: Chapman and Hall, 1983.

Sharpe, Deborah T. *The Psychology of Color Design.* Chicago: Nelson-Hall, 1974.

Shinsha, Kawade S. and James Stockton. *Designer's Guide to Color: Volume 2.* San Francisco: Chronicle Books, 1984.

Shinsha, Kawade S. *Designer's Guide to Color: Volume 3.* San Francisco: Chronicle Books, 1986.

Shinsha, Kawade S. and James Stockton. *Designer's Guide to Color: Volume 4.* San Francisco: Chronicle Books, 1989.

Shinsha, Kawade S. and James Stockton. *Designer's Guide to Color: Volume 5.* San Francisco: Chronicle Books, 1991.

Sidelinger, S. K. *Color Manual.* Englewood, New Jersey: Prentice-Hall, 1985.

Sonsino, Steven. *Packaging Design: Graphics, Materials, Technology.* New York: Van Nostrand Reinhold, 1990.

Stanziola, Ralph. *Colorimetery and the Calculation of Color Difference.* New Jersey: Industrial Color Technology, 1994.

Stockton, James. *Designer's Guide to Color: Volume 1.* San Francisco: Chronicle Books, 1984.

Summer, F. C. "Influence of Color on Legibility of Copy." *Journal of Applied Psychology 16* (April 1932), pp. 201–204.

Contributors

Taylor, Cornelia D. "The Relative Legibility of Black and White Print." *The Journal of Educational Psychology 8* (November 1934), pp. 560–579.

Tinker, Miles. A. "The Effect of Color on Visual Apprehension and Perception." *Genetic Psychology Monographs 11* (February 1932), pp. 459–461.

Tinker, Miles. A., and D. G. Paterson. "Studies of Typographical Factors Influencing Speed of Reading." *Journal of Applied Psychology 15* (October 1931), pp. 241–247.

Traxler, Arthur E. "The Relation Between Rate of Reading and Speed of Association." *The Journal of Educational Psychology 8* (November 1934), pp. 357–365.

Wang, Larry. *What Is New in Barrier Packaging for Food and Non-Food Products. Business Opportunity Report, P-085N.* Norwalk, Connecticut: Business Communications Co, 1991.

West, Suzanne. *Working with Style: Traditional and Modern Approaches to Layout and Typography.* New York: Watson-Guptill Publications, 1990.

Whitehouse, Roger. *The Americans with Disabilities Act White Paper.* Cambridge, Massachusetts: SEGD, 1992.

Wisniewski, Agnes M. *The Influence of Color and Figure-Ground Patterns on Target Accuracy.* Smith College, 1973.

Wong, Wucius. *Principles of Color Design: Designing with Electronic Color.* New York: John Wiley and Sons, 1997 (2nd edn).

Wyszecki, Gunter and W. S. Stiles. *Color Science.* New York: John Wiley and Sons, 1967.

Zwimpfer, Moritz. *Color, Light, Sight, Sense.* Pennsylvania: Schiffer Publishing Ltd., 1988.

Studios

1972dg
3PART designteam
AG Adriano Goldschmied
Alian Design
Aloof Design
Arcadia Studio SF
Articulate Solutions®, Inc.
Artiva Design
Bohoy Design
Bright Strategic Design
Camacho Associates
CF NAPA
chuckie-boy records
Curiosity
David Lefler Photography
DESer
design@qirk.com
Design B
DESIGNLAB
Design Team One, Inc.
dododesign.se
Domot Antistudio
Doyle Partners
Dustin Edward Arnold
Dustin Edward Arnold/
DL&Co.
Elf Design, Inc.
el recordo records
estudiocrop
Estudio Iuvaro
estrus records
Exhibit A: Design Group
FiF DESIGN
first american records
fourillusion
Fuelhaus
Gouthier Design
a brand collective
The Grafiosi
Graham Hanson Design

Greydient
The Hively Agency
ICAN DESIGN
International
in the red records
Irving
Jefferson Acker
jerden records
L.A. Salgado
Kara Brennan Photography
LIGHT PUBLICITY CO., LTD.
Mary Hutchison Design LLC
media9 studio
Midnite Oil
milkxhake
Mostardesign Studio
Nita B. Creative
norton records
One Lucky Guitar, Inc.
Phoenix Creative
Positiu Design Consultants
Poulin + Morris
Principle
RED8 Comm
REFLECTUR.COM
Reisigl Associates
Ruadesign
SandorMax
schönereWelt! swelt.com
SGDP
SOLUTIONS Branding &
Design Companies
sub pop records
The People's Design
Twointandem
Typework Studio
Wallace Church
WE RECOMMEND
XO Create!
Zemma & Ruiz Moreno

Individuals

Sara Abdi
Jefferson Acker
Dan Adams
Lydia Adi
Salvatore Aduchi
Sam Aloof
Savio Alphonso
Dustin E. Arnold
Letty Avila
Bradley W. Baker
Fabian Barral
Dan Bittman
Quentin Blake
Kathrin Blank
Johanna Bohoy
Renita Breitenbucher
Kara Brennan
Christopher Brown
Mark Brown
John Bruno
Kelly Bryant
Maria F. Camacho
Anne Carls
Marco Cavallo
Kyung Jin Cha
Art Chantry
Cyrille Charbonnier
Marcos Chavez
Crystal S. Chin
Stan Church
Inyoung Choi
Rob Clarke
Jeremy Creighton
Dave Crider
Zoltan Csillag
Heather Darwall-Smith
Daniele De Batté
Gabriela Lopez De Dennis
Jini Dellaccio
Jens Dreier

Andrea Egbert
Fanny El Tom
Elisava Escola de Disseny
Rodrigo Estacio
Dean Ethington
Thiago Fantinatti
Aldo Bastos Filho
Katherine Filice
Jason Feltz
Erin Ferree
Edwin Fotheringham
Martin Fredricson
Andi Friedl
Bettina Gabriel
Etel Garaguay
Simone Gauss
Daryl Geary
Ally Gerson
Danny Giang
Mariano Gioia
Nin Glaister
Micha Goes
Karel Golta
Steve Gonsowski
Kyle Goodwin
Olivier Gourvat
Jonathan Gouthier
Pia Grumeth
Isabelle Guérin-Groelz
Lawrence Haggerty
Zeina Said Hamady
Graham Hanson
Bryce Hendry
Gwendolyn Hicks
Flavio Hobo
Jon Hodkinson
Darren Hoffman
Dan Hoy
Mary Chin Hutchison
Kimiko Ida

Kimiko Ida
Catalin Ilinca
Carlo Irigoyen
Sachi Ito
Cecilia Iuvaro
Mongkolsri Janjarasskul
Beto Janz
Dusan Jelesijevic
Jan Jentsch
Virginia Johnson
Susannah Jonas
Sanver Kanidinc
Elena Ruano Kanidinc
Shun Kawakami
Matt Kelley
Nikolaj Knop
Chris Komashko
Ko-Zou
Camilla Kristiansen
Spy Lan
David Lefler
Michael Levine
Oswaldo S. Lima
Dorothy Lin
Douglas Little
Boris Ljubicic
Oriol Llahona
Angelino Lopez
Gabriela Lopez De Dennis
Jason Lowe
Donovan Mafnas
Carlos Marques
Igor Masnjak
Jordan Mauriello
Babette Mayor
Dejan Mauzer
Simon McBride
Kat McCluskey
Susan McKeever
Mary Ann McLaughlin

Clare Melinsky
John Minton
Javin Mo
Renan Molin
Maki Mori
Ann Muir
Fernando Munoz
Sarah Munt
Karen Murray
Mark Naden
Robyn Neild
Gwenazi Nicilas
Morten Nielsen
Nina Ng
Marcus Norman
Diogo Paulo
Rachel Pearson
Saulius Pempe
Valerie Pena
Charles Peterson
Pornprapha Phatanateacha
M. Piotrowski
Dado Queiroz
Piero Quintiliani
Tanya Quick
Clare Reece-Raybould
James K. Reisigl
Christopher Rimel
Cory Ripley
Julian Roberts
Michael J. Robins
Daniel Rodgers
Lucila Marina Ruiz Moreno
Glenn Sakamoto
Yu-Ki Sakurai
Camilla Saufley
Fabiano Schroden
Kellie Schroeder
David Schwemann
Andrew Scrase

Ian Shimkoviak
Sakae Soeda
Annahita Soleymani
Gaylord Somera
Davide Sossi
Isabeile Soulier
Brenda Spivack
Robert Spofforth
Michael Stapleton
Sven C. Steinmeyer
Jonathon Stewart
Mashael Al Sulaiti
Jennifer Sukis
Pushkar Thakur
Stuart Thompson
Augusta Toppins
Chapman Tse
Tadashi Ura
Chris Waiden
Chen Wang
Ty Webb
Martin Weber
Kimberly Welter
Theo Williams
Andrew Wong
Ikuma Yamada
Kristine Yan
Sebastián Yáñez
Akira Yasuda
Rhawn York
Marianne Young
Yoza
Santiago Zemma
Pamela Zuccker

Index

Abdi, Sara 53
Aceites Varietales Familia Zuccardi 20
Adams, Dan 60, 102, 104
additive color theory 132, 165
additives 147
Adi, Lydia 32, 52
Adobe 73, 76, 78, 80, 142, 145
AG Adriano Goldschmied 174
age 187–88
Alian Design 33, 47, 49
Alison Price 11
Aloof Design 11, 39, 114
Aloof, Sam 11, 39, 114
Alphonso, Savio 17
alternative inks 70–71
Amari Wines 20
Americans with Disabilities Act 145, 177–78
Andrew's Ties 46
Anheuser-Busch Lemon Tattoo Beer 54
antistatic packaging 127, 129
appetite ratings 190–209
Apple 142
Aquatanica Spa 15
aqueous coating 94–95
Arcadia Studio SF 42
Arla Maelk 29
Arnold, Dustin E. 14, 87, 92–93, 100, 182
AromaFloria 29
Art Kit 53
Art Nouveau 42
Articulate Solutions, Inc. 68
Artiva Design 16
ascenders 168–69, 177
aseptic packaging 128
Ashford Eye Drops 13
Assign Profile 135–36
Avila, Letty 168
Avon Plant Spa 32

B-flute 104
Babu 28
Baker, Bradley W. 170
banding 110, 152
The 12 Bar 11
Barral, Fabian 128
Becker Surf + Sport 13
Belle Hop Travel Accessories 46
beveled dies 90
bitmaps 142
Bittman, Dan 108
black 206
Blake, Quentin 50, 53
Blank, Kathrin 186
bleeding 22, 97
blend steps 152
blind emboss 90–91
blister packaging 104
blistering 93
blocking 86
blow molding 106
blown film 104
blue family 203–5
Bohoy Design 13, 19, 39
Bohoy, Johanna 13, 19, 39, 183
Bols Liqueur 54
bond 102
bottles 106–7, 116, 120, 124
brass dies 90
Breitenbucher, Renita 46, 50–51, 53
Brennan, Kara 28, 54
Briannas 36
Bright Strategic Design 67
brightness rating 100, 133, 148, 161
bristol 102–3
Brown, Mark 60
Bruno, John 33
Bryant, Kelly 46
bulk density 127
burn point 123
butte registering 87

C-flute 104
calibration 83, 131–42, 145
California Blossoms 56
California Sunshine 56
capitals 168–69, 171
Capsoles 11, 15
Captain Morgan Private Stock 37
card stock 102–3
cardboard 103
Carls, Anne 126
carriers 114
Cavallo, Marco 96
Caves Vidigal 20
CF NAPA 36–37, 86
Chakana Andean Wines 20
Chantry, Art 66, 68, 71, 76–78, 80–83, 132,
147–48, 155–56, 158–60
Chapman, Tom 60
characterization 141
Charbonnier, Cyrille 176
Charlie & the Chocolate Factory 50
Charlie's Notes 53
Chavez, Marcos 15, 162
Chen Wang 19
childproofing 127
Chin, Crystal S. 128
choking 147
Choklad Platts 29
chroma values 100, 136–37, 158–59, 165,
176, 186–89, 191–205
Church, Stan 13, 20, 33, 37, 55, 127, 153
Ciao Bella 13
CIE (Commission Internationale de L'Eclairage) 145
clamshell 104
Clarke, Rob 147
client proofs 76–79, 81–82
CMYK document calibration 135–37
coatings 94–95
color association 184–209
color balance 152, 154
color correcting 152–54, 157
color densities 73
color drifting 66, 68
color guides 155
color information 153
Color Picker 133, 158
Color Settings 135–36
color shading 161
color syncing 132
color theory 132, 165, 176
color wheel 135–38, 148
color work flow 141–42
color-study files 101, 103
Colors dialog box 80–81
ColorSync setting 145
ColorThink Pro 77, 79, 83, 142
ColorThink v2 77, 79, 83
competitors 124
computerized machine tooling 90
condensation 89, 120
Confection Breath Mints 17
conscious response 186
containers 124, 128–29
contaminants 117, 127
context 124, 190
continuous tone 152, 160
contrast 152–53, 162–63, 176–79, 188
convergence 174, 178
conversion 141–42
cool colors 186, 189
Copper Mountain Beer 124–25
cover 102–3
crates 116
Crew 15
crush resistance 103–4, 115, 119
Csillag, Zoltan 37, 54
Curiosity 19
Curious Sofa 10
Curves dialog box 157
Custom Colors 133
customs 128
CVD (Color Value Differential) 145, 148, 150–51, 161, 188

Dahesh Museum of Art 13
dark trapping 147
Darwall-Smith, Heather 94
Day-Glo inks 70, 118
De Batte, Daniele 16
debossing 90–91
Deep Herbal 33
Default Colors dialog box 155
delivery systems 124
Dellaccio, Jini 155
depth 182, 187, 190
descenders 168–69, 177
DESer 33, 36, 106
Design B 34
Design Team One, Inc. 108
design@qirk.com 35, 132
DESIGNLAB 176
Destination Space 145
1972dg 54, 141, 152
die cuts 96–97, 105
DigitalColor Meter 143, 145
display effects 116–17, 124
distance 180
DL&Co 87, 100
document calibration 135–40
dododesign.se 29
Domot Antistudio 70
dot gain 152–53
double-fluted cardboard 103
Doyle Partners 15, 58
dpi (dots per inch) 73
Dreier, Jens 29
Drew, John T. 11, 17, 24, 30, 32, 52–53, 56, 67,
82, 94, 97, 107, 110–11, 125, 168
Droobles Bubble Gum 30
dropout 152–53
dry stamping 86
dry trapping 94–95
Duotone Options dialog box 158
duotones 152, 154–60
dyne count 88

E-flute 104
early bind 142
Echoes of Summer 39
effect foils 87
Egbert, Andrea 46
Egekilde 18
electronic mechanicals 76–77, 81, 149, 161
Elf Design, Inc. 175
Elias & Grace 11
embossing 89–91, 105, 110
emission issues 128
empirical studies 124
engraving 92–93
environments 117–25, 127, 129, 165
Epona 33
Epson 142, 145
ergonomics 99, 118–19, 121–22
Estacio, Rodrigo 111
Estudio Iuvaro 20–21, 57
estudiocrop 20, 28, 48, 181
Etched Turkey Thanksgiving Wine 20
Ethington, Dean 24
Evian 19
Exhibit A: Design Group 11, 13, 15, 67, 124, 139
Expect 57
expertise 115, 127
expiration dates 118, 126
extrusion blow molding 106
eye testing 173, 178–79
Eye-One Display 2 system 142, 145
Eye-One Pro 146
Eyedrop tool 79, 143

F-flute 104
fake duotones 152, 154–60
Fantinatti, Thiago 166
Feltz, Jason 102
Ferree, Erin 175
FiF DESIGN House Team 52, 186
Filho, Aldo Basto 180

Filice, Katherine 68
The Fine Cheese Co. 22–23
The Fine Cheese Co. English Fruits 19
fixation points 167, 170
flat stamping 86
flexible plastic packaging 104
flexography 66–67, 70, 104–6, 109–10, 120
flood varnish 95
flooded images 97
Flora 46
Focus 31
foil imprinting 86
foil stamping 86–89, 91–92, 105, 109
folding 103
folding box board 104
fonts 175, 177–78
Foreground Color dialog box 143–45
form/silhouette 176–79, 190
Fotheringham, Edwin 71, 76–78
fovea 167
Franck Coffee, Zagreb 34
Fredericson, Martin 129
freshness dates 118–19
Friedl, Andi 29, 51
Fuelhaus 11, 33, 189
Furillusion 166

Gabriel, Bettina 106, 127
gamma 68, 77–79, 83, 138, 145, 155–59
gamut 141–42
Ganesh and Krishna Kits 47
Gauss, Simone 121
Geary, Daryl 35, 132
gender 187–88
Gerson, Ally 28, 54
gestalt 9, 116
Giang, Danny 171
Gioia, Mariano 20–21, 57
Glaister, Nin 37
glandular response 186–88
glass 107–10, 118, 124, 129
glazing 91
gloss emboss 91
glues 120–21
Godiva Chocolatier 52
Goes, Micha 29, 51
gold family 209
Goldstein 189
Golta, Karel 126
Gonsowski, Steve 11, 125
Goodwin, Kyle 94
Gourvat, Olivier 31
Gouthier Design 17, 50, 88–89, 118, 142
Gouthier, Jonathan 17, 50, 88–89, 118, 142
gradients 152
The Grafiosi 47, 183
Graham Hanson Design 122
grain 96, 103
gravure 92
gray family 207–9
grayscale 152–53, 156–59
green family 198–201
GretagMacbeth 142, 145–46
Greydient 15
Grumeth, Pia 105, 121
Guérin-Groelz, Isabelle 42
guidelines 148, 155–57, 179

Haggerty, Lawrence 153
Hamady, Zeina Said 141
handling 115, 119
Hanson, Graham 122
hard proofs 79, 142, 145
harsh environments 118–23
Heinz Heritage 55
Helvetica 172
Hemingray Company 107
Hendry, Bryce 68
hermetic sealing 128–29
Hexachrome system 68
Hicks, Gwendolyn 56, 162
highlights 153
The Hively Agency 36, 140
Hobo, Flavio 166
Hodkinson, Jon 11, 39, 114
Hoffman, Darren 137
holographic foils 87–88
hot stamping 86
How To Make Your Own Candle 30

Hoy, Dan 17
hues 165, 176, 189–90
humidity 89, 117
Hutchinson, Mary Chin 15, 50

I Am Imagination 50
ICAN DESIGN 91
iconic signifiers 9, 62, 125
Illustrator 73, 76, 78–80, 100, 135–38, 148–49, 152
Imageódesign 51
InDesign 73, 76, 78–80
indexical signifiers 9, 62, 124
Information dialog box 153
injection stretch blow molding 106
Ink Colors dialog box 158
ink systems 65–69, 77, 79, 133, 135, 138, 148, 159
insurance 115
intaglio 92
International 38, 59
Interstate Paper 12
introverts 189
Inyoung Choi 46
Irigoyen, Carlo 169
irony 125
irradiation 128
Irving 19, 22, 60, 69, 94–95, 101–4, 107–9, 116–19, 133–35, 147
italics 169
Ito, Sachi 30
Iuvaro, Cecilia 20–21, 57
Iuvaro, Estudio 20

Jacqueline Kennedy: The White House Years 46
Janjarasskul, Mongkolsri 13, 52, 56, 87, 105
Janz, Beto 48
Jefferson Acker 13, 105
Jelesijevic, Dusan 149
Jentsch, Jan 105
Johnson, Virginia 46
Jonas, Susannah 13
justified type 167

Kanidinc, Elena Ruano 51
Kanidinc, Sanver 51
Kawakami, Shun 62
Kelley, Matt 31, 101
Key Underwear Packs 33
King Delight: Grilled Chicken Wrap 29
kiss die cut 97
kiss fit 87
knock outs 87, 149, 161
Knop, Nikolaj 129
Ko-Zou 62
Komashko, Chris 166
Kristiansen, Camilla 20
Kyung Chin Cha 107

L*a*b* equivalents 137–38, 143, 145–46, 158
L.A. Salgado 48
labeling 106, 109–10, 120, 124–25, 189
lamination 94, 105
laser cuts 96–97
late bind 142
Layers dialog box 73, 78, 80, 149, 156
leading 167
leaf stamping 86
leafing 86
Lefler, David 57
legibility 147–48, 161, 163, 165, 172–83
letterforms 166–74, 177–79
letterpress 105
Levine, Michael 76
Levi's Flu Sports Clothes and Apparel 62–63
life cycle 118, 120, 126–29
Lima, Oswaldo S. 48
Lin, Dorothy 122
line art 90, 93
line length 167
Lip Glaze 53
litho lamination 104
lithography 66–67, 70, 92, 104–6
Little, Douglas 87, 92, 100
Ljubicic, Boris 17, 34, 38, 55, 59
Llahona, Oriol 176
Lopez De Dennis, Gabriela 47, 150
Love Glove 30
lowercase 168, 171
Luxelab Blonde-Aid Masque 14

McCluskey, Kat 46
McKeever, Susan 80
McLaughlin, Mary Ann 30, 141
MacNeill Group 17
macro color associations 190–209
Macs 143–45
Mafnas, Donovan 11
manual color syncing 82–83
manufacturers 115, 118, 122, 127
marbling 60–61
marketplace 124, 152
Marques, Carlos 54, 141, 152
Marshall Field's 51
Martha Stewart Everyday 58
Mary Hutchinson Design LLC 15, 50
Masnjak, Igor 34
Matches 60–61
matrices 73–75, 78–79, 81–82, 132, 163
Mauriello, Jordan 128
Mauzer, Dejan 29
Mayor, Babette 171
mechanicals 76–77, 80–81, 121, 149, 160–61
metallic foils 87
metallic inks 70
metallic papers 101, 103
metaphor relationships 125
Meyer, Sarah A. 82
micro color responses 186–89
Midnite Oil 13, 52, 56, 87, 105
milkxhake 15, 90, 163
Mint Collection 17
Minton, John 31
Miron violet glass 107, 109
Mocafe 50
molding 106
Molin, Renan 20
monitors 131–33, 141, 143–45, 158
morgue folders 103
Mori, Maki 110
Mossback 36
Mostardesign Studio 31
motion 180, 187, 190
motor response 186–88
muddy/dirty hues 72, 208
Muir, Ann 60
Multiply feature 73–74, 78, 80, 101, 149, 156
Munoz, Fernando 29, 32
Munt, Sarah 36, 140
Murray, Karen 22

Naden, Nick 162
Neild, Robyn 46
Nestlé (Thai) Ltd 52
New England Cranberry 19
Ng, Nina 174
Nicilas, Gwenazi 19
Nielson, Morten 15
Nita B. Creative 46, 50–51, 53
nonleafing 86
normal environments 118–23
Norman, Marcus 46
44° North Vodka 20
numbers 169

Okumura, Akio 72
One Lucky Guitar, Inc. 31, 101
ophthalmology 173
Opium 19
optimum reading distance 167, 172–73, 178–80
orange family 194–95
overprinting 70–83, 136–37, 147, 149, 152, 156, 158
Overprinting dialog box 158

packing 113, 115–16
Paddywax: Classic 57
Paddywax: Destinations 28
Paddywax: Jolie 28
Paddywax: Journey of the Bee 54
Palmistry 49
Pantene Pro-V Hair conditioner 122
papers 83, 88, 90–91, 93–96, 100–103, 118, 120–21, 123, 129, 133, 153, 161, 163
parody 125
3PART designteam 18, 116
Paulo, Diogo 161
Pazzo 21
Pearson, Rachel 30
Pena, Valeria 67
The People's Design 166
perishable products 118, 126

Perla Beer   36
Peterson, Charles   80, 156
Phoenix Creative   169
photochromic inks   70
photoreceptor cells   162, 173–74, 177–80
Photoshop   73–74, 76, 78–80, 100, 133, 135–38, 142–43, 148–49, 152–60
picas   167
pigment foils   87
pink family   193
Piotrowski, M.   33, 36, 106, 187
plastic bottles   106
plastic tubes   106
plastics   104–6, 118, 120–23, 129
points system   115
poisons   189
polymorphous paper   105
polypropylene packaging   104–5
Pophaus Type Foundry   32
position   167
Positiu Design Consultants   176
positive associative responses   190–209
The Possum Trot Orchestra *Harbor Road*   31
Poulin + Morris   13, 66
press proofs   73, 76, 80–81, 132, 152–53, 159, 161
pressure-sensitive labeling   106
price point   118–19
primary containers   128
Principle   28, 54, 57
The Private Press   47
profile settings   136–37, 140, 142, 145
proof set-up   76–79
psychological response   187–89
puckering   89–90
Pure & Natural Revitalising Moisturiser   56
pure hues   72, 147, 161
Puria   19
purple family   201–3

QuarkXPress   155–56
QuarkXPress 6.5   78–79, 81
QuarkXPress 7   73, 76, 78–80
Queiroz, Dado   20, 28, 48, 181
Quick, Tanya   29, 32
Quintilliani, Piero   96

radiation   128
Rasta Mind International   28
Raster Image Processor (RIP)   141
readability   147, 161, 163, 166–72, 174, 177–78
reading distance   167, 172–73, 178–80
reading speed   169, 171–72
rectangular Marquee tool   73
RED8 Comm   187
Red Ambrosia: Collection Sensual de Corps   42–43
red family   191–93
Red Rover 2004 Merlot   21
Reece-Raybould, Clare   127
reflectance disparity   101
REFLECTUR.COM   10, 56, 162
refractive engraving   91
registration   161
regresses   167
Reisigl Associates   138, 180
Reisigl, James K.   138, 180
repackaging   115
research   124
retail context   124
retinal-cone fatigue   162
retortable pouches   129
reversals   161
RGB equivalents   137–38, 143, 145
Right Guard (The Dial Corporation)   33
rigid box board   105
Rimel, Christopher   128
RIP (Raster Image Processor)   78, 81
Ripley, Cory   11, 13, 15, 67, 124, 139
Roberts, Julian   19, 22, 60, 69, 94–95, 101–4, 107–9, 116–19, 133–35, 147
Robins, Michael J.   120
Rock Street Journal   47
Rodgers, Daniel   91
Ruadesign   161
Ruiz Moreno, Lucila Marina   20–21
Rush   17

Sakamoto, Glenn   13, 67, 105
Sakurai, Yu-Ki   62
sample sheets   122
sample strips   73

SandorMax   37, 54
Sandy's Sweets   24–25
Saufley, Camilla   68
Scarborough & Co   13
schönereWelt! swelt.com   171
Schroden, Fabiano   28, 48, 181
Schroeder, Kellie   11, 33
Schwemann, David   21, 36–37, 86
score folds   103–4
scoring   96
Scrase, Andrew   11, 39, 114
scratch-off foils   87–88
sculptured dies   90
secondary containers   128
sell-by dates   118
semipure hues   72, 147, 161
Séptima Rosé Wine   21
Set Foreground Color   133
SF Jazz Collective for Nonsuch Records   32
SGDP   46
shelf impact   119, 124–25
shelf life   126
Shimkoviak, Ian   33, 47, 49
shipping   114–15, 117, 119
Shoot Better   15
short lines   167
signage   167, 172, 178
silhouette/form   187
silkscreening   66–67, 70, 103–6, 109, 147–48
silver family   209
simile   125
simultaneous contrast   162–63
single-fluted cardboard   103
skin response   187
SMS   38
SMS Jam   59
Snellen, Hermann   173–74, 178–79
Soeda, Sakae   62
Solutions   51
SOLUTIONS Branding & Design Companies   105–6, 186
Somera, Gayford   97
Sossi, David   16
Soulier, Isabelle   78
split-fountains   152
Spofforth, Robert   11, 13, 15, 67, 124, 139
spot-color document calibration   133, 138–40
spot-color matrices   73–75, 78–79, 81–82, 132, 148–49, 163
spot-color verification   155
spreading   147
Spy Lan   12
stacking   115, 119
Standardized Eye Chart   173, 178–79
Stapleton, Michael   56
Steinmeyer, Sven C.   171
sterilization   128
Stewart, Jonathon   133
storage effects   116–17, 119
stresses   127
strobing   162
stroke width-to-height ratio   177–78
structural factors   168
subtractive color theory   132–33, 165, 176
Sukis, Jennifer   28
Al Sulati, Mashael   30
surface tension   88
swatch books   68–69, 122, 132, 135, 137–38, 156
System Preferences dialog box   143

tamper-resistance   127
target audience   118, 189
tarnishing   86
taste   188–209
tertiary containers   129
tests   136–37
text stock   102–3
textured emboss   91
Thakur, Pushkar   47, 183
thermochromic inks   70
thermoforming   106
thermography   92–93
thermoplastic sheets   106
Thompson, Stuart   95
three-dimensional color theory   132
three-dimensional shapes   96, 131, 165
time limitations   167
tins   110–11
tint leaf combination   91
Tom, Fanny El   106
tonal range   152

Toppins, Augusta   46
tracking   167
translucent papers   101, 103
Transparency dialog box   149
transportation effects   114–15, 117
trapped blister packaging   104
trapping   147–51
tristimulus values   145, 150–51, 176
tritones   152, 154–60
Tse, Chapman   30, 57
tubes   106
Turning Leaves Thanksgiving Wine   37
Twointandem   51
type   161
Typework Studio   102

Ukiyo-e   42
U'luvka Vodka   11, 39
Ura, Tadashi   62
US Web Coated SWOP v2   142–43
Utrecht University   173
UV coatings   94
UV light blocking   107–9

vacuum forming   106
vacuum packaging   128
Valle Escondido Winery   21
varnishing   86–87, 90–91, 94–96
Vida Orgánica   57
The Vines of Ilok   55
Virgil's Fine Soaps   11
viscosity   117
visual acuity   172–75, 182
visual angle   167, 173–74, 177–79
visual clarity   172
visual impact assessment   124
visual separation   9
Vivil, Sugar-Free   51
Vivr   17

Walden, Chris   28
Wallace Church, Inc.   13, 20, 33, 37, 55, 104, 127, 153
warm colors   186, 189
wasp   35
wavelengths   165, 174, 186
WE RECOMMEND   129
Webb, Ty   33
Weber, Martin   106, 186
weights   102–3, 129
wells   92
Welter, Kimberly   46, 50, 53
wet trapping   94
white   206
white space   167
width-to-height ratio   177–78
Wild Bites   13
Williams, Theo   177
Wong, Andrew   12
word count   167
word pictures   169–72
Wow   15
written instructions   77, 81

X-rite   142
XO Create!   120, 136, 188

Yamada, Ikuma   62
Yan, Kristine   17
Yáñez, Sebastián   20–21, 57
Yasuda, Akira   20
yellow family   195–99
Yoplait   118
York, Rhawn   82
Young, Marianne   138, 180
Yoza   62

Zemma & Ruiz Moreno   20–21, 37
Zemma, Santiago   20–21
Zenz Therapy   15
Zuccker, Pamela   28, 54, 57
Zummer   52